Harmonizing Work, Family, and Personal Life

When designed well, effective work–life balance practices can improve employee productivity and firm success, while enriching employee engagement and life satisfaction. These practices are not just the *right thing to do* for employees – they are the right thing to do for an organization's bottom line. *Harmonizing Work, Family, and Personal Life* examines the organizational challenges of introducing work–life policies and practices from both an individual and a managerial perspective. Drawing on state-of-the-art academic literature and studies of a broad range of companies around the globe where such policies have been implemented, this book is a practical guide for policy design and implementation.

Harmonizing Work, Family, and Personal Life is essential reading for human resource managers, consultants, and coaches, as well as students and researchers in the fields of human resource management, organizational behavior, or career management.

STEVEN A. Y. POELMANS is Assistant Professor of Managing People in Organizations at IESE Business School, Barcelona, where he is co-founder and Academic Director of the International Center of Work and Family. Professor Poelmans is also the coordinator of the second phase of the Collaborative International Study on Managerial Stress (CISMSII), the first international study of work–family conflict in twenty-six countries.

PAULA CALIGIURI is Professor of Human Resource Management in the School of Management and Labor Relations at Rutgers University, where she is the Director of the Center for Human Resource Strategy (CHRS). As a consultant, Professor Caligiuri is the President of Caligiuri and Associates, Inc., a consulting firm specializing in the selection, performance assessment, and development of global leaders.

Harmonizing Work, Family, and Personal Life

From Policy to Practice

STEVEN A. Y. POELMANS AND PAULA CALIGIURI

CAMBRIDGE
UNIVERSITY PRESS

HD
4904.25
.H38
2008

CAMBRIDGE UNIVERSITY PRESS
Cambridge, New York, Melbourne, Madrid, Cape Town, Singapore, São Paulo, Delhi

Cambridge University Press
The Edinburgh Building, Cambridge CB2 8RU, UK

Published in the United States of America by Cambridge University Press, New York

www.cambridge.org
Information on this title: www.cambridge.org/9780521858694

First published 2008

Printed in the United Kingdom at the University Press, Cambridge

A catalogue record for this publication is available from the British Library

Library of Congress Cataloguing in Publication Data

Harmonizing work, family, and personal life: from policy to practice/[edited by]
    Steven Poelmans [and] Paula Caligiuri.
        p.   cm.
    Includes bibliographical references and index.
    ISBN 978-0-521-85869-4 (hbk.)
    1. Work and family.   I. Poelmans, Steven A. Y., 1968–
    II. Caligiuri, Paula.   III. Title.

    HD4904.25.H38 2008
    658.3′12–dc22

                                                            2008007714

ISBN 978-0-521-85869-4 hardback

I dedicate this book to my dear friends and colleagues who inspired me to study the work–family interface over the last decade: Marc Buelens, Nuria Chinchilla, Pablo Cardona, and Tammy Allen.

In my heart I dedicate this book to my dear wife and daughter, Lilia and Elisa, who reward me every day for my balancing act with their joy and optimism.

– Steven

I dedicate this book to the individuals who have helped shape my own sense of work–life balance:
To my parents – by example, they taught me what matters most in life
To Don – an everlasting reminder that life is precious and short
And
To George – a muse for my work, a joy in my life, who brings balance to my days.

– Paula

Contents

Figures

Tables

Contributors

Tammy D. Allen is Associate Professor of Psychology at the University of South Florida. Her research interests include work and family, career development, and mentoring. Her work on these topics has appeared in journals such as the *Journal of Applied Psychology*, *Personnel Psychology*, *Journal of Management*, *Journal of Vocational Behavior*, and *Journal of Organizational Behavior*. She is an associate editor for the *Journal of Occupational Health Psychology* and serves on the editorial boards of the *Journal of Applied Psychology*, *Personnel Psychology*, and *Journal of Vocational Behavior*.

Anne Bardoel is Associate Professor in the Department of Management, Faculty of Business and Economics at Monash University, Melbourne, Australia. The current focus of her research is organizational strategies for work and family balance and she has published a number of articles in academic journals on this topic. She is recognized as one of Australia's leading researchers in the work–family area and is the founder of the Work–Life Research Program (part of the Australian Centre for Research in Employment and Work). She is also the President of the Work–Life Association in Australia. She has extensive consulting experience with a wide range of public and private sector organizations including undertaking company work–life assessments, organizational cultural audits, and benchmarking quality management programs.

Barbara Beham holds a Master's degree in business administration and a PhD in business sciences/organizational behavior (University of Linz, Austria). For two years she worked as a researcher at the International Center of Work and Family at the IESE Business School in Barcelona, Spain. Her research focuses on organizational citizenship behavior, work–family conflict, and family-friendly human resource policies. She is currently working as a post-doctoral research fellow at the University of Hamburg, Germany.

Paula Caligiuri is Professor of Human Resource Management Department in the School of Management and Labor Relations at Rutgers University, where she is the Director of the Center for Human Resource Strategy (CHRS). She has lectured in numerous universities in the United States, Asia, and Europe. Paula researches, publishes, and consults in three primary areas: strategic human resource management in multinational organizations, global leadership development, and global assignee management.

Paula Caligiuri was listed among the most prolific authors in the field of international business according to a 2005 study conducted by Michigan State University. Her academic publications include several articles in the *International Journal of Human Resource Management, Journal of World Business, Journal of Applied Psychology, Personnel Psychology*, and *International Journal of Intercultural Relations*. Consonant with her interest in action-oriented research, she has also published on the topic of psychometric statistics in the *Handbook of Statistics* and *Statistics and Probability*. Paula is on numerous editorial boards for academic management journals. She holds a PhD in industrial and organizational psychology from Penn State University.

Paula is also the President of Caligiuri and Associates, Inc., a consulting firm specializing in the selection, performance assessment, and development of global leaders. Her clients include several US-based and European-based global organizations.

Helen De Cieri is Professor of Management and Director of the Australian Centre for Research in Employment and Work (ACREW) in the Department of Management at Monash University. She has held visiting appointments at universities in Australia, China, Malaysia, Hong Kong, and the USA. Her consulting experience includes projects with Australian and international organizations across private and public sectors. Helen's current research activities include strategic human resource management (HRM) in multinational enterprises, HRM issues in the Asia-Pacific region, and work–life management issues.

Helen has co-authored two books and published over seventy book chapters, monographs, and journal articles in leading international academic publications. From 1996 to 2002, Helen was the editor of the *Asia Pacific Journal of Human Resources*, the leading regional journal in the HRM field. Helen is a departmental editor (strategic human resources and international industrial relations) for the *Journal of International Business Studies* and serves on the editorial boards of several academic journals, including the *Academy of Management Journal* and *Human Resource Management*.

Joan Gentilesco-Giue is currently an HR consultant with the IBM Corporation, Sales & Distribution. Formerly, Joan spent six years as Technology and Communication Project Manager for the Work–Life, Flexibility, and Mobility Project Office with IBM, where she provided leadership and counseling on new and existing IBM work–life programs and initiatives. More specifically, in this role, Joan was responsible for identifying global technology solutions in support of a workforce flexibility executable plan to address employees' expressed needs in the area of work–life balance and workload. She was also responsible for developing and implementing employee and management cultural training consistent with an approved flexibility strategy. Additionally, Joan has created a methodology consistent with IBM Human Resources Research practices to measure results. Joan originally joined IBM in Valhalla, New York in 1980. She has held various positions including Corporate Business Transformation Senior Project Manager, Marketing Operations Manager, and Human Resources Advisory Professional.

Joan also holds a Master's degree in human resource management. Joan is married and currently resides in Somers, New York. She enjoys spending time with family and friends and volunteering at local schools to promote students' interests in technology.

Nicole Givelekian is Research Fellow with the Center for Human Resource Strategy at Rutgers University in New Jersey, USA. Nicole has worked with Schering-Plough Corporation to develop recommendations for a comprehensive work–life balance program for their employees in the United States. Previously, Nicole had worked in human resource management for Siemens Corporation in the United States in the areas of staffing and employee relations. Nicole holds a Master's degree in human resource management from Rutgers University and a BA in labor and employment relations (Rutgers University, Douglass College). Her current research interests include work–life balance program composition and implementation and strategic human resource management.

Mila Lazarova is Assistant Professor of International Business at Simon Fraser University, Canada. She received her PhD in industrial relations and human resource management from Rutgers University in New Jersey, USA. She also holds a Master's degree in international economic relations from the University of National and World Economics in Sofia, Bulgaria. Mila's research interests include expatriate management, with a focus on repatriation and the career impact of international assignments, work–life balance issues related to assignments, global careers, and the role of organizational career development and work–life balance practices on employee retention. She is currently involved in a study of global virtual teams. She was recently awarded a SSHRC-INE grant for an international comparative study of training and development practices. Mila's work has been published in outlets such as the *Journal of World Business* and the *International Journal of Human Resource Management*. She has also contributed chapters to several books on international human resource management and global leadership.

Aline D. Masuda received a Master's degree at Missouri State University and a PhD from the University at Albany, State University of New York in industrial organizational psychology. She has consultant experience in the area of organizational surveys working at International Survey Research, a global consultant firm in Chicago, and at IBM in the areas of workforce research and marketing intelligence. She has been conducting research in the area of work–family balance, motivation, and leadership with emphases in cross-cultural studies. She has published in the areas of leadership and motivation. Currently, she is working as a post-doctoral researcher at IESE Business School, Barcelona.

Shilpa Patel is currently Technical Support and Training Manager for MTL Instruments Group plc. She is responsible for the development of both internal and external customers in Europe, the Middle East and Asia, and for rolling out the training and support function through these regions. At the time of working on the material in this chapter, she was engaged as a consultant in the Department of Organizational Behavior in IESE Business School, University of Navarra. Her role was to build on the previously defined methodology for measuring, assessing, and improving the performance of companies in terms of work–family balance, by developing a practical guide for organizations to follow.

Oana Petrescu is currently Work–Life Programs Manager for IBM Europe, Middle East, and Africa (EMEA). In this role, Oana is working closely with the EMEA Diversity team, providing support in all work–life related areas, from strategy definition to project design and implementation, from data analysis to managing budget and financial processes. In addition, she is responsible for all pan-EMEA Global Work–Life Fund projects related to dependent care. Oana joined IBM in 1996, since then holding positions as human resources manager, human resources and administration manager, and HR specialist. Oana holds a Master's degree in engineering, a Master's in business administration from Henley Management College, and a certification in human resources management from the Romanian–American Post-Graduate School of Business in cooperation with the University of Washington. Oana is married, has one son and currently resides in Bucharest, Romania. Her free time is spent with family and friends, travelling, reading, and playing bridge.

Steven A. Y. Poelmans is currently Academic Director of the International Center of Work and Family and Assistant Professor in the Managing People in Organizations Department of IESE Business School. He has a Master's in organizational psychology (University of Louvain, Belgium), a Master's in marketing management (Vlerick Management School, Belgium), and a PhD in management/organizational behavior (IESE Business School, University of Navarra). His research focuses on work–family conflict, managerial stress, and family-friendly human resource policies.

He teaches organizational behavior, career management, managerial communication, and self-management to MBA students and executives. In his research, teaching, and consulting practice he has developed a cross-cultural approach, doing collaborative international research on managerial stress and work–family conflict, teaching executives in European multinationals in English, Spanish, and Dutch, and consulting in Europe, Central America, and Africa.

He is a founding member of the European Academy of Management and a member of AOM and SIOP. He is editor of the book *Work and Family: An International Research Perspective* (2005) and has published in journals such as the *Human Resource Management Review*, *Personnel Psychology*, *International Journal of Cross-Cultural Management*,

Applied Psychology – An International Review, *Academy of Management Journal*, and *Journal of Organizational Behavior*.

Olena Stepanova holds a Master's degree in the psychology of intercultural actions (University of Nancy 2, France). She graduated in psychology after studying in Ukraine and the USA, and has worked in a personnel consulting company. She has also collaborated with various academic and social institutions.

Currently she is working as a research assistant in the International Center of Work and Family (ICWF) at IESE Business School, University of Navarra. Her research focuses on cultural change, family-friendly policies, work–family and cross-cultural issues, coaching and mentoring.

Cynthia A. Thompson is Professor of Management in the Zicklin School of Business at Baruch College, City University of New York. She teaches undergraduate, MBA, and doctoral courses in organizational behavior, human resource management, and work–life balance. She has been studying work–family issues for over twenty years and has presented her research at numerous national and international conferences. Her work has been published in both scholarly and practitioner journals, including the *Journal of Applied Psychology, Journal of Vocational Behavior, Journal of Occupational and Health Psychology, Sex Roles, Journal of Management Education, Community, Work and Family*, and *Journal of Employee Assistance*. Two of her articles were nominated for the Rosabeth Moss Kanter Award for Excellence in Work–Family Research. Her current research interests are focused on the structural antecedents of work–life culture. In addition to her research and teaching, she has worked as a consultant to the Center for Work and Family in Boston and as Senior Research Associate at the Families and Work Institute, where she co-authored the *2002 National Study of the Changing Workforce*.

Introduction

STEVEN A. Y. POELMANS
IESE Business School, Spain

In the last few decades we have witnessed a trend in the international labor markets that from a historical point of view can be considered as a revolution, as it has caused dramatic shifts in the lives of people and created a new social and economic reality. The percentage of women in the active work population has increased rapidly in the USA, Europe, and Australia, as in many other regions around the world, to reach what seems to be its saturation point in most Scandinavian countries and dramatic increases in some southern European countries such as Spain. As a consequence we have seen the proliferation of dual-income families where role expectations toward men and women, both in their work activities and their domestic responsibilities, have radically changed (Bond, Galinsky, & Swangberg, 1998).

The male model of work prescribes an ideal employee who is male, full-time, and continuously at work from the end of the education, fully committed to the organization, and without any responsibilities outside of work (Lewis, 1997). This model is no longer valid and has become outdated (Bailyn & Harrington, 2004). In addition, we can also observe a change in attitudes toward what constitutes a successful career, especially among the generations X and Y. Young talents have started to question old assumptions about how work is done, how to show commitment, where and when to work, and how to advance in the company. Having a highly paid job and a career no longer seems to be the most important and central objectives of these individuals in life. They strive for a more "complete" life that includes both a successful professional and a personal life. Parallel to these changes in the workforce, work itself has undergone major changes over the last decades. With the introduction of IT and telecommunication technologies work has become more complex and fragmented. Technology has created a sense that life is moving faster and that more and more activities are squeezed into shorter amounts of time. New technologies have made it possible to perform job tasks from everywhere at any time, and have increased the number of interruptions during work as well as expectations of speedy replies, fragmenting time and indirectly, affecting productivity. Employees, especially in professional and managerial work settings, feel increasingly pressured to not only work faster but also to work longer hours (Milliken & Dunn-Jensen, 2005).

We still need to come to grips with the positive and negative consequences of the massive integration of women in the workforce. Among the positive effects are the increase in nations' productivity, the wealth and consumption power of families, the financial independence of women, and an improvement of gender equity. On the other hand, as both men and women are working, family time is coming under pressure. Due to this new mix of gender equity, shifting role expectations, and family time scarcity, many men and women are required to find a new modus vivendi quite different from the traditional breadwinner model. Judging from the high rate of separations and divorces, many couples seem to struggle with the new reality. Separations of couples have resulted in an increasing prevalence of new family forms, like mono-parental and mixed families, in which two single parents together raise their children of previous marriages. In these families, working men and women are experiencing increasing levels of work–family conflict.

In order to avoid or cope with work–family conflict and the resulting strains, couples have started to postpone and control their procreative activity, resulting in an increasing average first childbearing age and a considerable reduction in fertility (most western European countries now have fertility rates below the substitution rate). Only immigration maintains the necessary levels of productivity. In sum, it is clear that although the incorporation of women is improving productivity in the short and mid term, it may have a detrimental effect on the workforce in the long term since there will be a gap between available talent and demand, unless solutions can be found for combining work and caring responsibilities.

We do not need to wait for the next generation to see the clash between this socio-demographic trend and economic reality. Already we see that employers and employees are in opposite camps when they claim more flexibility. For employers, flexibility means availability for the firm, mobility, and willingness to work beyond "nine to five" to meet fluctuations in customer demands. For many employees this translates into long working hours, extra time, and weekends. Employees on the other hand have a kind of flexibility in mind that is almost diametrically opposed to this concept. They refer to availability for the family, working closer to home or at home, and the possibility to interrupt or reduce work to attend family needs and emergencies.

In order to deal with this new paradox, firms have started to adopt what have been coined "family-friendly" or "work–life" human resource policies. This reflects that today's business community increasingly recognizes the importance and value of finding a healthy harmony between professional and personal responsibilities, both in terms of meeting the needs of individual employees and the demands of stakeholders to balance social and economic interests. It has become a critical element within the management of human capital – a vital aspect of corporate governance – to secure a prosperous future for the firm through the management of attraction, retention, promotion, and succession of highly skilled and motivated personnel. With the aging of the work population and the resulting scarcity in certain labor markets, the "war for talent" will only become more intense in the decades to come. Therefore we can expect that work–life policies will only continue to proliferate in firms in the future. Many leading organizations have taken steps to implement comprehensive strategies to aid work–life harmony; these begin with a move to introduce policies and practices that help to alleviate conflict between work, family, and personal responsibilities. However, if such policies and programs are only superimposed on "ideal worker" practices they may not sufficiently contribute to an improved work–life integration of their employees (Bailyn & Harrington, 2004). Policies need to progressively develop into actions centered around engineering a positive cultural change, that is, steps toward creating a strong, supportive, and well-equilibrated professional environment.

The title of the book

Inspired by leading scholars like Susan Lewis and Rhona Rapoport we have become aware that words are not neutral. Therefore a short note on the terms in the title is warranted.

Harmonization

The central term in the title of the book is *harmonizing*. We use the term harmonization to refer to both *relieving conflict* and *seeking enrichment* between the domains of work, family, and personal life. Two competing arguments dominate the scholarly discussion about outcomes associated with the engagement in multiple life roles. According to the scarcity argument, individuals have limited resources and energy. Engaging in multiple roles means competition for these limited resources, thereby causing psychological distress and role strain, since there is only a finite amount of resources and energy available to the individual (Goode, 1960). Based on this argument work–family conflict has been defined as a type of inter-role conflict which is experienced by an individual when the role demands stemming from one domain (work or family) are incompatible with role demands stemming from another domain (family or work) (Greenhaus & Beutell, 1985).[1] Since the late nineteen sixties, hundreds of studies and books have been published, generally or implicitly based on the scarcity argument/role theory, focusing on the antecedents and

---

[1] Work–family conflict has been related to important individual and organizational problems such as absenteeism, intentions to leave work, decreased organizational commitment, and decreased job, family, and life satisfaction (Allen, Herst, Bruck, & Sutton, 2000; Aryee, 1992; Bedeian, Burke, & Moffet, 1988; Higgins, Duxbury, & Irving, 1992; Kossek & Ozeki, 1998; Lyness & Thompson, 1997; Netemeyer, Boles, & McMurrian, 1996; Thomas & Ganster, 1995). In addition, negative mental and physical health outcomes (e.g. depression, stress, job burnout) have been associated with high levels of work–family conflict (Boles, Johnstone, & Hair, 1997; Frone, 2000; Parasuraman, Purohit, Godshalk, & Beutell, 1996). More recently scholars have called for a more balanced approach that recognizes the positive effects of combining work and family roles (e.g. Barnett & Hyde, 2001; Frone, 2003). Experiences in one role can produce positive experiences and outcomes in the other role. Greenhaus and Powell (2006) refer to this mechanism as work–family enrichment. Work–family enrichment as well as work–family conflict is bi-directional; work can interfere with family (referred to as work-to-family conflict or work-to-family enrichment when work experiences improve the quality of family life) and family can interfere with work (referred to as family-to-work conflict or family-to-work enrichment respectively; Frone, Russell, & Cooper, 1992; Greenhaus & Powell, 2006). In addition, time-based, strain-based, or behavior-based work–family conflict can be distinguished (Greenhaus & Beutell, 1985). Time-based conflict occurs when role pressures stemming from the two different domains compete for the individual's time. For example, an employee who is unexpectedly asked to travel abroad may fail to attend a sick child. Strain-based conflict occurs when the strain experienced in one role domain interferes with effective performance of role behaviors in the other domain. For instance, a father who had to deal with a mounting conflict at work may come back home irritated and bad-tempered, resulting in shouting at his children. Behavior-based conflict is described as conflict stemming from incompatible behaviors demanded by competing roles. An example is a military officer commanding her children as if they were little soldiers.

consequences of work–family *conflict*. Until very recently, it was the dominant paradigm. Over the last decade, the work–family literature has begun to pick up the argument of enhancement theory (e.g. Barnett & Hyde, 2001; Frone, 2003; Greenhaus and Powell, 2005). Very much in the spirit of positive psychology, followers of the enhancement theory (Marks, 1977; Sieber, 1974) work on the premises that engaging in multiple roles can have a positive and enhancing effect on the individual. Their argument is based on the assumption that multiple roles generate social and economic resources. Accordingly, involvement in multiple roles often generates social support, added income, increased self-complexity, and opportunities to experience success, which in turn can create a satisfactory self-image and life situation (Barnett & Hyde, 2001). Experiences in one role can produce positive experiences and outcomes in the other role. From our point of view both the conflict and enrichment perspectives are relevant for designing policies in the firm. Therefore we integrate them under the term *harmonization*.

Work, family, and personal life

In this book some authors use the terms work–family and work–life policies interchangeably, although one may argue that these are not neutral terms and reflect the degree of inclusion of different employee groups: employees with families (work–family policies) or both employees with and without families (work–life policies). Many firms see the issue as even broader and speak of diversity policies, to include employees of different gender orientation, race, and culture. We choose to distinguish family and personal life, although many could argue that family is part of personal life, for two reasons. First, we want to recognize and stress that when designing policies, we need to keep in mind both groups, employees with families and employees without families. Many firms focus on – or give priority to – employees with families, as they are considered to be more in need of firm support given their responsibility over others. The degree of inclusion is an ethical and strategic decision of the firm, and often reflects the socio-cultural set-up of the labor force or client base and stakeholders of the firm. Second, even if firms decide to focus on employees with families alone, it is recommended they think of work–family policies encompassing benefits that directly enhance the personal life of the employee, as activities aimed at personal development and harmony will indirectly impact the employee's family life.

The purpose of the book: from policy to practice

The purpose of the book is to provide the reader with ideas and guidelines on how to create a working environment that encourages the harmonization of work, family, and personal life, while respecting the bottom line. Although many books on individual work–family conflict and dual-income families have been published, few of them pretend to offer a practical guide to managers who want to develop work–life policies and practices in the firm. This book points at the strengths and pitfalls associated with different types of work–life policies, and explains the necessity of a supportive culture, and the development of work practices that promote this harmonization. By going beyond formal policies, and emphasizing the need for practice, we recognize the fundamental importance of the support and accountability of middle managers, an often strongly underestimated source of failure in implementing these policies. The book is very practical in nature, illustrating different points with cases and examples, and helping firms to assess themselves on different dimensions by providing easy-to-use checklists and questionnaires. The scope of the book is clearly international, with contributions from authors from three continents. We pretend to offer ideas and advice that is neutral to the specific legislative context of the firm, which falls outside the scope of this book. We encourage our readers from different parts of the world to take inspiration from the many examples given throughout the book and to take innovative initiatives that are compatible with their labor markets and legal contexts. This is a book for (human resource) managers who are about to embark on developing work–life policies, or who want to deploy policies in subsidiaries of their firms in different regions around the world. Second, it will be of interest and use to a broad range of practitioners, teachers, consultants, and coaches who want to advise their clients or students in the development of these policies.

The content of the book

In this book, we are covering a broad spectrum of concerns for human resource scholars, managers, and consultants who are interested in (the theme of) adopting, designing, and implementing work–life policies. The book is organized into three parts. In the first part – "Describing different work–life policies, policy development, and pitfalls," comprising Chapters 1 to 5 – the authors describe various work–life policies introduced in different working environments and their role in the harmonization of work, family, and personal life. In the second part – "Policy design, implementation, and deployment," comprising Chapters 6 and 7 – implementation and policy development is presented and commented upon. In the third part – "Cultural change," comprising Chapters 8 and 9 – the authors present ideas on how to plan and implement change, as well as barriers to a successful employment of change.

With Chapter 1 – "Strategic HR and work–life balance" – Paula Caligiuri and Nicole Givelekian (both Rutgers University, USA) open the book with a broad strategic HR perspective, focusing on employees who occupy critical or core positions in the organization and excel in them. As a result of the centrality to a firm's success, core positions tend to be associated with high stress, long working hours, and constant spillover from work to personal life. In order to reduce the risk of stress and burnout, prevent decreased job satisfaction and occupational commitment, and ultimately improve firm productivity, the authors argue in favor of promoting work–life balance among core employees. The authors affirm the importance of taking into account individual differences and personal characteristics as they affect employees' perceptions of their work–life balance, when they feel out of balance, the amount of spillover they are comfortable with, etc. As core employees tend to be achievers and high-performers it is crucial for the company not to over-utilize them, causing stress, ill-effects, and turnover intentions. The authors suggest several ways to promote greater balance in core employees, like services helping reduce the non-work hassles, wellness programs to increase employees' physical and psychological well-being, and recreational activities.

In Chapter 2 – "Reviewing policies for harmonizing work, family, and personal life" – Steven Poelmans (IESE Business School, Spain) and Barbara Beham (University of Hamburg, Germany) analyze traditional human resource policies and practices aimed at improving the work–family balance of employees in organizations. In order to guarantee that the review of these policies and practices does not remain at a purely theoretical level, the authors provide examples of work–life

programs and policies successfully implemented in various companies.
First, they briefly address the adoption decision. Second, they describe
the human resource policies known for possibly improving work–life
balance, providing practical examples of companies which have
implemented single policies as well as bundles of work–life arrangements. They offer a detailed overview of flexibility policies, leave
arrangements, care provisions, supportive arrangements, and conventional provisions for job quality and compensations/benefits. They also
provide useful checklists stating the business benefits, advantages, and
disadvantages of these work–life arrangements. Finally, the authors
point out the importance of creating a family-supportive organizational
culture and introduce a new paradigm for work–life harmonization.

In Chapter 3 – "Integrating career development and work–family
policy" – Tammy Allen (University of South Florida, USA) examines
the intersection between individual and organizational career development with that of work–family needs and policies. First the author
reviews the literature examining career implications for individuals as a
function of their family structure and use of family-supportive benefits.
She gives examples of various studies showing ample evidence that
family and using family-supportive benefits may be detrimental to an
employee's career, resulting in fewer promotions, smaller salary
increases, and decreased involvement in training opportunities. Next
she offers recommendations for integrating work and family with
employee development. For instance, she suggests expanding ideas
regarding flexibility by constructing the flexibility concept so as to
encompass the entire career course. This way, taking a few months/
years should not be a barrier to future career advancement prospects.
Also, she proposes to implement mentoring programs as a way to
increase a company's competitive advantage through employee
learning and development. In addition, supervisors' support in meeting
non-work demands is introduced as a way of alleviating employees'
work–family conflict. Therefore training supervisors in employee
family concerns might encourage the usage of work–family programs
and help both supervisors and employees improve their quality of life.
It can also help the former acquire such skills as flexibility, promoting
cross-training among employees, communication, coordination, and
team-building.

In Chapter 4 – "Work–life balance on global assignments" – Paula
Caligiuri (Rutgers University, USA) and Mila Lazarova (Simon Fraser

University, Canada) address the importance of companies supporting employees on global assignments in managing their work–life balance as both the employee and the family are going through an adaptation phase. Therefore to contribute to the successful outcome of the assignment, these organizations must become more involved in the non-work aspects of their assignees and families (e.g. help establish social ties, find communities, re-establish hobbies, sports, and places of worship in the host countries.). In the first part of the chapter the authors complete an important informative task by tackling in detail the adjustment difficulties the expatriate, and his/her partner and children might experience during relocation. They also bring into the discussion a new category of "assignees" – "non-traditional expatriates" or "flexpatriates" – and describe personal and family challenges they are facing. Then they highlight some examples of the practices organizations have developed to enhance global assignees' work–life balance. The practices comprise pre-departure decision-making; cross-cultural training, including language skills training; in-country support – including various networks and services, but also special in-company policies; career assistance, accompanying partner support, and general work–life assistance. In addition to covering the difficulties emerging on global assignments, the authors make sure to mention the positive outcomes for the assignees as well as their families.

In Chapter 5, Joan Gentilesco-Giue and Oana Petrescu (both IBM) present an IBM case study, a story about changing mindsets at IBM. A globally conducted survey showed the existing need of balancing the work and life of IBM's employees. Therefore it required the application of new management strategies that would "empower" the employees in the workplace and help adapt their needs of balancing work and life to the place of work. First, the authors describe the existing work–life strategy and work–life programs. Next they concentrate on the concrete steps IBM took on the global level. Besides the introduction of different work–life benefits, they address change of unnecessary/ unproductive work practices and the improvement of the workplace, so that employees feel comfortable there. Nevertheless, the authors mainly focus on the change of the mindset of both managers and employees relative to the acceptance of a flexible work environment at IBM and different supporting tools provided by the company.

In Chapter 6 – "Stages in the implementation of work–family policies" – Steven Poelmans (IESE Business School, Spain), Shilpa Patel

(MTL Instruments Group, UK), and Barbara Beham (University of Hamburg, Germany) discuss how work–life policies can be implemented and applied in general (implementation) and in specific cases (allowance) to reduce conflicts between responsibilities at work, in the family, and in personal life. They focus on how to identify a realistic path for development; where to begin when introducing initiatives; what challenges companies face; and what pitfalls some organizations have already encountered in the implementation of improvement opportunities. The authors introduce the four-phase "Family Responsible Company Development Model," based on five consecutive national surveys of work–life policies in organizations in Spain, which defines the organization's present status in terms of family responsibility. The phases are described through the lenses of the four fundamental elements of change that are: policies, practices, culture, and enablers. The model, being an instrument of change, is complemented by on-line evaluation and diagnostic tools designed to help assess the needs and priorities of the organization in its development towards a family responsible firm.

In Chapter 7 – "Policy deployment across borders: a framework for work–life initiatives in multinational enterprises" (MNEs) – Anne Bardoel and Helen De Cieri (both of Monash University, Australia) discuss the advantages of a global work–life strategy and the challenge of work–life policies introduction across a global context with the consideration of local conditions. Most significantly, the chapter provides practical advice to organizations, especially to human resource practitioners in MNEs. The authors develop a framework that can be used to guide managers' decision-making to build a global work–life strategy and they illustrate how this framework can be applied, by analyzing approaches to work–life strategy in several MNEs. To highlight the challenges that managers may face, the authors compare an MNE that is at an early stage of developing a work–life strategy with other firms that are well advanced in this area. In this way they provide examples of strategies in which managers deal with such challenges.

In Chapter 8 – "Barriers to the implementation and usage of work–life policies" – Cynthia Thompson (Baruch College, CUNY, USA) addresses the causes of (non-)usage of work–life policies, such as poor communication, fears of detrimental career effects, improper implementation of programs, or absence of technical and management support. The author reflects on potential barriers that may impede the successful implementation and utilization of work–life programs. First she discusses the underlying assumptions and values that influence the way employees and employers think about work and family. Then she spells out specific barriers that may occur at the planning and implementation stage of work–life programs. Finally, she presents a model that highlights barriers at each of the following levels: organization-level (e.g. organizational culture), work-group level (e.g. supportiveness of co-workers and supervisors), and individual-level (e.g. knowledge of work–life programs). Throughout the chapter examples are provided of organizations that have struggled with these issues, and of how they overcame them.

In Chapter 9 – "Proposing a model for cultural change" – Steven Poelmans and Olena Stepanova (both of IESE Business School, Spain) propose a model for cultural change, with the ultimate goal of reaching work–personal life integration which would satisfy both the needs of the employees and those of the company. First, they introduce the main concepts that support the process of change. Then they give a short overview of what impacts the process of change and describe the existing models of cultural change. By addressing employees' assumptions regarding work–life balance, fears towards innovations, existing values, myths, and practices, and by working with resistance, the authors build up a model for cultural change based on Collaborative Interactive Action Research. The presented model consists of two main parts: preparation for change and introduction of the change process. The authors illustrate in detail the whole process of change by describing different practices used in real cases, like framing the project as an experiment, using pictures and metaphors, reinforcing different behaviors, using role models, and creating a working atmosphere impregnated by certain meanings and values.

Acknowledgments

The very first seeds of this book project were academic and practical in nature and were sown in 2003. At that time I was writing books on work–family research and practice for academics (Lawrence Erlbaum, 2005) and a broad audience (Lannoo, 2004; McGraw-Hill, 2005) and decided to complete the "trilogy" with a book for (human resource) managers and consultants. I found support for these initial ideas from

Petra Vandendriessche and Sonia Van Ballaert, at that time respectively Senior Consultant and Partner Human Capital Management at IBM Business Consulting Services in Belgium. We organized a small seminar for human resource managers and felt strengthened in our faith that little by little, companies were starting to get interested in the theme, but lacked guidance. Later on Karla Bousquet and Ingrid De Bock, both of IBM, made sure the project received continuing support and lifted the project up from a regional to a global level. This would ultimately result in the IBM case study in this book, written by Joan Gentilesco-Giue and Oana Petrescu of the IBM Corporation.

In the following years I presented the book project to several publishers. After having received the generous support of an American-based publisher for the academic volume (Lawrence Erlbaum) I wanted to collaborate with a European-based publisher with a strong reputation in the academic press but with ambitions for divulgating academic work relevant for practice. Cambridge University Press united both characteristics and was kind enough to lend its support. I am deeply grateful for the confidence and patience I have received ever since. I would like to especially mention the different editors that accompanied the project from its beginning (Katy Plowright) to the end (Paula Parish).

This book would have been impossible without the contributions of the authors. When I started conceptualizing the book I asked for the support of Paula Caligiuri as co-editor and co-author, as I wanted the book to have a distinct human resource management focus. Paula took responsibility for two chapters for which she collaborated with Nicole Givelekian and Mila Lazarova respectively. Her moral support throughout the project has proven to be vital. As a group, the authors work in three different continents (America, Europe, and Oceania), have backgrounds in management, industrial and organizational psychology, human resource management, project management, change management, engineering and IT technology, and deal with work–life issues, either as academics, consultants, or industry experts. Together they form an excellent, multidisciplinary and multicultural team answering a broad but very practical question: How can I turn my organization into a company that offers solutions to the increasing conflict between work, family, and personal life? Tammy Allen and Cynthia Thompson started working on their chapters during their sabbatical visit to the IESE Business School in the summer of 2005.

Anne Bardoel and Helen De Cieri joined the group later on, after the founding conference of the International Center of Work and Family in Barcelona, as their research on the globalization of policies fit well with the international scope of the book. Barbara Beham and Shilpa Patel contributed to various chapters with the literature research they conducted as part of projects at the International Center of Work and Family. Throughout the process the authors were backed up by an extraordinary team of people. Without their support the book would have been a mere idea: Olena Stepanova and Aline Masuda, my dear research and editorial assistants at IESE Business School, who coordinated the multiple stakeholders involved in this project, in addition to contributing with their own writing and editing of various chapters. The quality of the book has been safeguarded thanks to the patient work and feedback of the reviewers: Jean-Luc Cerdin, Ariane Ollier-Malaterre, Oana Petrescu, Wendy Andrews-De Waal, Joy Schneer, Helen De Cieri, Herminia Sanz, Montse Moliner, Consuelo Leon, Joan Giue, Sebastian Reiche, Javier Quintanilla, Anne Bardoel, Sara Moulton Reger, Jaime Pereira, and Aline Masuda. Their names reflect a cultural diversity I wanted to respect to make the chapters relevant from any (Western) point of view. Last but not least I would like to thank my employer IESE Business School/University of Navarra, and more specifically my mentor and colleague Nuria Chinchilla, Director of the International Center of Work and Family, for their support and enlightening example in the fight for a worthy cause: making our lives and the lives of our families compatible with having a fulfilling career.

Thank you, all of you, those who have I mentioned and those I was negligent enough to not mention.

Steven Poelmans
Barcelona, May 2007

References

Allen, T.D., Herst, D.E.L., Bruck, C.S., & Sutton, M. (2000). Consequences associated with work-to-family conflict: A review and agenda for future research. *Journal of Occupational Health Psychology*, 5, 278–308.

Aryee, S. (1992). Antecedents and outcomes of work–family conflict among married professional women: Evidence from Singapore. *Human Relations*, 45, 813–37.

Bailyn, L. & Harrington, M. (2004). Redesigning work for work–family integration. *Community Work and Family*, 7, 197–208.

Barnett, R. C. & Hyde, J. S. (2001). Women, men, work, and family. *American Psychologist*, 56, 781–796.

Bedian, A. G., Burke, B. G., & Moffett, R. G. (1988). Outcomes of work–family conflict among married male and female professionals. *Journal of Management*, 14, 475–491.

Boles, J. S., Johnston, M. W., & Hair, J. F. (1997). Role stress, work–family conflict and emotional exhaustion: Inter-relationships and effects on some work-related consequences. *Journal of Personal Selling & Sales Management*, 1, 17–28.

Bond, J. T., Galinsky, E., & Swangberg, J. E. (1998). *The 1997 National Study of Changing Workplace*. New York: Families and Work Institute.

Burke, R. J. (1988). Some antecedents and consequences of work–family conflict. *Journal of Social Behavior and Personality*. 3(4), 287–302.

Frone, M. R. (2000). Work–family conflict and employee psychiatric disorders: The National Co-morbidity Survey. *Journal of Applied Psychology*, 85, 888–895.

Frone, M. R. (2003). Work–family balance. In J. C. Quick & L. E. Tetrick (eds), *Handbook of Occupational Health Psychology* (pp. 143–162). Washington, DC: American Psychological Association.

Frone, M. R., Russel, M., & Cooper, M. L. (1992a). Antecedents and outcomes of work–family conflict: Testing a model of the work–family interface. *Journal of Applied Psychology*, 77, 65–78.

Goode, W. J. (1960). A theory of role strain. *American Sociological Review*, 25, 483–96.

Greenhaus, J. & N. Beautell (1985). Sources of conflict between work and family roles. *Academy of Management Review*, 10, 76–88.

Greenhaus, J. H. & Powell, G. N. (2006). When work and family are allies: A theory of work–family enrichment. *Academy of Management Review*, 31(1), 72–92.

Higgins, C. A., Duxbury, L. E., & Irving, R. H. (1992). Work–family conflict in the dual-career family. *Organizational Behavior and Human Decision Processes*, 51, 51–75.

Kossek, E. E. & Ozeki, C. (1998). Work–family conflict, policies, and the job–life satisfaction relationship: A review and directions for organizational behavior–human resources research. *Journal of Applied Psychology*, 83, 139–149.

Lewis, J. (1997). Lone mothers: The British case. In J. Lewis (ed.), *Lone Mothers in European Welfare Regimes – Shifting Policy Logics*. London: Jessica Kingsley.

Lyness, K. S. & Thompson, D. (1997). Above the glass ceiling? A comparison of matched samples of female and male executives. *Journal of Applied Psychology*, 82, 359–375.

Marks, S. R. (1977). Multiple roles and role strain: Some notes on human energy, time and commitment. *American Sociological Review*, 42, 921–936.

Milliken, F. J. & Dunn-Jensen, L. M. (2005). The changing time demands of managerial and professional work: implications for managing the work–life boundary. In Kossek, E. E. & Lambert, S. J. (eds). *Work and Life Integration: Organizational, Cultural, and Individual Perspectives* (pp. 43–59). Mahwah, NJ: Lawrence Erlbaum Associates.

Netemeyer, R. G., Boles, J. S., & McMurrian, R. (1996). Development and validation of work–family conflict and family–work conflict scales. *Journal of Applied Psychology*, 81, 400–410.

Parasuraman, S., Purohit, Y. S., Godshalk, V. M., & Beutell, N. J. (1996). Work and family variables, entrepreneurial career success, and psychological well-being. *Journal of Vocational Behavior*, 48, 275–300.

Poelmans S. A. Y. (ed.) (2005). *Work and Family: An International Research Perspective*. Mahwah, NJ: Lawrence Erlbaum Associates.

Sieber, S. D. (1974). Toward a theory of role accumulation. *American Sociological Review*, 39, 567–578.

Thomas, L. T. & Ganster, D. C. (1995). Impact of family-supportive work variables on work–family conflict and strain: A control perspective. *Journal of Applied Psychology*, 80, 6–15.

PART I

Describing different work–life policies, policy development, and pitfalls

1 Strategic human resources and work–life balance

PAULA CALIGIURI and NICOLE GIVELEKIAN
Rutgers University, USA

Ways to improve the firm's financial success and market competitiveness are a top priority for business executives. Ways to improve employees' work–life balance, unfortunately, tend to be much lower on the priority lists of most executives. Today, however, two trends in combination have pushed the need for greater work–life balance further up the priority list: the *changing demographics of today's workforce* and the *increase in incidences of stress and burnout*. Work–life imbalance and the associated conflict have been shown to be related to decreased feelings of well-being (Kinnunen & Mauno, 1998), increased psychological and physical complaints (Frone, Russel, & Cooper, 1992), and increased job and life dissatisfaction (Netemeyer, Boles, & McMurrian, 1996). Maintaining the work–life balance of key employees helps reduce the risk of stress and burnout (Bacharach, Bamberger, & Conley, 1991) and can ultimately improve firms' overall success (Arthur, 2003; Konrad & Mangel, 2000; Meyer, Mukerjee, & Sestero, 2001; Perry-Smith & Blum, 2000). The effects of burnout from extreme stress not only encompass physiological, psychological, and behavioral consequences for employees, but may also include decreased job satisfaction, occupational commitment, and overall work success. Together, these negative factors can directly affect a firm's bottom line, especially when present among a firm's key employees.

Over the past twenty years, workforce demographic shifts have been profound, with some of these shifts having the potential for a negative influence on work–life balance. For example, in almost all developed nations around the world, dual-earner families are commonplace, populations are aging, and birth rates are declining (see Bond, Thompson, Galinsky, & Prottas (2003) and the OECD (2001) for reviews of the changing demographics affecting work–life balance). These demographic trends suggest that individuals have less of a traditional support at home (i.e. one spouse taking care of the home), less of a child-centered family life (i.e. children being a diversion from work), and more work centrality, especially among well-educated career professionals (i.e. self-worth may be originating more from work roles than other life roles). Independently, these three trends are *not necessarily* problematic for individuals' sense of personal work–life balance. (There are many well-balanced married or single childless career-oriented people.) However, these three trends *in combination* with demands for greater productivity at work may be negatively affecting individuals' work–life balance. In other words, while changes in workplace demographics may have created the potential for a strain on work–life balance, the demands of the work itself have made achieving work–life balance more difficult and stress and burnout more prevalent.

Researchers from Europe define workplace stress as the relationship between psychosocial work characteristics, such as high demands, low control, and low support, and general health and safety in policy areas such as productivity, labor market forces, company image, and total quality management (Kompier & Cooper, 1999). Similarly, the American Institute of Stress defines job stress as the harmful physical and emotional responses that occur when the requirements of the job do not match the capabilities, resources, or needs of the worker. Burnout is the result of prolonged exposure to these stressful environments where an employee does not have control over changing or complex work situations and is unable to perceive benefits despite his or her increased effort. Ongoing exposure to this type of stressful working condition is particularly dangerous for individuals' physical and mental well-being. The negative outcomes of stress are tangible and beginning to be well documented.

The cover of *Fortune's* November 2005 issue was dedicated to the stress and burnout of the most elite group of employees within organizations today – the executive level. In this issue, senior male executives were surveyed about their issues of work–life balance.[1] While 49 percent of the respondents were self-described workaholics,

---

[1] This *Fortune Magazine* poll (November 28, 2005) is unique for two reasons. The first is that the sample was of senior executives. The second was that it focused on men. In the past, work–life balance issues tended to be viewed as a predominantly "female" topic and more relevant for those in less professional careers.

64 percent stated that at this stage of their life they would choose more time over money. While a request for greater work–life balance was once considered a sign of weakness, 80 percent of the members from this high-powered group of survey respondents agreed with the following statement: "I am comfortable talking with my boss about the issue of balancing work and the things outside of work that are important to me." With a heightened sensitivity for work–life balance issues, 98 percent said that they are sympathetic to requests from their own direct reports for a better work–life balance. The most profound result was that 87 percent of the respondents agreed that the companies that restructure senior management jobs in ways that would both increase productivity and make more time for a life outside the office would have a **competitive advantage** in attracting talent.

Labor market issues affecting strategic offering of work–life benefits

Before we begin our discussion of the organizational factors affecting whether companies select to offer work–life benefits, it is important to discuss the factors that are out of the firms' control – the contextual factors embedded in the environment where the firms operate. These contextual factors are often either labor market related factors (e.g. a tight external labor market, competitors offering work–life benefits, labor markets with a high percentage of women) or country-level factors (e.g. cultural differences in norms toward work–life balance, and government regulations). Both of these sets of contextual factors, labor market related and country-level, are briefly described in this section (see Poelmans & Sahibzada (2004) for a comprehensive review).

Labor market related contextual factors

While McKinsey's *The War for Talent* (1997) study was originally published in the late 1990s, attracting and retaining the best talent who can successfully fill the most strategic positions continue to be the most competitive significant challenges facing organizations today. Not much has changed in ten years – in certain labor markets, in certain sectors, the availability of talent is scarce so the inducements needed to attract, recruit, and retain are increased. The clearest example of this is in the company SAS, a software company based out of North Carolina.

As a result of the global trend towards increased use and development of technology, the labor market has an ever-increasing demand for individuals with backgrounds in technical development. As this is a profession that requires extensive education and training, the labor market supply is often scarce, making the employees holding these positions feel overworked as they attempt to compensate for the lack of peers in their field.

Being that SAS is a private software company whose success thrives upon attracting and retaining the best employees in the computer technology field, they have designed their company and community to provide exceptional work–life benefits to their employees, allowing them to be more successful individually and collectively within the company. For example, SAS practices a 35-hour workweek and offers flexible work arrangements within those workweeks as well. The company uniquely offers an on-site work–life department that is run by social workers, a 50,000 square yard fitness center that employees can use on work time to relieve stress, and a staff of doctors, nurses, and physical therapists available to the employees at any time, all at no expense to the employee. As a result of these work–life balance implementations, the company enjoys an extremely low turnover rate of 3 percent, low absenteeism, and high employee and customer satisfaction. The company believes in feeding the spirit of their employees so that they will be more creative and dedicated to enhancing the success of the company, which is a goal they appear to be achieving through the implementation of their unique work–life balance benefits.

Country-level contextual factors

Cultures differ on the extent to which they focus on career success over quality of life, or vice versa. Status-motivated societies believe that career success in its own right is valuable and will expend much effort to achieve, even at the expense of a personal life. In these status-motivated cultures, you are more likely to observe people who opt to work on weekends, take fewer and shorter vacations, answer emails and make work-related calls from home. Balance-motivated societies believe that different spheres of one's life may co-exist but should not interfere with each other, if at all possible. While professional careers may be equally important to people in these balance-oriented cultures, individuals tend to be motivated by the intrinsic rewards of the career. For example, in some balance-motivated cultures additional compensation is not as motivating a reward as compared to additional vacation. It is not uncommon for people in balance-oriented cultures to take summer vacations ranging from two to four weeks, which may seem an excessive number of consecutive vacation days for those in status-oriented cultures.

In addition to cultural factors, government regulations will also influence the work–life practices a firm will offer. For example, in the United States, the average employee works 1,976 hours per year, roughly the equivalent of a 40-hour work week for 50 weeks of the year. In contrast, the average German employee works 1,556 hours per year, or the equivalent of 35 hours per week for less than 45 weeks. The country with the lowest average annual hours worked is the Netherlands, where the average employee works 1,368 hours per year, or the equivalent of 35 hours per week for 39 weeks of the year. One factor that drives up the US annual hours relative to the other countries is that most European workers are entitled to many more vacation days than US workers are. Also playing a crucial role in the reduction of hours in the workweek internationally are governmental regulations. In France, for instance, the 35-hour workweek became law for firms with more than 20 employees as of 2000. In 1997, Belgium's prominent labor and academic leaders called for a shift to a 35-hour workweek and the main trade unions and the Socialist Party endorsed a 4-day, 32-hour workweek. In Italy, the workweek has reduced from 40 hours to 35 hours as of 2001 through legislation and financial incentives that guide collective bargaining in this locale (Jacobs & Gornick, 2001).

Organizational issues and the strategic offering of work–life benefits

With an understanding of the contextual necessity in the previous section, the balance of this chapter is dedicated to the competitive advantage which can be achieved through human talent. This section will focus on the choices firms make to differentially adopt and offer work–life benefits in order to become more competitive. There are three primary reasons companies should take a strategic view of their work–life balance practices: (1) *attracting and retaining key talent*;

(2) *increasing the time capacity of key talent*; and (3) *maximizing the performance of key talent*. These three will be reviewed below with some illustration of the strategic offering of work–life balance benefits.

Attract and retain key talent

Companies that are able to offer greater work–life balance to their high-functioning core employees are more able to attract and retain top talent. Several studies have demonstrated the link between attraction, retention, and citizenship of talent and organizational work–life balance practices (e.g. Aryee, Luk, & Stone, 1998; Grover & Crooker, 1995; Kossek & Nichol, 1992; Lambert, 2000; Osterman, 1995). Thus, *companies best able to offer highly-motivated high-performing individuals (who occupy core positions) opportunities to achieve within their chosen professions – in a manner consistent with their definitions of "work–life balance" – will achieve a competitive advantage by attracting and retaining the best talent.*

One company that provides an excellent example of this is Verizon Wireless. This US-based telecommunications company places a great deal of emphasis on its employees having the opportunity to advance within the company so that they can achieve their individual professional goals in the professional area of their choice. For example, the company is consistently growing in size, market share, and profitability, and encourages their employees to grow with them. What this entails for the employees is the opportunity to develop their individual talents in different areas of the organization so that they have the knowledge and experience to achieve their professional goals while bringing the organization to higher levels of success. Employees with the motivation and desire to achieve their highest goals within their profession will have the opportunity to do so through their performance within the company. Actually, some of the company's top executives began their careers in the company's entry-level call center positions and broadened their experience throughout the company's various functional areas to the point where they continually accepted more responsibility and rose to the rankings of an executive, displaying the company's opportunities for extensive advancement. By doing this, the company is able to attract the best employees into the organization, and then develop them to be even better. A critical contributor to the Verizon Wireless's success with this initiative is the extensive work–life balance options that are provided to employees. Some elements of these options include generous tuition assistance, emergency back-up dependent care, a 24-hour resource and referral center, flexible work arrangements, and a self-service environment where employees are provided the tools and resources to find and utilize all information that they may need.

Increase the time capacity of key talent

Every job has more and less desirable tasks. For those in core positions, organizations should consider reducing the non-productive aspects of the jobs to allow more time for the important aspects of the jobs. This is important because the elimination of non-productive activities would limit core employees' work time, but not diminish their productivity. Operating under intense time pressure, or in what Perlow (1999) refers to as a *time famine*, can create a feeling of overwork, which can lead to stress and job dissatisfaction, possibly creating strain-based work–family conflict (Greenhaus & Beutell, 1985; Kossek & Lambert, 2005). If either side of the work–life balance equation is disproportionately swayed, there is going to be a natural converse effect on the other role. For example, work–life balance is achieved when an individual is able to successfully fulfill the demands and responsibilities associated with his or her professional work while fulfilling the demands of his or her personal life in such a way that neither priority is neglected.

When an employee experiences higher levels of stress in his or her professional role, his or her personal role will suffer from negative repercussions. Likewise, if an employee experiences above average stress levels in his or her personal role, his or her professional role will reflect this negative imbalance. Therefore, to reduce the level of stress that employees encounter on the job, organizations are encouraged to reconstruct core jobs so that key employees are working smarter hours, not longer hours. Flextime, for example, may enable employees to have greater control and less stress associated with the freedom to allocate their work and life time (e.g. Christensen & Staines, 1990; Scandura & Lankau, 1997). Time-based practices (such as flextime) or "family-friendly" policies have the added benefits of increasing employee satisfaction, improving retention, and increasing performance (Grover & Crooker, 1995). Other practices help employees expand their time allocation by allowing spheres of their lives (e.g. work and family) to comfortably co-exist. For example, on-site daycare centers may be convenient for employees with small children, but they also enable working parents more time with their children, improving and perhaps ultimately giving them a greater sense of perceived balance.

Another way to improve individuals' time famine is to help reduce their life hassles. Picking up the dry cleaning, going grocery shopping, paying bills are, for most people, less desirable and time-consuming activities. Some organizations, in an attempt to improve work–life balance have tried to offer services to help reduce the non-work hassles that encroach on employees' free time. Among these emerging work–life benefits that are more frequently being offered are on-site credit unions and ATMs, on-site dry cleaning and shoe repair services, prepaid legal services, on-site mailing services, and pick-up/drop-off programs for car repairs, oil changes, and inspections. In addition to offering services for these less desirable activities, organizations are also offering services for employees to accomplish other non-work activities that employees view as important, however, because of work–life imbalance, may not be accomplished to the extent that is desired.

Common services that are being offered to address this need are financial planning or personal financial consulting, college coaching, and elder-care resource and referral programs. Additionally, these services have the capability to identify resources in any community across the country to meet employees' needs and provide customized referrals to match individual needs. For example, a parent who is interested in locating a child development center for their toddler that offers bilingual instructors, cultural outings, and is located within five miles of their place of work can contact the third-party resource and referral service at any time of the day or night to be provided with a detailed list of centers meeting their specifications. This allows the employee to utilize his or her time away from the workplace more effectively because they no longer need to spend time researching all of the local child development centers which may or may not fulfill their needs or take time off from work to accomplish this task. Therefore, their employer has successfully reduced the employee's non-work hassles, allowing the employee to have a greater sense of work–life balance. In a survey used to assess the effectiveness of this third-party resource and referral service, 98 percent of respondents rated the service as good or excellent and said they would utilize it again

(New York State Family Benefits Program, 2006). Regarding the impact that this program has on work–life balance, employees utilizing the service stated that it has helped to reduce their stress and save them time, thereby allowing them to be more productive in both their professional and personal lives.

Maximize the performance of key talent

Individuals' feelings of work–life balance can also be affected by the amount of perceived time employees have for the maintenance of their own health, wellness, and fitness. In the work–life balance equation, many firms have developed wellness programs in an attempt to improve individuals' work and personal lives by increasing their physical and psychological well-being. In other words, improve the mental and physical health of employees for them to achieve more from their hours on and off work. In fact, these programs have demonstrated to be a sound financial investment. Some research has shown that employer-sponsored wellness programs have a positive impact on the sponsoring firms' bottom line and that companies can expect a return of $2 to $10 for every dollar invested in wellness programs. This return is based on an increase in productivity, and a decrease in disability days, sick leave, absenteeism, and workers' compensation (Corporate Leadership Council, 2003).

Both the quality of time (increased productivity) and the quantity of time (decreased absenteeism) can improve with wellness programs. Realizing this potential, companies such as AstraZeneca have begun offering programs designed to ensure physical and psychological well-being. Merck, for example, currently offers comprehensive employee assistance and behavioral healthcare programs and a Health Alliance program. Similarly, Schering-Plough offers an employee assistance and behavioral healthcare program, while also offering on-site medical services, medical screenings, immunizations, and wellness lectures. Johnson & Johnson, moreover, offers a unique benefit aimed at encouraging and supporting the wellness of nursing mothers. Available in some of their locations is a quiet and comfortable facility staffed with trained professional counselors to assist new mothers at successfully breastfeeding while returning to work.

The aim of these and other such wellness programs is two-fold. First, companies seek to decrease the amount of time away from work due to disability, sick leave, or unspecified absenteeism. Secondly, companies aim to improve the health of employees so that they are able to work more effectively and efficiently on the job. By doing so, the result of decreased costs for the organization is seen in fewer workers' compensation claims, less lost productivity, and lower healthcare expenses. The *Journal of Occupational and Environmental Medicine* cites that healthcare expenditures are nearly 50 percent greater for workers who report high stress levels, so by reducing the level of occupational stress for employees, the company stands to benefit from significantly decreased healthcare expenses. Regarding absenteeism, the US Bureau of Labor Statistics found that a median of twenty-five days away from work occurs because of occupational stress, which is over four times the median absence for all injuries and illnesses. This finding serves to support the immense gains resulting from decreased costs and increased productivity that companies can benefit from by focusing on their employees' wellness. Organizations also stand to benefit from a workforce that is better able to deal with job-related stressors, as well as able to concentrate on job-related tasks and issues without losing focus due to personal matters on their mind. Decreases in stress also lead to less fatigue, anxiety, or other adverse psycho-physiological consequences being experienced, allowing the quality of both professional and personal life to increase.

Similar to wellness programs, companies are currently offering a variety of opportunities for relaxation and recreational activities to improve the physical and mental wellbeing of their employees. By offering their employees the opportunity to partake in these physical activities, organizations are providing an outlet for employees to increase their health, reduce their stress, and develop their personal interests. This particular type of benefit aims at improving employees' personal lives, so that the company may benefit from an improvement in employees' professional lives as a result. More specifically, employees who utilize the available opportunities for recreation feel that they are more relaxed, healthier, less prone to using sick leave, less prone to injury resulting in disability leave, and more mentally prepared to handle the stress associated with either their personal or professional lives. This increase in morale and physical and psychological wellbeing has been shown to positively affect the workforce through increased job satisfaction, increased intention to stay, increased productivity, decreased absenteeism, decreased turnover, and fewer employee relations conflicts.

Understanding the positive impact that can be actualized from offering opportunities for recreational activities, some major corporations are offering work–life benefits applicable in this arena. For example, Schering-Plough offers employees matching grants towards volunteer organizations and activity. Pfizer offers access to health and fitness facilities, as well as discounts and free admission to cultural offerings such as museums and performing arts performances. Similar to Pfizer, Novartis offers on-site fitness centers and sports facilities for their employees to access. Novartis also offers a camera club, a cultural forum, and music groups and bands. Their cultural forum offers its members a diverse and ever-changing program of cultural events including excursions, visits, and viewings of rehearsals at the theatre or in museums. A unique benefit that Novartis offers is access to the company-sponsored band. Their brass band, composed of a group of Novartis employees, plays at various functions including the company's annual general meeting.

Genentech currently offers matching charitable donation and fitness programs similar to other leading companies, but also puts an interesting spin on their employee wellness and recreation benefits. As part of their company culture, Genentech hosts at least one "ho-ho," or kegger party, every Friday night for their employees. The company also firmly believes in celebrating every milestone that the company reaches with a party and commemorative T-shirt. For especially significant achievements, Genentech celebrates with an even bigger party, as seen through a celebration which warranted turning the company's main parking lot into the site for a rock concert (*Fortune*, 2006).

Strategic differentiation and work–life balance offerings

Most of the developed world shares a value of greater egalitarianism – the desire for all people to be treated equally and fairly. While we share that value, it might be too idealistic to believe that companies can create environments for employees where everyone is achieving the same high level of work–life balance. It would be more prudent for firms to differentiate their workforces and ensure the work–life balance of those in the most critical positions. Strategic human resources (HR) expert Richard Beatty,[2] who has worked with numerous global firms

[2] Personal communication, January, 2006.

on their overall workforce strategy, notes that *"you can go out of business trying to satisfy your employees. You should not try to satisfy all of your employees. In fact, your firm might be better if some employees were so dissatisfied that they left."*

For certain positions in a company, particularly those that are supportive in nature and require knowledge, skills, or abilities that are easily obtainable, elevated levels of turnover are expected and do not have a significant impact on the business's functional success as these positions are easily refillable and have minimal amounts of training and compensation associated with them. From the economic standpoint, it would not be advantageous for a company to incur the expense of providing extensive and possibly costly work–life benefits for this particular group of positions, as it is unlikely that they will see a return on their investment, as these positions do not contribute to their core competencies or competitive advantage. The cost of the work–life benefits for this segment of positions would most likely not outweigh the benefits obtained from retaining employees in positions that are easily refillable and do not require hard to obtain or replicate knowledge, skills, or abilities.

Following along these lines, it would be economically advantageous for a company to invest its resources in providing comprehensive, and possibly tailored, work–life benefits to employees with positions that are hard to replace, hard to replicate, and cannot be easily substituted. Individuals in core positions contribute directly to the company's competitive advantage and are extremely costly to replace. Therefore, a company may need to offer additional work–life benefits for core employees to better *attract and retain them, increase their productive capacity*, and *maximize their performance.*

Core positions have a direct and significant impact on the organization's overall success, therefore is critically important to retain these individuals so that the company's competitive advantage is not jeopardized. Since offering work–life benefits has been shown to increase intention to stay and decrease turnover, it would be in the company's best interest to dedicate their resources towards providing work–life benefits to the core positions within the company. In the following section, we will review the three most common value propositions for firms: operational excellence, product leadership, and customer intimacy. Each value proposition requires a different set of workforce competencies, cultures, and employee mindsets. Each value proposition will have different HR practices or similar HR practices used in different ways (Ulrich & Beatty, 2001). Each value proposition, therefore, suggests a differential application of work–life balance practices.

Although we advocate for this type of strategic differentiation, it is important to note that when designing tailored work–life programs, it is essential to take some precautions to avoid feelings of unfairness in the workplace which could lead to a negative work climate (Greenberg, 1987). For example, procedures should be in place to ensure that employees understand the rationale for the different work–life benefits.

Work–life practices and an operational excellence strategy

In operational excellence firms, lowering cost is critical for sustainability and competitiveness. Organizations competing with this value proposition may include low-cost, high-value retail stores (e.g. Costco and Tesco plc). Core talent in these firms is the professionals in operations and distribution through the value chain and employees who are satisfied and willing to help customers when needed. With an emphasis on efficiency, work–life benefits in firms with an "operational excellence" strategy tend to be available broadly for employees and have (at least in part) the goal of reducing employees' hassles and making it easier for employees to come to work on time and ready to work. For example, Costco, a US-based warehouse-style retailer, offers a program called WorkLife. Costco's WorkLife program provides information on a wide variety of topics to help employees manage both their work and home priorities, including child and elder care, legal issues, children, and family concerns. The program helps workers become more productive and helps them balance their demands at home with their time spent at work. Another example is from Tesco plc, a UK-based retailer. Tesco plc offers flexible working arrangements such as job sharing, shift swapping and part-time working. This program has an emphasis on helping employees work the way they wish to work, to ultimately have a more satisfied, committed, and reliable workforce.

Work–life practices and a product leadership or innovation strategy

In product leadership firms, innovation is critical for sustainability and competitiveness of the firm. Organizations competing with this value proposition may include pharmaceutical, biotech, and high-technology firms. Core talent in these firms is often the scientific and engineering staff. This group, in particular, may have a perceived or very real need to update their skills and to stay connected to their professional community outside of their employing organization.

Given the centrality of their professions for scientists and engineers, opportunities to connect with their professional community should be encouraged. A top research scientist may feel more balance and life satisfaction with the opportunity to attend professional conferences, write research articles, etc., the very activity which, while time-consuming, may encourage innovation that would have a positive benefit on the firm's core business. An example of such a benefit is the option for an educational leave, where an employee is granted permission to take a leave of absence from their position for a set duration of time to pursue further educational achievements and then return to their position upon completion of the educational pursuit. Although the company is at a disadvantage during the educational leave because they do not have access to the particular core employee's competencies nor his or her productivity, the company benefits from an overall gain upon the employee's return from the leave, as he or she has additional knowledge, skills, or abilities that can be applied to the job and the company. This allows the employee to be more productive upon his or her return from the educational leave, where the employee may be performing at a level much higher than they would have naturally progressed to through the course of the job without additional educational pursuit. This benefit is currently being offered at Eli Lilly and Company, a pharmaceutical company that thrives on the educational advancement of their core employees so that this particular segment of their human capital may serve as a competitive advantage.

Firms that are in direct competition with universities for their core talent (i.e. those with PhDs in the technical or scientific fields) will sometimes offer sabbatical programs to mirror the benefit offered in the university setting. The sabbatical programs currently offered in many companies allow eligible employees (those of a certain level in the company who have also worked with the company for at least a particular number of years) the opportunity to conduct research or to complete a research project that is directly relevant and applicable to the project work they are currently working on. Differing from an educational leave, sabbatical programs have specific requirements regarding the research to be completed, which has to be approved by a committee that includes the employee's direct supervisor and other managerial figures who supervise the employee's research during the course of the sabbatical.

Companies generally offer six-month to twelve-month sabbatical programs to employees who have a minimum number of years of service with the company and are within departments where sabbatical research could have a measurable impact on the current work the employee engages in. Often sabbatical programs are used for the purpose of learning new scientific techniques or methods, conducting research projects, or gaining additional skills in a current discipline, or building collaborative relationships with other institutions. By providing this opportunity for their core talent, companies reduce the competition for these individuals from other research institutions, such as universities. By having the ability to pursue this type of educational advancement, employees are more likely to remain with the company and experience increased job satisfaction resulting from having control over the work they are doing, as well as the flexibility of how the work is being completed, so that the employee can decide how to best obtain their optimal work–life balance during this period of time. *Fortune* found that twenty-five of their "100 Best Companies to Work For, 2006" offer fully paid sabbaticals, demonstrating how the best companies are finding it critical to update their employees' technical skills, as a means to retain this pool of core talent.

Work–life practices and a customer intimacy strategy

In customer intimacy firms, tailoring solutions is critical for sustainability and competitiveness. Organizations competing with this value proposition may include consultancy (e.g. McKinsey and PWC) and firms involved in customized software solutions (e.g. EDS). The professionals who have customer facing roles are the core talent in these firms. This group, in particular, may have an increased pressure to be available whenever the client demands and are less in control of their own schedule (e.g. on the road and traveling for many days each year).

Given that being "present" for clients is important for the customer intimacy value proposition, absenteeism is especially detrimental. Aon Consulting conducted a study to identify absenteeism rates, the most common causes for absenteeism, and the effects that are commonly felt in organizations. They found that employees missed more than eleven days per year to handle personal and family matters. The study also further showed that more than 80 percent of employees who miss work due to stress are also missing work to handle daycare, elder care, and other personal issues. Ultimately, these pressures lead to employee burnout with corresponding declines in productivity, attendance, and job satisfaction (Corporate Leadership Council, 2000). By providing such work–life benefits as outsourced resource and referral services and on-site convenience services, employees are able to handle personal issues without having to be absent from the workplace. This allows the organizations relying on employee presence to benefit from decreased absenteeism rates.

Travel to client sites is also important for the customer intimacy value proposition. This is a concern because time spent away from home, by definition, will negatively impact work–life balance. Jet lag, physical exhaustion, overwork, and burnout are common complaints among frequent business travelers. In an effort to try to have a positive effect on frequent business travelers, corporations will often attempt to provide alternative work arrangements to these critical employees. Some efforts include offering a flex day off, an opportunity to flex one's hours the days before and after travel, and the ability to work from home after returning from a business trip. These options allow business travelers to compensate for the time spent away from the home during travel by having additional time spent at home upon return.

Conclusion

Satisfy some, dissatisfy others

Offering work–life benefits impacts employees' well-being and also gives a competitive advantage to companies by retaining and attracting talent. In this chapter we emphasize that it is economically advantageous for a company to invest their resources in providing comprehensive, and possibly tailored, work–life benefits to employees with positions that are hard to replace, hard to replicate, and cannot be easily substituted. As these positions have a direct and significant impact on the organization's overall success, it is critically important to retain these individuals so that the company's competitive advantage is not jeopardized. Since offering work–life benefits has been shown to increase intention to stay and decrease turnover, it would be in the company's best interest to dedicate its resources towards providing work–life benefits to the core positions within the company.

From this strategic perspective, not all positions should be managed equally. As discussed in this chapter, the process of attraction and retention of core talent is of interest in a strategic discussion of work–life balance for three very important reasons. The first is that employees in wealth-creating positions tend to hold positions which require greater demands on their intellectual capabilities and emotional energy – potentially decreasing their mental downtime from work. The second is that wealth-creating positions, by definition, tend to be associated with greater responsibility – usually resulting in longer hours and greater spillover of work activities to personal time. The third is that employees in wealth-creating positions tend to have more achievement orientation and a higher degree of career centrality (i.e. the amount of themselves they identify by their career) and may have a blurred line between work and life that they themselves induce (if not encourage). An example of this can be seen with critical care nurses. In this particular profession, it is common to see these employees working in significant excess of the standard 40-hour workweek in part because of the labor demand, but also because of their emotional dedication to their line of work. Naturally, having this much emotional and physical demands set forth by a position can lead to burnout, which the industry has seen in an average rate of voluntary turnover for nurses hovering consistently around 20 percent over the last six years.

For these three reasons, reduced mental downtime, increase spillover from work to home time, and increased need for achievement, those in core positions may be particularly susceptible to a decrease in work–life balance. While most firms turn a blind eye on the confluence of these issues, there has been a plethora of research suggesting that it may be time to take notice. Decreases in work–life balance have been linked to higher unwanted turnover, lower physical and psychological well-being, lower productivity, greater stress-related ailments, and the like. When these negative factors are taken together – especially among core employees – they may contribute to a negative impact on firm success. The most critical people in most organizations are the very people who tend to be most susceptible to the ill-effects when they do not have the appropriate level of work–life balance.

References

Arthur, M. M. (2003). Work–family initiatives and share price reaction: An institutional perspective. *Academy of Management Journal*, 46, 497–505.

Aryee, S., Luk, V., & Stone, R. (1998). Family-responsive variables and retention-relevant outcomes among employed parents. *Human Relations*, 51(1), 73–87.

Bacharach, S. B., Bamberger, P., & Conley, S. (1991). Work–home conflict among nurses and engineers: Mediating the impact of role stress on burnout and satisfaction at work. *Journal of Organizational Behavior*, 12, 39–53.

Bartolome, F. & Evans, P. (1980). Must success cost so much? Reprinted in *Harvard Business Review on Work–Life Balance*, pp. 31–60.

BenefitNews (March 2006). Work–life issues pushing one in five to quit. *Employee Benefit News*, 3.

BNA's Human Resources Library. Health Promotion, Wellness, and Medical Programs. The Bureau of National Affairs, Incorporated.

Bond, J. T., Thompson, C., Galinsky, E., & Prottas, D. (2003). *Highlights of the 2002 National Study of the Changing Workforce* (No. 3). New York: Families and Work Institute.

Christensen, K. & Staines, G. (1990). Flextime: A viable solution to work/family conflict? *Journal of Family Issues*, 11, 455–476.

Corporate Leadership Council. (2000) Work–Life Balance Policies in Support of Innovative Cultures.

Corporate Leadership Council (2003). Maintaining a Work–Life Balance in the Professional Services Industry.

Costco Corporate Website. www.costco.com.

Frone, M. R., Russell, M., & Cooper, L. M. (1992). Prevalence of work–family conflict: Are work and family boundaries asymmetrically permeable? *Journal of Organizational Behavior*, 13, 723–729.

Genentech Corporate Website. www.gene.com

Greenberg, J. (1987). Reactions to procedural injustice in payment distributions: Do the means justify the end? *Journal of Applied Psychology*, 72, 55–61.

Greenhaus, J. H. & Beutell, N. J. (1985). Sources of conflict between work and family roles. *Academy of Management Review*, 10, 76–88.

Grover, S. L. & Crooker, K. J. (1995). Who appreciates family-responsive human resource policies? The impact of family-friendly policies on the organizational attachment of parents and non-parents. *Personnel Psychology*, 48, 271–288.

Jacobs, J. & Gornick, J. (2001). Hours of Paid Work in Dual-Earner Couples: The U.S. in Cross-National Perspective. Working paper, University of Pennsylvania.

Kinnunen, U. & Mauno, S. (1998). Antecedents and outcomes of work–family conflict among employed women and men in Finland. *Human Relations*, 52, 157–177.

Koesten, J. (2005). Reducing stress and burnout for financial planners. *Journal of Financial Planning*, 64–74.

Kompier, Michael & Cooper, C. (1999). *Preventing Stress, Improving Productivity: European Case Studies in the Workplace*. London: Routledge.

Konrad, A. M. & Mangel, R. (2000). The impact of work–life programs on firm productivity. *Strategic Management Journal*, 21, 1225–1237.

Kossek, E. E. & Lambert, S. J. (2005). *Work and Life Integration: Organizational, Cultural, and Individual Perspectives*. London: Lawrence Erlbaum Associates.

Kossek, E. E. & Nichol, V. (1992). The effects of on-site child care on employee attitudes and performance. *Personnel Psychology*, 45, 485–509.

Lambert, S. (2000). Added benefits: The link between work–life benefits and organizational citizenship behavior. *Academy of Management Journal*, 43(5), 801–815.

Levinson, H. (1981). When executives burn-out. Reprinted in *Harvard Business Review on Work–Life Balance*, pp. 61–80.

McKinsey *et al.* (1997) The war for talent. *The McKinsey Quarterly*, 3, 44–57.

Meyer, C. S., Mukerjee, S., & Sestero, A. (2001). Work–family benefits: Which ones maximize profits. *Journal of Managerial Issues*, 13, 28–44.

Netmeyer, R. G., Boles, J. S., & McMurrian, R. (1996). Development and validation of work–family conflicts and work–family conflict scales. *Journal of Applied Psychology*, 81, 400–410.

New York State Family Benefits Program (2006). www.familybenefits.lmc.state.ny.us.

Novartis Corporate Website. www.novartis.com

OECD (2001). *OECD Employment Outlook*. Paris: Organization for Economic Cooperation and Development.

Osterman, P. (1995). Work–family programs and the employment relationship. *Administrative Science Quarterly*, 40, 681–700.

Perlow, L. A. (1999). The time famine: Toward a sociology of work time. *Administrative Science Quarterly*, 44, 57–81.

Perry-Smith, J. E. & Blum, T. C. (2000). Work–family human resource bundles and perceived organizational performance. *Academy of Management Journal*, 43, 1107–1117.

Pfizer Corporate Website. www.pfizer.com

Poelmans, S. & Sahibzada, K. (2004). A multi-level model for studying the context and impact of work–family policies and culture in organizations. *Human Resource Management Review*, 14, 409–431.

Scandura, T. A. & Lankau, M. J. (1997). Relationships of gender, family responsibility and flexible work hours to organizational commitment and job satisfaction. *Journal of Organizational Behavior*, 18, 377–391.

Schering-Plough Corporate Website. www.schering-plough.com

Tesco Corporate Website www.tesco.com.

Ulrich, D. & Beatty, R. (2001). From partners to players: Extending the HR playing field. *Human Resource Management*, 40, 293–308.

2 | *Reviewing policies for harmonizing work, family, and personal life*

STEVEN A. Y. POELMANS
IESE Business School, Spain
and
BARBARA BEHAM
University of Hamburg, Germany

In order to better align business needs to the needs of employees with caring responsibilities, companies have started to implement family-supportive human resource (HR) policies over the last years referred to as work–life policies, work–family policies, or work–family arrangements in this chapter. Work–life policies and benefits are the most visible indicators of a family-responsible workplace and can be defined as any employer sponsored facilities and benefits, designed to support the combination of paid work and family responsibilities of its employees (den Dulk, Van Doorne-Huiskes, & Schippers, 1999). Work–life policies aim at enhancing the ability of employees to manage competing demands from work and personal interests and to alleviate work–family conflict.

Poelmans and Sahibzada (2004) proposed a model of four main decisions that managers need to consider when thinking about the implementation of a work–life program in their company. The central question of the first decision, the *adoption decision*, is whether and when to start incorporating work–life programs. Companies do not exist in a vacuum. The social, economic, legal, and technological contexts as well as the political dimension need to be carefully reviewed and incorporated into this decision. In the *design decision*, the right constellation of human resource policies needs to be selected according to business requirements and workforce needs. The *implementation decision* focuses on how to implement and diffuse these policies within the firm, how to secure managerial support for the program, and how to stimulate cultural change within the company. Once a company has moved through the different stages of adopting, designing, and implementing work–family policies and practices, it still has to actually

39

decide whether and when to approve the request of a certain work–family benefit to an employee. The *allowance decision* often is the responsibility of the direct supervisors of an employee and is influenced by various individual, group-level, and organizational factors (e.g. employee characteristics, supervisor's experience, team size, task inter-dependency among team members, official decision-making rules, etc.) (Powell & Mainiero, 1999; Peters & den Dulk, 2003). The approval process is an important determinant of the success of a work–life program because only when employees actually can make use of work–family policies and their real needs and expectations are met, can we talk about a successful implementation of the program (see Table 2.8 for a checklist including the main issues that need to be considered when implementing work–life programs).

In this chapter we will provide a review of a variety of human resource policies and practices aimed at harmonizing work, family, and personal life of employees in organizations. We will focus specifically on the adoption and design questions, i.e. which policies to adopt and implement. In Chapter 6 we will elaborate on the concerns regarding the implementation and allowance of those policies. First, we will briefly address the adoption decision. Second, we will describe various human resource policies that improve work–life balance and provide practical examples of companies that have implemented single policies as well as bundles of work–life arrangements. We will discuss flexibility policies, leave arrangements, care provisions, supportive arrange-ments, and conventional provisions for job quality and compensations/benefits. Finally, we will point out shortly the importance of creating a family-supportive organizational culture and conclude with what we understand as the new paradigm of harmonization between work and personal life. Throughout the whole chapter, useful checklists for the implementation of work–life programs are provided.

The adoption of work–life policies

The extent to which companies provide work–life policies differs widely by country and the level of national family policy provision. There is a lively discussion among work–family researchers whether the presence or absence of public policies stimulates the implementa-tion of company-sponsored work–life programs. While some scholars argue that the absence of governmental provision stimulates the creation of work–life programs in organizations, the alternative argument is that public provision creates a climate in which employers become active and supplement basic entitlements (Lewis, 1997a). Den Dulk (2001) used Esping-Andersen's (1999) typology of welfare state regimes (such as the social-democratic, conservative, and liberal welfare state regimes) to study differences and similarities in organizational policy provision in the Netherlands, Italy, the UK, and Sweden. She concluded that it is the (near) absence of public provisions that leads to larger employers' involvement rather than the presence of advanced public provisions. Organizations in different types of welfare state regimes focus on different work–family arrangements, and the level of involvement of organizations varies between and within countries. Den Dulk concludes active government involvement does not necessarily mean that the incentive for employers to develop facilities themselves disappears. When taking both statutory and employers' provisions into account, Sweden still has the highest level of provisions. In the other three countries, employers are on average more active, but never fully substitute statutory provisions. From an organizational point of view, even within a social-democratic regime, it can be profitable to supplement statutory provisions to a higher degree than one's competitors. Nevertheless, if we look at actual data provided by the OECD (Organization for Economic Cooperation and Development), neither companies in countries with the highest level of national provision (e.g. the European Nordic countries), nor those in countries where national provision traditionally has been relatively low (e.g. UK, Spain), have filled the gap sufficiently (OECD, 2001).

Poelmans and Sahibzada (2004) systematically reviewed the literature looking at all factors that may influence the adoption decision. They argue that the probability that an organization will be more effective in improving performance by reducing work–family conflict is a function of the macro-context in which an organization operates. Whereas the legislative and cultural context will influence individuals' sense of entitlement to receive family support from their organizations, the labor market context will influence individuals' choice and negotiation power, thus increasing the pressure on firms to adopt work–life policies.

According to research on organizational motives for the implementation of work–life programs, companies respond to both external pressure (e.g. regulations, laws, norms, social expectation of shareholders, labor market situation) and internal pressure (e.g. dependence on female employees, talented high-potentials) (Goodstein, 1994). Human resource managers act as the interpreters of institutional pressure and choose which and how many work–family friendly polices are being implemented in the company. Research revealed that organizations are more likely to offer benefits when work–family issues are salient to senior HR staff, but research on the topic is not conclusive (Kossek, Dass, & DeMarr, 1994; Milliken, Martins, & Morgan, 1998; Poelmans, Chinchilla, & Cardona, 2003). The rationale of those managers is a function of the recognition that workforce characteristics (specifically workforce care responsibilities) may impact productivity (Milliken Dutton, & Meyer, 1990; Morgan & Milliken, 1992). This is especially true when products or services offered by organizations require high commitment and creativity of employees (Osterman, 1995; Poelmans *et al.*, 2003). Knowledge workers in general and specifically in the service sector are prone to have concerns about family care responsibilities. Work-related responsibilities compete for the same resources: attention, psychological commitment, processes of creativity, problem-solving, and customer-orientation (Poelmans & Sahibzada, 2004). The knowledge worker *is* the most important processor and container of knowledge. The service provider *is* the service. Therefore it should not surprise us that companies active in sectors like healthcare, finance, insurance, real estate technology, and consulting are more inclined to adopt family-friendly policies (Poelmans *et al.*, 2003; Morgan & Milliken, 1992). Morgan and Milliken (1992) suggested that differences between industries in adopting work–family policies can be traced back to the average skill level and related training costs.

In 1991 Procter & Gamble (P&G) conducted a study of employee turnover and uncovered an alarming trend: two out of every three good performers who left P&G were women. Whereas a small percentage of them dropped out of the workforce, the majority moved on to high-profile, high-stress jobs similar to their previous jobs. Interestingly, almost half of the women were surprised to learn that P&G regretted the loss (Poelmans & Andrews, 2001). These findings created the impetus for P&G to develop flexible work arrangements in the USA and EMEA (Europe, Middle East, and Africa). This example illustrates that companies that operate in tight labor markets can profit from adopting work–family policies to attract and retain employees.

Table 2.1. *Macro-context factors that influence organizations' policy adoption decision*

COUNTRY LEVEL
- *Extensive government-supported policies, as in social-democratic countries.*
- *Egalitarian gender-role ideology*
- *Low in masculinity*[1]
- *Low in power distance*[2]
- *Countries high in individualism*[3]

LABOR MARKET
- *Scarcity of talent or skills*
- *High diffusion of work–family benefits*
- *High percentage of women in the active population*
- *High reliance on knowledge work*
- *High reliance on quality of customer service*

---

[1] Masculinity = level of aggressiveness, tenacity, and focus on material success
[2] Power distance = level of equality in power among individuals
[3] Individualism = level of differentiation from others and individuality

Academic scholars have also suggested that companies make a rational choice by calculating the inputs and outcomes of work–life arrangements for the company (den Dulk, 2005; Poelmans & Beham, 2005a). In terms of inputs, the firm may have to invest in setting up home offices for teleworkers, creating personnel administration systems which allow for dealing with a wider range of (part-time) contracts and salary levels, stimulating and training managers in management by objectives (MBO), and coaching employees in meeting these objectives. These inputs are weighed off against the reduced costs of turnover, absenteeism, and demotivation in employees. Furthermore, managers may consider the extent to which a work–family arrangement disrupts the conduct of work (occasional work disruption, as it is the case for a short-term leave to care for a sick child, versus longer disruptions, as for parental leave) (Powell & Mainiero, 1999). If the overall benefits exceed the implementation costs, then the employer will adopt these arrangements (Poelmans, 2001).

To summarize, the macro-context factors shown in Table 2.1 are associated with higher levels of sense of entitlement and negotiation power and thus create a stronger pressure for companies to adopt these policies.

The design of work–life programs – the right fit

Formal versus informal policies – justice and prudence

Organizations who decide to implement work–life programs have to choose between formal, written policies available to all employees or informal arrangements only available to certain employees in specific situations. In cases where work–family policies are not available to all employees in the company (e.g. only to employees with a permanent contract or to female employees), perceptions of inequity and unfairness need to be considered by HR managers. According to European Union directives, it is illegal to exclude certain groups (e.g. men) from these arrangements (den Dulk *et al.*, 1999). Research on organizational justice and work–life programs suggests that work–family programs can create a "backlash" among employees who cannot use these policies (Rothausen, Gonzalez, Clarke, & O'Dell, 1998). They compare their situation with those employees who can make use of these policies and may perceive unfair treatment (Grandey, 2001). Resentment, frustration, and negative attitudes toward the organization may be the consequence (Kossek & Nichol, 1992; Rothausen *et al.*, 1998). Thus, it is recommended to define objective criteria for inclusion and allowance and to be consistent in the application process. Whereas the virtue of justice is important for establishing the minimum entitlement and clarifying the degree of inclusiveness of the policies, the virtue of prudence is probably more relevant when considering the actual allowance of a benefit to an employee. Each case is different, and in order to be able to respond to unique needs in employees, companies are recommended to develop cafeteria-style benefits, where employees can trade off free time against salary, and choose benefits that correspond with their specific family or personal situation.

Bundling work–life policies

Not all work–life policies are equally suitable to a company's business model and/or the actual needs of its workforce. Companies need to carefully evaluate the potential of various types of policies, and choose those that fit best its business model and the actual needs of its workforce.

Companies, for example, who require employees to be flexible across the natural boundaries of work and family in order to attend fluctuating client needs and quickly solve work-related problems outside of working hours may opt for flexible work arrangements. However, this flexibility required by the company's business model may or may not be compatible with care responsibilities of employees. Hence, the provision of supportive and flexible childcare arrangements (e.g. emergency childcare arrangements, financial compensation for a babysitter) may need to be considered in addition to the flexibility arrangements in order to support employees when a call for duty comes unexpectedly and/or outside of working hours and childcare hours.

When companies decide to combine two or more disparate work–life policies into a group of interconnected and overlapping policies aligned with one another and the overall HR strategy we can talk about a work–family *bundle* (Perry-Smith & Blum, 2000). Offering extensive family-friendly HR bundles is often aimed at addressing a wide variety of needs. The implicit assumption which lies behind this effort is that the more is the better (Perry-Smith & Blum, 2000). However, research has also shown that not all policies have the same impact on firm profitability and some policies are more beneficial than others. Offering paid sick days when family members are ill increases profits just by the virtue of being offered. Telework, on the other hand, was found to increase a firm's profitability only when the use is generalized within the company (Meyer, Mukerjee, & Sestero, 2001). Companies who seek policy effectiveness need to develop a specific and unique bundle of policies, tailor-made for the specific work–family needs of its workforce and aligned with the company's business model. The right "fit" is the relevant approach (Poelmans, 2003).

Types of work–family policies

Although there is no single, widely accepted approach to classify work–family policies, it is possible to categorize them in five basic groups (Poelmans & Beham, 2005a): (1) flexibility policies, (2) leave arrangements, (3) care provisions, (4) supportive arrangements, and (5) conventional provisions for job quality and compensations/benefits. Each group will be discussed and illustrated with practical examples in the following sections.

Flexibility policies

Under the broad umbrella of flexibility policies all organizational initiatives are summarized that allow the adaptation of working hours and locations to the needs of the employee. Flexible work arrangements allow employees to accomplish their work duties outside of the traditional and/or spatial boundaries of a standard working day (Rau, 2003). Although there is no universal definition of a "standard working day" due to different legislation on total working hours across countries, we can broadly assume that the traditional work schedule is defined as a 40-hour and five-day working week within certain time limits that may vary across countries, industries, organizational policies, and social norms. France for instance reduced the standard working week to 35 hours in 2000. In principle, this frees up a considerable amount of hours for caring needs. In countries like the UK, where in addition to a longer standard working week a generalized culture of overtime is very common, companies have a higher incentive to adopt flexible work arrangements.

In general, a distinction is made between arrangements that create flexibility in terms of time (e.g. flexible working hours, part-time work, and compressed work weeks) and those that allow for flexibility in space, such as satellite offices and telework (see Table 2.2 for advantages of flexibility policies for organizations).

Flexibility in time

Flexible working hours

Flexible working hours (also referred to as flextime or flexitime) allow employees to vary their work schedule within certain ranges and dimensions in accordance to their differing needs (Hyland, 2003). Employees can enter and leave work within certain margins, as long as they work eight hours a day. No prior approval from supervisors is required. Frequently these arrangements include core hours – the daily hours during which employees must be at work – and a bandwidth – the earliest and latest starting and stopping times to which employees can adjust their schedules (Christensen & Staines, 1990).

Whereas work is organized around clock time rather than task time, care giving responds to the needs of a person and may not follow a predefined schedule (Bailyn, 2002). Hence, allowing employees to adjust their job to task time will help employees to better integrate

Table 2.2. *Advantages of flexible work arrangements for companies*

✓ Enhanced recruitment and retention of valuable employees and associated recruitment and training cost savings.

✓ Improved employee morale, satisfaction, commitment, and productivity resulting from support for personal work style preferences.

✓ Creation of a favorable view of the job, company, and workload.

✓ Reduced stress, absence, tardiness, and turnover through the ability to better balance work and personal responsibilities.

✓ Improved coverage and scheduling (e.g. of peak workloads) for the department.

✓ (Un)interrupted time for creative, repetitive, or highly detailed work.

✓ Savings in office space and equipment through more office space options and expanded use of equipment.

✓ Improved transportation and parking options; time lost in traffic jams can be invested in work.

✓ Government schemes or incentives available to encourage flexible employment driven by concerns about transport networks, air quality, etc.

---

work and family lives. Policies which guarantee employees a higher level of flexibility have indeed been found to be related to a variety of positive individual and organizational outcomes. Flexible hours were found to improve employees' satisfaction with the work schedule, overall job satisfaction, job involvement, and productivity (Dunham, Pierce, & Castanda, 1987), and to decrease absenteeism, stress, and work–family conflict (Baltes, Huff, Wright, & Neuman, 1999; Shinn, Wong, Simko, & Ortiz-Torres, 1989; Thomas & Ganster, 1995). Studies that examined outcomes at the organizational level found bundles of work–family policies, including flextime, to be related with higher perceived organizational performance (Perry-Smith & Blum, 2000). Policy announcements of human resource decisions in the press, including flextime, were associated with increased shareholder return (Arthur, 2003). In addition, work schedule flexibility was reported to be related to job pursuit intentions of employees, thereby suggesting that organizations which offer flexible work arrangements are more attractive to job seekers (Casper & Buffardi, 2004). In times where more and more employees aim at both a successful work and family life, these arrangements constitute a competitive advantage in securing talented applicants and retaining valuable employees.

Table 2.3. *Advantages of flexibility arrangements for employees*

✓ Greater freedom to manage time and tasks.
✓ Ability to better manage family responsibilities while keeping the job.
✓ Increased job satisfaction.
✓ Fewer co-worker interruptions and distractions.
✓ Improved efficiency and productivity.
✓ Fewer hours committed to the work day (such as time spent organizing, dressing, and commuting), without actually working fewer hours.

Flexible hours are consistently rated as the most valuable work–life arrangement among employees. (See Table 2.3 for a list of advantages of flexibility arrangements for employees.) In the context of full-time jobs, flextime is ranked ahead of reduced-time schedules, because many employees with family responsibilities do not want or simply cannot afford to work less (Rodgers, 1992). Flextime is already widely implemented in a large number of companies. To give a few examples: IBM*[1] offers its employees individualized work schedules. Employees can vary their work time up to two hours before or two hours after the normal location start and stop times. At Deutsche Bank* about 50 percent of its employees used flextime in 2004, and at Bristol-Meyers Squibb* about 72 percent of those who worked flexible hours in 2003 were female.

Nevertheless, not all jobs may be suitable for flextime. Jobs with set costumer service hours or those in production (shift work) may have limited compatibility with flextime. In such cases, other flexible arrangements such as staggered compressed work weeks (see section on reduced working schedules), other types of work–life policies, or a combination of different policies need to be considered. At the plants of Pearson NCS* in Columbia/US, for example, additional off-shift service days are offered to employees who work the second or third shift. These are extra paid days off provided by the company in recognition of employees who work non-traditional and fixed hours and who may need extra time off to take care of personal business or attend family events. An employee is eligible for two off-shift days during the first

---

[1] References to all items marked with an asterisk (*) can be found in a separate list at the end of the chapter.

four years of employment. During years five through nine, the time rises to three days; ten to fourteen years of service garners four days; and those with fifteen or more years of service have five days.

Part-time work

Employees on a part-time schedule work a specific number of hours below the standard work week on a regular basis (Galinsky, Friedman, & Hernandez, 1991b). In the European Union part-time work usually refers to working weeks of less than 31 hours (den Dulk *et al.*, 1999). According to the US Bureau of Labor Statistics, less than 35 hours per week is considered a part-time schedule. The share of part-time employment varies significantly across European countries. The Netherlands, for example, scores highest with nearly 36% of all employees working part-time, followed by the United Kingdom and Germany with almost 23% and 20%. In the new member states and in southern European countries the part-time rate is below 10% (e.g. the Czech Republic 2.8%, Greece 1.9%) (Plantenga & Remery, 2005). Part-time jobs tend to be mostly occupied by women (e.g. 93% of all part-timers in Luxembourg are women, 86.9% in Austria, and 76.0% in the Netherlands). Motherhood and part-time work are often strongly linked. With the arrival of children many women shift to part-time work (Blackwell, 2001). But part-time work not only may attract women, it may be also a valuable option for older workers (men and women equally) who want to reduce work before retirement. Nevertheless, it needs to be pointed out that not all employees are voluntarily employed on a less-than-full-time basis. Especially women often take on part-time jobs because affordable childcare facilities are not available, or because they could not find a full-time position that offered flexible working hours. Part-time jobs often tend to be found in low-paying industries (e.g. retail, sales, etc.), and offer less benefits, and limited career advancement opportunities. A study comparing part-time work in New Zealand, the Netherlands, and Denmark, Rasmussen, Lind, and Visser (2004) found that part-time jobs tend to be concentrated in low-paying service sectors and in construction; part-time employees tend to participate less in job-related training than full-timers (OECD 2001); and there are fewer opportunities to create long-term career paths. Only recently, companies have started to create part-time jobs in professions and management that have adequate salaries and benefits, and allow climbing the career ladder

(Barnett, 2003). Despite some of the clear disadvantages, in the Netherlands, thanks to its generalized use, part-time work has become a culturally accepted alternative, also for men, to standard work schedules. This example shows that more role models in professional and managerial jobs are definitively needed to counteract the bad reputation of part-time work. Governments and organizations however should also assure through legal arrangements or sectorial negotiations with labor unions that part-time workers are sufficiently protected and have social security and salary levels at least proportional with their reduced working schedule. In Spain, Gres de Valls,* a production company in the ceramic industry, pays its part-time workers proportionally more than their schedule, in order to encourage take-up and increase the firm's labor force flexibility.

Reduced working schedules
Reduced working hours is a rather new term that has been introduced to mark the development of "good" part-time jobs (Barnett, 2003). Employees with reduced working schedules work part-time on a weekly basis, with a working time reduction (anything between 50% and 100%) spread over a week, resulting for instance in an employee working three days a week (60%). While reduced hours options are typically voluntary and arranged on a case-by-case basis, conventional part-time jobs are generally negotiated on a formal basis. A special type of reduced hours is *V-time* (Christensen & Staines, 1990). In a V-time arrangement, the agreed hours worked are scheduled throughout the year in such a way that some weeks might require 45 or more hours, whereas other weeks require substantially less hours.

Another form of reduced working schedule is referred to as *compressed workweeks*. While flexible working hours and part-time work are defined on a day-to-day basis, compressed work weeks offer flexibility on a week-to-week basis. Under a compressed workweek arrangement, employees typically work a standard 40-hour week but may only work three or four days a week. One day they put in more than eight hours per day, compensating it with a proportional time off another day, for instance on a Friday afternoon (Rau, 2003). Compressed workweeks allow employees to continue to work the same amount of hours, but attend punctual or recurring private responsibilities like picking up children from school, or attending a part-time course on Friday afternoon.

With respect to organizational outcomes, there is growing consensus that employees working reduced hours are at least as productive as their full-time counterparts (Barnett, 2003). Studies suggest that absenteeism and turnover is lower among employees working reduced hours compared to full-time employees (Blank, 1990). In addition, part-time workers tend to take fewer breaks and less personal time while on the job (Epstein, Seron, Oglensky, & Saute, 1999). Moreover, increased organizational commitment (Scandura & Lankau, 1997) and an increased likelihood to return to one's job after a leave of absence have been associated with schedules of reduced hours (Barnett, 2003).

Recently reduced hours and compressed workweeks started to become more common among companies. At General Mills,* for example, more than 6,000 of its 18,000 workers opted for a compressed workweek in 2004, including a summer-hours program when work is not as busy as during the rest of the year. At Manor Group,* a 11,000-employee department store chain in Switzerland, employees can reduce their working hours to a minimum of 10 percent of a full schedule. JetBlue* CEO David Neeleman is experimenting with compressed work schedules for senior executives. One of his executive vice-presidents works on a four-day week at reduced compensation, and another request from a crucial player is under consideration (Miller, 2005).

> *"It's also important that managers provide a role model for healthy work–life balance. I work a four-day week and our CEO takes Wednesday mornings off to attend a reading class at his daughter's school."*
>
> Cathy Busani, managing director of Happy Ltd* training company, London.

In a legal services agency in the US, where a high proportion of attorneys are women committed to social services, who can accept low salaries because of high-earning husbands, and who want flexible work arrangements to spend time with their families, a complementary staggered compressed work schedule was introduced. Two employees work a full-time schedule but in four days a week, with one out on Monday and one out on Friday. This schedule provides employees with more flexibility, but also guarantees that the office is covered all days (Bailyn & Harrington, 2004). (See Table 2.4 for a list of the costs associated with flexible work arrangements.)

Table 2.4. *Costs of flexible work arrangements*

- Initial start-up costs (e.g. setting up the contract, equipment for teleworkers, setting up telework office, etc.).
- Running costs (e.g. telecommunication and Internet access, maintenance of home office equipment, additional software licenses, data security).
- Additional administrative duties/time for managing different schedules, organizing meetings and trainings, workload management.
- Increased communication demands between co-workers because of varying time schedules, distance to teleworkers, etc.
- Recruitment and training expenses for new employees (e.g. job-sharing partner, additional part-time worker).

Job sharing

Job sharing can be described as a specific form of part-time work or reduced working schedule where two employees share the same job, but fill a full-time job or even more between the two of them. From the employer's point of view the job function is still completely covered, but by two people. Job sharing is usually introduced when organizations want to maintain consistency with respect to its clients but it may also be an interesting option for highly demanding jobs like executive assistant or school director, that often extend well beyond eight hours a day (Barnett, 2003). Sharing the job allows two part-timers to work a reasonable schedule (e.g. two times 60 percent) while covering a 120 percent job. The success of a job-sharing arrangement largely depends on the level of communication and cooperation between the two part-timers, their flexibility, and polyvalence.

Royal Bank Financial Group* (RBFG), one of Canada's largest employers with 60,000 employees in 1,500 branches and offices across the country and a workforce that is constituted of approximately 75 percent women, has the highest percentage of job-share teams in Canada. Starting in the early 1990s with a transformation of informal and ad hoc initiatives into a foundation of formal policies and programs, job sharing has undergone successful permutations of its original definitions and concepts at RBFG. Job-share teams of three employees sharing two jobs, for example, have been established. Job sharers and job-share teams have been promoted, and managers with supervisory responsibilities are successfully job sharing (Tombari &

Spinks, 1999). At the University of Marburg* in Germany, two professors in the psychology department are sharing a full-time senior professor position, and at the Technical University in Berlin* a senior professor is sharing his full-time position with an assistant professor. In the Netherlands "duobanen" (duo-jobs) for school directors are being widely promoted in the primary school system. A special website (http://primaironderwijs.duojob.nl/) was developed where school directors can apply for a duo-job. An organization helps them with finding an adequate position and partner. An example for a successful job-sharing initiative at the executive level is provided by Fleet Financial* in Boston Group which offered two employees to share the position of the vice-president for global markets foreign exchange (Miller, 2005). Each one worked three days a week on the trading desk. Whoever was at work dealt with whatever came up. They had one set of goals and one performance review. Instead of working 50–60 hours a week, due to their shared role they could reduce their working hours to 20–25 hours each. However, when Bank of America acquired Fleet and the department was eliminated, they were looking for a new job together, but could not find another company who was willing to proceed with their successful job-sharing model.

Flexibility in space – telework

Telework, or telecommuting, is a subset of flexible work arrangements that allows employees to conduct work at an off-site location (e.g. from home or at a satellite office) during regular work hours by using telecommunications technologies, including computers, video and telephone systems, fax machines, and high-speed data lines for transferring data (Galinsky & Johnson, 1998). Usually, we talk about telework when an employee works at least parts of the week from home. Working occasionally from home (e.g. once a month) or work done "on the road" (e.g. sales) is not considered telework. In addition, it is important to distinguish between telework and flexible working hours. Although many teleworkers have a flexible work schedule, some are expected to work a fixed schedule (e.g. the need to be available between 9.00 a.m. and 5.00 p.m.) (Kossek, 2003).

According to the US Department of Labor (2000), the typical teleworker is a college-educated, 34–55-year-old male who earns more than $40,000 a year. Telework is best suited for jobs that are information-based, predictable, and portable, and/or require a high level of privacy and concentration. Approximately 25% of the working population in the US are teleworkers, compared to 13% in the European Union (including self-employed people who work from small offices in homes in Europe) (SIBIS, 2003). At IBM,* for example, about 30% of employees are permanently mobile. The company sponsors socials and teas to bring telecommuters together and to give them the feeling that they belong to a community. Half of Manor Group's* administrative staff in Switzerland (approximately 400 employees) are teleworkers. Vaude,* a leading mountain sports gear manufacturer, offers its 200 employees at the headquarters in southern Germany the opportunity to telework during parental leave and only come to the office for meetings. Allianz,* a German life insurance company, offers parents the opportunity to work from home for up to four days a week and only come to the company for meetings. And the Washington DC area is considered to have 50,000 additional people working at home (or at telecommuting centers near home) or at least one day a week to reduce traffic congestion (Kossek, 2003).

Among scholars there is no consensus yet whether telework actually decreases work–family conflict and enhances work–life balance, or if telework itself is one of the root causes of work–family conflict. While some scholars argue that by reducing commuting time to the office and/ or avoiding traffic jams, time can be saved and used for other activities such as childcare or household tasks (Peters & den Dulk, 2003), others believe that teleworkers often work longer hours compared to employees in other arrangements, and/or have difficulties in keeping work and private hours apart due to a lack of physical barriers between private life and work. As a consequence, they may experience higher levels of work–family conflict (Rau & Hyland, 2002). Nevertheless, telework often implies more control over work schedules which may positively affect the work–life balance of employees (Gottlieb, Kelloway, & Barnham, 1998; Thomas & Ganster, 1995). Being allowed to work from home may create favorable views of the job and the firm, and thus the employee may evaluate the workload associated with the job more positively (Poelmans & Beham, 2005a). Research on the profitability of work–life policies suggests that a company only enjoys significant positive benefits if a considerable amount of employees work from home (Meyer *et al.*, 2001). A possible explanation for these findings is that telework works better if it is accepted and supported

Table 2.5. *Special issues for consideration when offering telework*

- Nature of the job (e.g. required physical presence of the employee, level of supervision involved).
- Contractual arrangements for teleworker and taxation.
- Health and safety arrangements at employee's home.
- Provision of furniture and technical equipment.
- Specific systems requirements (e.g. remote access to company databases and applications).
- Information security.
- Expenses and allowances (e.g. for home heating and lighting), additional travel (e.g. for business meetings).
- Human resources for recruitment, training, and career progression.
- Personal support (e.g. ensure that teleworker does not become isolated).

within the firm, if training and managerial support are provided, and if teleworkers have gone through a learning curve of teleworking "wisely." (See Table 2.5 for a list of issues that need to be considered when implementing telework.)

Leave arrangements
Contrary to flexible work arrangements, which allow for flexibility on a day-to-day or week-by-week basis, leave arrangements have the objective to dismiss employees from work for a longer period of time. Leave arrangements allow employees to return to their jobs after temporarily shifting their attention to their family or personal life. When taking a leave is seen as an alternative to quit employment, it improves outcomes for leave takers (Poelmans & Beham, 2005a). The availability of liberal, even unpaid-leave policies, has been found to increase the likelihood of returning to work after childbirth (Hofferth, 1996). In addition, leave policies have been found to be positively related to loyalty and productivity, and reduced employee turnover (Lambert, 1990; Waldfogel, 1998).

In the majority of European countries leave arrangements for parents are regulated by local law, and therefore differ in duration, monetary refunds, and job protection (see Table 2.9 for an overview). They aim at helping employed women to fulfill family roles, increase the low birth rates, or encourage mothers to return to paid work

(Lewis & Astrom, 1992). Statutory arrangements in Europe mainly include maternity, paternity, and parental leaves that allow parents to take time off from work to care for an infant or young child, as well as short-term leaves to care for a sick child or the elderly. In the United States the only federal law that gives employees a right to job-protected leave is the Family and Medical Leave Act of 1993 (FMLA). The FMLA guarantees eligible employees (having worked a total of twelve months for a covered employer or at least 1,250 hours during the last twelve months) who work for a covered employer (local, state, and federal agencies with more then 50 employees) twelve weeks of unpaid leave in a twelve-month period. During these twelve weeks the employer must maintain the employee's group health coverage and reinstate the employee to his or her former position or an equivalent after his/her return (Nowicki, 2003).

The near absence of governmental leave provision in the US has forced companies to become proactive in the provision of unpaid and paid leave arrangements in order to retain especially their female workforce. A wide variety of leave arrangements are offered by US companies today. Just to give a few examples: Avon Cosmetics,* a company active in the cosmetic industry, with nearly 75 percent of its more than 7,000 employees being women, offers new mothers eight weeks of paid leave, and adoptive parents receive $10,000 toward adoption expenses. Employees at JPMorgan Chase* also get a reimbursement of $10,000 toward adoption expenses and twelve weeks of fully paid maternity leave. Abbott* expanded its parental leave policy very recently in 2004: fathers get two weeks of paid leave, and adoption leave for primary caregivers may now be taken either before or after the adoption (for travel or to complete the process). Credit Swiss First Boston* employees (moms, dads, and adoptive parents) get at least twenty weeks off, job-guaranteed, to look after their child. Upon return they can spend eight weeks phasing back into work on a part-time schedule. In addition, employees can take a sabbatical with full pay for the first month and partial pay for the remaining two months. Parents who want to take the summer off to spend time with their kids may use this arrangement.

Although these examples look impressive and are well intended, the discretionary system of the US has several downsides. It has led to a fragmented system of leave provisions that lacks uniformity, consistency, and equal access to such benefits. Types of arrangements vary by employer size, industry type, public or private sector, and union status. Employees most likely to enjoy paid and extensive leave arrangements are mainly the most highly educated, highest-paid ones working at top-ranked companies (Grosswald, Ragland, & Fisher, 2001).

Compared to the United States, European governmental leave policies are very generous. Paid parental leaves, for example, range from three to thirty-six months depending on the country and can be split to a certain amount of weeks between mother and father. In Austria, for example, the thirty months parental leave including a universal childcare benefit can be extended for another six months, if the other partner (mainly the father) is taking these additional six months. In Norway fathers are eligible to one month of paid family leave reserved for them around the birth of the child, and up to 80 percent of fathers are indeed taking this month off. In Sweden, where approximately 3 percent of fathers took paid parental leave as early as in 1974, the number is now up to more then 50 percent who are taking at least some paid parental leave (Rudd, 2004).

While at a first glance these statutory leave policies in European countries look more generous than the US policies, they also bring along potential risks for leave takers as well as for companies. In some European countries, like Germany or Austria, women with young children stay at home for up to three years, and many young mothers never return to their jobs after having their first or second child. Especially in knowledge-intensive or high-tech businesses which require a permanent update of employees' knowledge and skills, women may face difficulties in returning to their old professions after these long leaves. Their knowledge is outdated at the time they return to work, and technologies or the way business is done may have changed. Permanent contact with the company during parental leaves and systematic knowledge updates help both women who want to return to their former profession and the company that will be able to retain a highly qualified employee. Allianz* regularly organizes come-together sessions for parents on leave at its offices in Germany. The meetings are aimed to keep in touch with parents on leave, exchange information and company news, and normally end with a common lunch. The Bosch Group,* a leading global manufacturer of automotive and industrial technology, consumer goods, and building technology, offers trainings and seminars for parents on leave, and provides regular information about part-time vacancies and temporary sickness and holiday replacements in which parents on leave or parents about to return after a leave may be interested. At Jones Lang LaSalle* unpaid career breaks of six or twelve months are available and are mainly used to extend maternity leaves. During these leaves the HR department actively tries to keep in touch with the employee in order to ensure that they receive company information and also to demonstrate a continuing interest in the employee returning to work.

In general, leaves and career breaks need to be well planned and be part of the career development program offered by the company as well as the business planning process. Judiesch and Lyness (1999) reported that performance ratings were lower during the year a leave was taken, the probability of promotion decreased, and merit salary increases were lower for managers who had been on a leave. The negative impact was equivalent for parental and medical leaves, male and female managers, short- and long-term leaves. These findings suggest that firms are strongly recommended to manage leaves well in terms of keeping employees informed and trained and plan the reincorporation of the employee well beforehand. As in repatriation, returning from a leave can be a traumatic experience for an employee and cause high costs, if the company and the employee did not manage well expectations about job content, workload, salaries, and bonuses. Returning employees may also be confronted with resentful co-workers who had to do double work for several months because the employee was not replaced. At least as important as the formal aspects of the job are the emotional aspects. If the personnel department or the direct supervisor does not support adequate contact with co-workers during the leave, and prepare reintegration upon return, the employee may feel isolated. This will most probably result in a reduction of productivity and well-being in the employee. (See Table 2.6 for a list of issues concerning leave arrangements.)

Care provisions

Care provisions refer to care functions which are performed by others during the time employees are at work and refer to both care for children and elderly people (den Dulk *et al.*, 1999). In terms of childcare, companies may offer on-site childcare centers that are owned and operated by the company or a third party, or collaborate with other companies nearby and run a common childcare center (e.g.

Table 2.6. *Special issues to consider with leave arrangements*

- Leaves need to be planned well beforehand, in order to replace the employee or redistribute the work over existing employees.
- Keep in touch with employees during leave and provide information on work–family policies available after returning to work. Many young mothers never return to their jobs after having a first or second child, because they perceive that combining their caring responsibilities with the demands of their job are incompatible.
- The support person for a pregnant woman or a parent on leave will not always be a husband or wife. But like a husband/wife, support people may be required to attend medical appointments, etc.
- Returns need to be planned beforehand.
- Communicate the degree to which the firm guarantees that the employee can return to the same or a similar job, maintaining the salary level and social benefits.
- Avoid side-tracking or demoting employees (mothers and fathers!) upon their return or taking them less seriously in their career aspirations.

---

in technology parks). On-site childcare or close-by facilities allow employees to reduce transport time by cutting distances. Instead of leaving early to pick up children from school, this time can be invested in an extra hour at work or at home. Communi Corp,* for example, a 200-employee company in Columbus/US offers two on-site childcare centers that provide infant care, kindergarten programs, after-school programs, and evening services on Saturdays. Parents are actively involved in the activities planned for their children, and the convenience of being so close to the center enables employees to leave work to attend planned activities, or just to drop in to check on the children. Schering-Plough* provides two childcare centers that accommodate about 190 kids and provide back-up, holiday, and before- and after-school care, thereby helping parents to manage asynchronous school hours, holidays, and working schedules. And Vaude* runs an on-site daycare center that is open the whole year round from 7.00 a.m. to 5.00 p.m. on weekdays.

On-site childcare is one of the most expensive policies, and only large organizations may have the scale to justify the provision of such a service. But even then, these services may only be available at the headquarters or in big subsidiaries. A less expensive option for small and medium-sized firms and subsidiaries is to provide employees with assistance in locating quality childcare, and/or reimburse the employees for childcare expenses of local childcare providers. Companies can negotiate discounts or reserved slots can be made available at local childcare centers close to the employer. By using the mere scale of the firm (quantity of employees using the services) as a negotiation argument, firms are able to negotiate lower prices with childcare centers than single employees. Discounts may not only signal concern of the employer towards employees but directly translate in tangible monetary value for employees (Poelmans & Beham, 2005a).

To give a few examples: Schering-Plough,* for example, offers those employees who do not have access to its on-site care centers discounts at two national childcare providers. At Citigroup* 10 percent discounts at national daycare chains are available to all US employees.

Companies may also offer assistance to employees when childcare falls through or provide emergency childcare facilities at the company site. The Castle Press,* Pasadena/US, with fifty-six employees, has set up a room for childcare emergencies. This space is equipped with a bed, chairs, television, VCR, children's books, and an abundance of toys. Fraport AG,* the owner and operator of Frankfurt Airport, offers its employees an emergency on-site childcare service, which is open 365 days a year from 6.00 a.m. till 10.00 p.m. When childcare falls through and/or in cases of unexpected calls for duties or emergencies, parents can leave their children at this care center.

Organizations that require high levels of business travel can offer financial reimbursement for childcare expenses incurred because of employees' business travel. Another option is to reduce business travel of employees when young children are around. Accenture,* for example, in 2004 launched the Flexible Career Arrangement, a pilot program that allows managers whose jobs involve frequent out-of-town travel to take local assignments for up to six months which allows them to spend more time with their families. If no such work is available, they can take an unpaid leave of absence.

Care arrangements are a less attractive option for many firms, because of the time that needs to be invested in negotiating these services and financial investments associated with setting up and organizing these services on the company premises. Firms fear the legal aspects of assuming the risk of childcare on-site, or the time of administrative staff spent in interacting with providers and constantly actualizing contracts and services. This can be avoided by radically outsourcing both the risk and the transaction costs by simply facilitating the contact between service providers and employees (Poelmans & Beham, 2005a). Research in Spain showed that merely facilitating information of childcare centers already has a positive impact on employee perceptions (Poelmans, Chinchilla, & Cardona, 2003). This may be the case in Spain, where at the time of the study little support existed, but not in northern European countries, where employees' sense of entitlement may extend beyond support with information to include the right to be financially supported when unexpected assignments force them to arrange childcare.

Supportive arrangements

Supportive arrangements cover a wide range of services which can either serve as a support for the actual implementation of all other policies, or directly support employees with information and training to improve their own work–life balance (Poelmans & Beham, 2005a). The first group of arrangements may include services such as a work–family handbook, an intranet web page that communicates the company's work–family policies, distribution of information to increase the awareness of work–family issues within the organization, like videos or leaflets, or a work–family coordinator who is responsible for work–family initiatives within the company. IBM's* Flexibility Brochure, for example, describes the range of flexible work options, and the two web-based tools *QuickCase* and *QuickView* display work–life scenarios that illustrate the use of IBM flexibility programs and policies. Royal Bank Financial Group* provides a Flexible Work Arrangement Handbook Series that describes the flexibility policies offered by the company and includes checklists for managers and employees. Bosch* provides checklists and information for the use of its flexible work arrangements via the company intranet.

Arrangements that are directly aimed at improving employees' work–life balance include work–family management trainings which provide management personnel with skills necessary to manage a diverse workforce and to implement family-responsive policies and programs; workshops/seminars for all employees on topics related to

Table 2.7. *Advantages and disadvantages of referral programs*

Advantages:
+ Relatively inexpensive to establish.
+ Can serve a broad range of dependent care needs.
+ Adapts to changing demographics of the workplace.
+ Stimulates program development in the community due to greater demand.
+ Fits multi-site companies or smaller departments.
+ Visible within the department.

Disadvantages:
− Initial costs for database generation (if developed in-house).
− Of less use in smaller population centres.
− Do not help families who cannot afford the existing childcare options.
− Costs (time and resources) associated with maintaining the database.

parenting, child development, and elder care; and employee counseling/assistance programs for substance abuse, and for work–family conflict (den Dulk *et al.*, 1999; Galinsky, Friedman, & Hernandez, 1991a). At Nike* in Spain, middle managers are offered time-management training as part of Nike's "24.3 Work-Life Program." In this training special attention is given to achieving harmony between personal and professional spheres. Top managers are offered personalized coaching sessions in order to improve their harmony between work, family, and personal life. They may serve as role models within the organization and create a truly supportive culture.

In terms of child and elder care, services helping employees to find reliable and qualified elder care, seminars and support groups, resource libraries, and information on emergency elder-care support may be provided (Galinsky *et al.*, 1991b). In Germany, for example, many companies including BMW, Lufthansa, and Deutsche Bank contracted the firm Familienservice pme,* a professional child and elder-care referral service which runs offices in all major German cities. Employees can directly contact this service for information on childcare, elder care, babysitters, and au pairs.

Compared to other employer-supported childcare options, information and referral services present the advantages and disadvantages shown in Table 2.7.

Wellness/health or stress management programs set up to prevent or address health issues could also be included here as yet another type of support for employees experiencing conflicts or stress in work, family, or personal life. These programs are mainly not introduced for the specific purpose of work–family balance, but aim at job quality and/or the well-being of the employee and therefore indirectly have a beneficial impact on an employee's personal life. Johnson & Johnson* (J&J) US, for example, pays special attention to the health and well-being of all employees. One of J&J's fitness goals 2006 was helping 90 percent of staffers reach their ideal blood-pressure level and another 85 percent to get their total cholesterol below 240. CEO William C. Weldon and other top J&J executives led a Campus Walk, urging workers to get physically active. Eli Lilly and Company* US recently expanded the hours of its on-site health services and cafeterias 'which now offer healthier meals' and introduced work-shops to help employees deal with work stresses. Novartis* Spain offers all its employees time and stress management seminars which are held during working hours. Prudential Financial* US organized an Adult Care Forum at company headquarters that gave employees the opportunity to speak to experts on aging to collect resource materials, and network. At Royal Bank Financial Group* Canada maternity/parental leave kits, and discounts on parenting/health-related books are available to employees. And a new Breastfeeding Buddies program of Abbott* US links employee mothers who have nursed while working with moms who are just starting out.

The costs involved for providing such services to employees can be optimized by carefully selecting the service provider, and by evaluating the impact and results of the program and training. Obviously the impact can be objectively increased if integrated in a more systematic health program in the firm, as is the case in employee assistance programs which can typically be found in the United States, Australia, and the UK.[2]

If information and training sessions for employees in harmonizing work, family, and personal responsibilities and needs are well set up by the company, they can increase the awareness and skills of employees reduce conflicts and stress and decrease indirectly costs associated with

[2] For more information on employee assistance programs see www.eapconsultants. ie/what_eap.htm.

absenteeism and "presenteeism," and less-than-optimal productivity on the job. A well organized and focused employee is undoubtedly more efficient, creative, and proactive. Nevertheless, in order to really favorably change perceptions in employees by offering these programs, companies need to present this information and training sessions as an expression of true concern of the firm for the well-being of the employee. If these sessions are offered in a period of organizational downsizing or a climate of employee antagonism these sessions can be welcomed with sarcasm. Arrangements that are merely a perk or a way of compensating or even facilitating long working hours may actually provoke turnover (Poelmans & Beham, 2005a). An unfortunate example is a software development firm that provided a wide variety of vending machines and domestic services like prepared meals and laundry services without counteracting the workaholic culture. They subsequently experienced serious problems with employee morale and turnover because their well-intended initiative was interpreted as a way to encourage employees to work even longer hours.

Conventional provisions and compensation/benefits

The last group of arrangements is comprised of conventional compensation and benefits/services provided by the company, and may include health insurances for employees and family members, life insurances, career development options, retirement plans, relocation services for the whole family, company cars, or company-based or outsourced services that help the employees with their domestic tasks, such as cleaning and ironing, shopping, or banking. These services can be offered by the firm or outsourced, off-site or on-site by renting out company office space to service providers, or virtually through links on the intranet. Such benefits traditionally form part of the personnel policy of a firm and have a direct monetary value for the employee. To give some practical examples, at Avon Cosmetics* US pension schemes, private healthcare and life insurances can be tailored to individual needs and preferences. At Land Registry* US, employees receive health screening and relocation packages and have access to an on-site gym. Compuware US helps employees to find care homes, schooling, and legal advice. Lilly Laboratorios* Spain provides dry cleaning and laundry services on site, a photo lab service, and on-line grocery shopping via its intranet. Hewlett Packard* Spain subsidizes parking and meals at its on-site restaurant up to 85 percent of the original price. Sales staff are provided with lunch tickets that can be used at selected restaurants. In addition it offers an on-site gym at headquarters and travel agency services.

Among these conventional policies, career development is an extremely valuable instrument. In order to attract and retain talented employees, and especially women, managers and HR professionals may have to rethink traditional career models. Instead of one predefined linear way of climbing the hierarchy, alternative career paths in which professionals can choose the speed of their promotions need to be offered. While some may choose to advance to vice-president level in five years, others may opt for ten years or more because of young kids, elder-care responsibilities, or to avoid heavy traveling or a relocation. A study among MBA students revealed that participants were more attracted to organizations that offered flexible career paths (Honeycutt & Rosen, 1997; see Chapter 3 in this volume for more details).

Creating a family-friendly company culture and work–life enrichment

The mere implementation of work–life programs does not necessarily guarantee the actual utilization of these policies and the creation of a family-friendly working environment (see also Chapter 8 in this volume and Table 2.8 for an implementation checklist). Several studies have shown that only if employees perceive their organizations as "family-supportive" will work–family policies actually reduce work–family conflict and enhance commitment and job satisfaction (Allen, 2001; O'Driscoll *et al.*, 2004; Thompson, Beauvais, & Lyness, 1999). The attitude of the direct supervisor thereby plays an important role, because he/she decides if and how formal procedures are implemented on a daily basis. Small day-to-day decisions and subtle reactions to employees prioritizing work over family or vice versa shaped the organizational culture.

> *"We plan flexible working arrangements at management level and line managers monitor performance against targets, but it has to become part of the company culture in order to work really well."*
> Andy Middleton, managing director, TYF Group,* UK.

Table 2.8. *Practitioner's checklist – how to get started*

___

(1) Consider the important issues:
- ✓ What impact will work–life policies have on your service to clients?
- ✓ What are the benefits for employees and the organization?
- ✓ What are the potential problems? Can you deal with them?
- ✓ What time, effort, and money will it take to make the arrangements successful?
- ✓ What is the legal situation?
- ✓ Is training required to be sure managers and co-workers have the knowledge and skills to make the arrangements work?

(2) Identify possible options:
- ✓ Ask employees, possibly in a survey, what they want.
- ✓ Consult widely – with other organizations, clients, board members, volunteers, staff.

(3) Formulate policies:
- ✓ Review options, consider strengths and weaknesses of these options.
- ✓ Choose options.
- ✓ Obtain support throughout the organization (all levels of management, trade unions, employee representatives, all staff).
- ✓ Develop written policies and procedures for implementation and monitoring.
- ✓ Allocate adequate resources to draw up and implement schemes.
- ✓ Allocate responsibility for maintaining an overview of the development of policies.

(4) Communicate the change:
- ✓ Communicate to board, clients, staff, volunteers, public.
- ✓ Ensure that the use of flexible work options is voluntary.
- ✓ Acknowledge that developing more flexible work patterns will be a slow process, and is part of a wider cultural change.
- ✓ Provide leaflets, posters, handbooks, etc.
- ✓ Illustrate the business needs for work–life programs and provide real examples to show how for example flexible work patterns work in practice.
- ✓ Use managers to convince other managers of the benefits.

(5) Run a pilot for a trial period and evaluate it:
- ✓ Give support to managers in their policy implementation by providing:
  - • training, written guidelines, a named contact for advice.

(6) Amend and/or extend the program if necessary.

Table 2.8. *(cont.)*

---

(7) Monitor and evaluate:
- ✓ Require managers to report on changes to their work practices as a result of policies and education.
- ✓ Ask employees affected by the policies to provide feedback or suggestions for improvements.
- ✓ Monitor the complaints received in order to determine whether or not they were successfully resolved.

Whether managers are supportive of employees' needs for work–life balance or not depends on various factors such as personal values and beliefs, their own life experiences and circumstances, and undoubtedly also on the way they advanced in their career (Poelmans & Beham, 2005a). Managers who often worked long hours by themselves and were required to sacrifice their family lives in order to climb the corporate ladder may demand the same commitment from their employees, thus making it virtually impossible to balance work and private life (Poelmans & Sahibzada, 2004). British Petroleum (BP), for example, takes a very creative approach to tackle the issue of managers not meeting employees' needs outside the office. Managers and employees are urged to sign contracts that outline work–life boundaries, and ensure that both agree to respect each other's time. We will discuss the policies aimed at a successful implementation and allowance in Chapter 6.

A family-friendly culture cannot be created overnight and (human resource) managers will face the same challenges as of any major organizational change (see also Chapter 9 in this volume). However, it seems that we have reached a point where society, companies, and managers are starting to become aware that they need to eliminate or avoid practices that are "systematically/structurally contaminating" the human ecology of the firm by upsetting the harmony between work, family, and personal life. On the contrary, firms should strive for policies and practices that create an enriching working environment (Poelmans, 2001). We use the term "enriching" because it goes beyond rationally allowing employees to take up their caring responsibilities. It refers to encouraging employees to actively participate in work and family roles and live a balanced and responsible life. In the end, by optimizing the harmony between the different life spheres of their employees, companies serve multiple purposes: economic, social, and ethical.

Table 2.9. *Statutory leave arrangements in Europe*

Leave Regulations in selected European countries

Country	Maternity leave	Payment	Parental leave (right)	Total parental leave	Payment
Belgium	15 weeks	30 days: 82% remaining: 75%	3 months (i)	6 months (26 weeks)	Flat rate: +/- 550 euro per month
Czech Republic	28 weeks	69% of income	156 weeks (f)	156 weeks	113 euro per month
Denmark	18 weeks	100% of wage with max. 419 euro per week	32 weeks (f)	64 weeks	90% of wage, limited to 32 weeks
Germany	14 weeks	100%	36 weeks(including maternity leave)	36 months	300 euro/month for the first 6 months; 7–24 months 300 euro/month but means tested; 25–36 no payment
Estonia	126 days normal (18 weeks)	100% of salary	239 days (f)	239 days (34 weeks)	100% with min. and max.
Spain	16 weeks	100%	36 months (f) including maternity leave	36 months	Unpaid
France	16 weeks	100% with max. 61.11 euro per day	36 months (f) including maternity leave	36 months	Unpaid (485 euro/ month for second and later child

Italy	5 months	Min 80%	10 months until child is 8 (f)	11 months (when father takes 3 months)	30%
Netherlands	16 weeks	100% with max of 165 euro per day	13 weeks (i)	26 weeks	Unpaid
Finland	17.5 weeks	43–82% of earnings (66% average)	26 weeks (f)	145 weeks (f) (including home care leave)	26 weeks: 66% average 119 weeks: about 300 euro per month
Sweden	12 weeks	80%	480 days (i)	960 days	390 days: 80% 90 days: 6.50 per day
United Kingdom	26 weeks	6 weeks: 90%; 20 weeks: flat rate £102.80 per week; 26 weeks unpaid maternity leave who worked at least 1 year at the same employer	13 weeks (i)	13 weeks (i)	Unpaid
Norway	9 weeks	80% (up to ceiling)	29 weeks/100%; 39 weeks' 80%; 5 weeks reserved for father. In addition, both mothers and fathers have an individual right as employees to one year of unpaid leave.	39 + 35 weeks	80% of previous earnings for first 39 weeks; rest of leave unpaid.

i = individual right; f = family right

References

Allen, T. D. (2001). Family-supportive work environments: The role of organizational perceptions. *Journal of Vocational Behavior*, 58, 414–435.

Allen, T. D., Herst, D. E. L., Bruck, C. S., & Sutton, M. (2000). Consequences associated with work-to-family conflict: A review and agenda for future research. *Journal of Occupational Health Psychology*, 5, 278–308.

Arthur, M. M. (2003). Share price reactions to work–family initiatives: An institutional perspective. *Academy of Management Journal*, 46(4), 497–505.

Aryee, S. (1992). Antecedents and outcomes of work–family conflict among married professional women: Evidence from Singapore. *Human Relations*, 45, 8.

Bailyn, L. (2002). Time in organizations: Constraints on, and possibilities for gender equity in the workplace. In R. J. Burke & D. L. Nelson (eds), *Advancing Women's Careers*. New York: Blackwell.

Bailyn, L. & Harrington, M. (2004). Redesigning work for work–family integration. *Community, Work & Family*, 7(2), 197–208.

Baltes, B. B., Huff, T. E., Wright, J. A., & Neuman, G. A. (1999). Flexible and compressed workweek schedules: A meta-analysis of their effects on work-related criteria. *Journal of Applied Psychology*, 84, 496–513.

Barnett, R. C. (2003). Reduced hours work/part-time work. Sloan Work and Family Research Network. Retrieved March 3, 2005, from www.bc.edu/bc_org/avp/wfnetwork/rft/wfpedia/wfpRHWent.html

Barnett, R. C. & Hyde, J. S. (2001). Women, men, work and family: An expansionist theory. *American Psychologist*, October, 781–796.

Bedeian, A. G., Burke, B. G., & Moffet, R. G. (1988). Outcomes of work–family conflict among married male and female professionals. *Journal of Management*, 14(3), 475–491.

Blackwell, L. (2001). Occupational sex segregation and part-time work in modern Britain. *Gender, Work & Organization*, 8, 146–162.

Blank, R. M. (1990). Are part-time jobs bad jobs? In G. Burtless (ed.), *A Future of Lousy Jobs?* Washington, DC: The Brookings Institute.

Boles, J. S., Johnstone, M. W., & Hair, J. H. (1997). Role stress, work–family conflict, and emotional exhaustion: Inter-relationship and effects on some work-related consequences. *Journal of Personal Selling and Sales Management*, Winter, 17–28.

Burke, R. J. (1988). Some antecedents and consequences of work–family conflict. *Journal of Social Behavior and Personality*, 3(4), 287–302.

Casper, W. & Buffardi, L. C. (2004). Work–life benefits and job pursuit intentions: The role of anticipated organizational support. *Journal of Vocational Behavior*, 65, 391–410.

Christensen, K. E. & Staines, G. L. (1990). Flextime: A viable solution to work/family conflict? *Journal of Family Issues*, 11, 455–467.

den Dulk, L. (2001). *Work–Family Arrangements in Organizations: A Cross-National Study in The Netherlands, Italy, the United Kingdom and Sweden*. Amsterdam: Rozenberg Publishers.

den Dulk, L. (2005). Workplace work–family arrangements: A study and explanatory framework of differences between organizational provisions in different welfare states. In S. Poelmans (ed.), *Work and Family: An International Research Perspective*. New York: Lawrence Erlbaum Associates Inc.

den Dulk, L., van Doorne-Huiskes, A., & Schippers, J. (eds). (1999). *Work–Family Arrangements in Europe*. Amsterdam: Thela Thesis.

Dunham, R. B., Pierce, J. L., & Castanda, M. B. (1987). Alternative work schedules: Two field quasi experiments. *Personnel Psychology*, 40, 215–242.

Epstein, C. F., Seron, C., Oglensky, B., & Saute, R. (1999). *The Part-Time Paradox: Time Norms, Professional Lives, Family, and Gender*. New York: Routledge.

Esping-Anderson, G. (1999). *Social Foundations of Postindustrial Economies*. New York: Oxford University Press.

Frone, M. R. (2000). Work–family conflict and employee psychiatric disorders: The national Comorbidity Survey. *Journal of Applied Psychology*, 85(6), 888–895.

Frone, M. R. (2003). Work–family balance. In J. C. Quick & L. E. Tetrick (eds), *Handbook of Occupational Health Psychology*. Washington, DC: American Psychological Association.

Frone, M. R., Russell, M., & Cooper, M. L. (1992). Antecedents and outcomes of work–family conflict: Testing a model of the work–family interface. *Journal of Applied Psychology*, 77, 65–78.

Frone, M. R., Russell, M., & Cooper, M. L. (1997). Relations of work–family conflict to health outcomes: A four-year longitudinal study of employed parents. *Journal of Occupational and Organizational Psychology*, 70, 325–335.

Galinsky, E., Friedman, D. E., & Hernandez, C. A. (1991a). *The Corporate Reference Guide to Work–Family Programs*. New York: Families and Work Institute.

Galinsky, E., Friedman, D. E., & Hernandez, C. A. (1991b). *Work–Family Programs*. New York: Families and Work Institute.

Galinsky, E. & Johnson, A. A. (1998). *Reframing the Business Case for Work–Life Initiatives*. New York: Families and Work Insitute.

Goode, W. J. (1960). A theory of role strain. *American Sociological Review*, 25(4), 483–496.

Goodstein, J. D. (1994). Institutional pressures and strategic responsiveness: Employer involvement in work–family issues. *Academy of Management Journal*, 37(2), 350–382.

Gottlieb, B. H., Kelloway, E. K., & Barnham, E. (1998). *Flexible Work Arrangements: Managing the Work–Family Boundary*. New York: John Wiley & Sons.

Grandey, A. A. (2001). Family friendly policies: Organizational justice perceptions of need-based allocations. In R. Cropanzano (ed.), *Justice in the Workplace: From Theory to Practice* (Vol. 2, pp. 145–173). Mahwah, NJ: Erlbaum.

Greenhaus, J. H. & Beutell, N. J. (1985). Sources of conflict between work and family roles. *Academy of Management Review*, 10(1), 76–88.

Greenhaus, J. H. & Powell, G. N. (2005). When work and family are allies: A theory of work–family enrichment. *Academy of Management Review*, 31, 1–21.

Grosswald, B., Ragland, D., & Fisher, J. M. (2001). Critique of U.S. work/family programs and policies. *Journal of Progressive Human Services*, 12(1), 53–81.

Higgins, C. A., Duxbury, L., & Irving, R. H. (1992). Work–family conflict in the dual-career family. *Organizational Behavior and Human Decision Processes*, 51, 51–75.

Hofferth, S. L. (1996). Effects of public and private policies on working after childbirth. *Work and Occupations*, 23, 378–404.

Honeycutt, T. L. & Rosen, B. (1997). Family friendly human resource policies, salary levels, and salient identity as predictors of organizational attraction. *Journal of Vocational Behavior*, 50, 271–290.

Hyland, M. M. (2003). Flextime. Sloan Work and Family Research Network. Retrieved March 1, 2005, from www.bc.edu/bc_org/avp/wfnetwork/rft/wfpedia/wfpFlxent.html

Judiesch, M. K. & Lyness, K. S. (1999). Left behind? The impact of leaves of absence on managers' career success. *Academy of Management Journal*, 42, 641–651.

Kahn, R. L., Wolfe, D. M., Quinn, R., Snoek, J. D., & Rosenthal, R. A. (1964). *Organizational Stress*. New York: Wiley.

Kossek, E. E. (2003). Telecommuting. The Sloan Work and Family Research Network. Retrieved 03.03., 2005, from www.bc.edu/bc_org/avp/wfnetwork/rft/wfpedia/wfpTCent.html

Kossek, E. E., Dass, P., & DeMarr, B. (1994). The dominant logic of employer-sponsored work and family initiatives: Human resource managers' institutional role. *Human Relations*, 47(9), 1121–1149.

Kossek, E. E. & Nichol, V. (1992). The effects of on-site child care on employee attitudes and performance. *Personnel Psychology*, 45, 485–509.

Kossek, E. E. & Ozeki, C. (1998). Work–family conflict, policies, and the job-life satisfaction relationship: A review and directions for organizational behavior–human resources research. *Journal of Applied Psychology*, 83(2), 139–149.

Lambert, S. (1990). Processes linking work and family: A critical review and research agenda. *Human Relations*, 43(3), 239–257.

Lewis, J. & Astrom, G. (1992). Equality, difference, and state welfare: Labor market and family policies in Sweden. *Feminist Studies*, 18, 59–73.

Lewis, S. (1997a). *European Perspectives of Work and Family Issues.* Boston: The Center for Work & Family.

Lewis, S. (1997b). Family friendly employment policies: A route to changing organizational culture or playing about at the margins? *Gender, Work & Organization*, 4, 13–23.

Lyness, K. S. & Thompson, D. E. (1997). Above the glass ceiling? A comparison of matched samples of female and male executives. *Journal of Applied Psychology*, 82, 359–375.

Marks, S. R. (1977). Multiple roles and role strain: Some notes on human energy, time and commitment. *American Sociological Review*, 41, 921–936.

Meyer, C. S., Mukerjee, S., & Sestero, A. (2001). Work–family benefits: Which one maximizes profits? *Journal of Managerial Issues*, 13(1), 28–44.

Miller, J. (2005). Get a life! *Fortune Magazine*, 152.

Milliken, F. J. & Dunn-Jensen, L. M. (2005). The changing time demands of managerial and professional work: Implications for managing the work–life boundary. In E. E. Kossek & S. Lambert (eds), *Work and Life Integration: Organizational, Cultural, and Individual Perspectives.* Mahwah, NJ: Lawrence Erlbaum Associates.

Milliken, F. J., Dutton, J. E., & Beyer, J. M. (1990). Understanding organizational adaptation to change: The case of work–family issues. *Human Resource Planning*, 13, 91–107.

Milliken, F. J., Martins, L. L., & Morgan, H. (1998). Explaining organisational responsiveness to work–family issues: The role of human resource executives as issue interpreters. *Academy of Management Journal*, 41(5), 580–592.

Morgan, H. & Milliken, F. J. (1992). Keys to action: Understanding differences in organizations' responsiveness to work-and-family issues. *Human Resource Management Journal*, 31, 227–248.

Netemeyer, R. G., Boles, J. S., & McMurrian, R. (1996). Development and validation of work–family conflict and family–work conflict scales. *Journal of Applied Psychology*, 81, 400–410.

Nowicki, C. (2003). *Family and Medical Leave Act.* Sloan Work and Family Research Network. Retrieved January 20, 2006, from http://wfnetwork. bc.edu/encyclopedia_entry.php?id=234&area=academics

O'Driscoll, M., Poelmans, S., Spector, P. E., Cooper, C. L., Allen, T. D., & Sanchez, J. I. (2004). The buffering effect of family-responsive interventions, perceived organizational and supervisor support in the work–family conflict–strain relationship. *International Journal of Stress Management*, 10(4), 326–344.

OECD. (2001). *Employment Outlook 2001*: OECD.

Osterman, P. (1995). Work–family programs and the employment relationship. *Administrative Science Quarterly*, 40, 681–700.

Parasuraman, S., Purohit, Y. S., Godshalk, V. M., & Beutell, N. J. (1996). Work and family variables, entrepreneurial career success, and psychological well-being. *Journal of Vocational Behavior*, 48, 275–300.

Perry-Smith, J. E. & Blum, T. (2000). Work–family human resource bundles and perceived organizational performance. *Academy of Management Journal*, 43(5), 1107–1117.

Peters, P. & den Dulk, L. (2003). Cross-cultural differences in managers' support for home-based telework. *International Journal of Cross Cultural Management*, 3(3), 333–350.

Plantenga, J. & Remery, C. (2005). *Reconciliation of Work and Private Life: A Comparative Review of Thirty European Countries*. Luxembourg: European Commission.

Poelmans, S. (2001). Cómo armonizar trabajo y familia en el nuevo siglo. In *Paradigmas del liderazgo [How to harmonize work and family in the new century. Paradigms of leadership]* pp. 195–211. Barcelona: IESE Publishing.

Poelmans, S. & Beham, B. (2005a). A conceptual model of antecedents and consequences of managerial work/life policy allowance decisions. Paper presented at the Inaugural Conference of the International Center of Work and Family, International Research of Work and Family: From Policy to Practice, Barcelona.

Poelmans, S. & Beham, B. (2005b). La gestion del equilibrio entre trabajo y familia. In J. Bonache & A. Cabrera (eds), *Dirección de personas* (2nd ed.). Madrid: Prentice Hall.

Poelmans, S., Chinchilla, N., & Cardona, P. (2003). Family-friendly HRM policies and the employment relationship. *International Journal of Manpower*, 24(3), 128–147.

Poelmans, S. & Sahibzada, K. (2004). A multi-level model for studying the context and impact of work–family policies and culture in organizations. *Human Resource Management Review*, 14, 409–431.

Powell, G. N. & Mainiero, L. A. (1999). Managerial decision making regarding alternative work arrangements. *Journal of Occupational and Organizational Psychology*, 72, 41–56.

Rasmussen, E. , Lind, J., & Visser, J. (2004). Divergence in part-time work in New Zealand, the Netherlands, and Denmark. *British Journal of Industrial Relations*, 42, 637–658.

Rau, B. L. (2003). Flexible work arrangements. Sloan Work and Family Research Network. Retrieved March 3, 2005, from www.bc.edu/ bc_org/avp/wfnetwork/rft/wfpedia/wfpFWAent.html

Rau, B. L. & Hyland, M. M. (2002). Role conflict and flexible work arrangements: The effects on applicant attraction. *Personnel Psychology*, 55, 111–136.

Rodgers, C. (1992). The flexible workplace: What have we learned? *Human Resource Management*, 31, 183–199.

Rothausen, T. J., Gonzalez, J. A., Clarke, N. E., & O'Dell, L. L. (1998). Family-friendly backlash – Fact or fiction? The case of organizations' on-site child care centers. *Personnel Psychology*, 51, 685–705.

Rudd, E. (2004). Family leave: A policy concept made in America. Sloan Work and Family Research Network. Retrieved January 20, 2006, from http:// wfnetwork.bc.edu/encyclopedia_entry.php?id=233&area=academics

Scandura, T. A. & Lankau, M. J. (1997). Relationship of gender, family responsibility and flexible work hours to organizational commitment and job satisfaction. *Journal of Organizational Behavior*, 18, 377–391.

Shinn, M., Wong, N. W., Simko, P. A., & Ortiz-Torres, B. (1989). Promoting well-being of working parents: Coping, social support, and flexible schedules. *American Journal of Community Psychology*, 17, 31–55.

SIBIS (2003). *SIBIS Pocket Book 2002/03*. Bonn: empirica GmbH.

Sieber, S. (1974). Toward a theory of role accumulation. *American Sociological Review*, 39, 567–578.

Thomas, L. & Ganster, D. (1995). Impact of family-supportive work variables on work–family conflict and strain: a control perspective. *Journal of Applied Psychology*, 1, 6–15.

Thompson, C. A., Beauvais, L. L., & Lyness, K. S. (1999). When work–family benefits are not enough: The influence of work–family culture on benefit utilization, organizational attachment, and work–family conflict. *Journal of Vocational Behavior*, 54, 392–415.

Tombari, N. & Spinks, N. (1999). The work/family interface at Royal Bank Financial Group: Successful solutions – a retrospective look at lessons learned. *Women in Management Review*, 14(5), 186–193.

US Department of Labor (2000). *Telework and the New Workplace of the 21st Century*. Washington, DC: Government Printing Office.

Waldfogel, J. (1998). The family gap for young women in the United States and Britain: Can maternity leave make a difference? *Journal of Labor Economics*, 16, 505–545.

References of cases

*Abbott – www.workingmother.com/abbott.html

*Accenture – www.workingmother.com/accenture.html

*Allianz – www.fast-4ward.de/base/show_article.php?a=355

*Avon – www.workingmother.com/avon.html

*Bosch Group – www.fast-4ward.de/base/show_article.php?a=238

*Bristol-Meyers Squibb – www.workingmother.com/bristolmyers.html

*Castle Press – Juggling Work with Life (2005). www.graphicartsfnonthlv.
   com

*Citigroup – www.workingmother.com/citigroup.html

*Communi Corp – Juggling Work with Life (2005). www.graphicartsfnonthlv.
   com

*Credit Swiss First Boston – www.workingmother.com/csfb.html

*Deutsche Bank – http://career.deutsche-bank.com/wms/dbhr/index.php?
   language=1&ci=3184

*Eli Lilly – www.workingmother.com/elililly.html

*Familienservice pme – www.familienservice.de/xi-400-0-1000-98-0-de.html

*Fleet Financial Group – Bailyn, L., Rayman, P., Bengtsen, D., Carré, F., &
   Tierney, M. (2001). Fleet Financial and Radcliffe explore paths of work/
   life integration. *Journal of Organizational Excellence*, 49–64.

*Fraport AG – Bundesministerium für Familien, Senioren, Frauen und Jugend
   (2003). *Betriebswirtschaftliche Effekte familienfreundlicher Maßnahmen.*

*General Mills – www.workingmother.com/generalmills.html

*Gres de Valls – Chinchilla, N. & Poelmans, S. (2001). *The Adoption of
   Family-Friendly HRM Policies: Competing for Scarce Resources in the
   Labour Market*. Research paper No. 438. Barcelona: IESE Publishing.

*Happy Ltd – Meet the needs of work–life balance. www.businesslink.gov.
   uk/bdotg/action/detail?r.s=sc&type=CASE%20STUDIES&itemId=
   1075431613#

*Hewlett Packard – Chinchilla, N., Poelmans, S., León, C., & Tarrés, J. B.
   (2005). *Guía de Buenas Prácticas de la Empresa Flexible*. Communidad
   de Madrid.

*IBM – Giue, J. & Petrescu, O. *The IBM Case*. Chapter 5 this volume.

*JetBlue – Miller, J. (2005). Get a life! *Fortune Magazine*, 152.

*Johnson & Johnson – www.workingmother.com/jnj.html

*Jones Lang LaSalle – Implementing work–life balance at Jones Lang LaSalle
   (2003). *HR at Work*, 2, 2.

JPMorgan Chase* – www.workingmother.com/jpmorgan.html

*Land Registry – Vowler, J. (2005). A flexible benefits scheme is key to staff
   loyalty. *Computer Weekly*.

*Lilly Laboratorios – Chinchilla, N., Poelmans, S., León, C., & Tarrés, J. B. (2005). *Guía de Buenas Prácticas de la Empresa Flexible*. Communidad de Madrid.

*Manor Group – www.familienplattform.ch/familienplattform/unternehmen-manor.htm

*Nike – taken from Professor Poelmans's consulting practice.

*Novartis – www.workingmother.com/novartis.html

*Pearson NCS – Juggling work with life (2005). www.graphicartsfnonthlv.com

*Prudential Financial – www.workingmother.com/prudential.html

*Royal Bank Financial Group – Tombari, N. & Spinks, N. (1999). The work/family interface at Royal Bank Financial Group: successful solutions – a retrospective look at lessons learned. *Women in Management Review*, 14(5), 186–193.

*Schering-Plough – www.workingmother.com/schering.html

*Technical University in Berlin – www.tu-berlin.de/presse/tui/95jun/jobshari.html

*TYF Group – Benefits of flexible working www.businesslink.gov.uk/bdotg/action/detail?type=CASE%20STUDIES&itemId= 1075398836&r.l3= 1074409708&r.l2=1073858908&r.t=CASE%20STUDIES&r.i=10 75431613&r.l1=1073858787&r.s=rg

*University of Marburg – www.tu-berlin.de/presse/tui/95jun/jobshari.html

*Vaude – www.fast-4ward.de/base/show_article.php?a=495

3 | Integrating career development and work–family policy

TAMMY D. ALLEN
University of South Florida, USA

Felice Schwartz made waves in her 1989 *Harvard Business Review* article that suggested that the costs of employing women in management was greater than the costs of employing men. Schwartz recommended that women be divided into two categories: "career primary" and "career and family." The article prompted a fierce controversy that included the accusation that Schwartz advocated a separate "mommy track" for women who were willing to give up higher pay and promotion opportunities in exchange for more flexible jobs that allowed them to attend to family needs.

The mommy track controversy was a foreshadowing of things to come. The vast majority of employees, both male and female, want to be able to lead fulfilling career as well as family lives. Indeed a recent Fortune 500 poll of senior male executives found that 84 percent reported that they want job options that allow them to realize their professional aspirations while having more time for things outside of work (Miller, Miller, & Zappone, 2005). Additionally, half of the men had questioned if the sacrifices they made for their careers were worth it. Although organizations have become more cognizant of the needs of employees who wish to balance their work and family lives, and are increasingly implementing policies and benefits designed to help them do so, organizational career development systems are still primarily based on outdated models that presume the career is all-important to all employees. One manifestation of this problem is that many employees are reluctant to use benefits such as flextime because they fear that using them will send a signal of less commitment and will jeopardize opportunities for future career advancement. The structure of career paths and the traditional practices used for developing managers need to be redesigned to better accommodate employees with families.

The purpose of this chapter is to examine the intersection between individual and organizational career development with that of work–family needs and policies. The chapter unfolds as follows. First I review the literature examining career implications for individuals as a function of their family structure and use of family-supportive benefits. Next, I provide a brief overview of career stages and organizational career systems. Finally, I offer suggestions for organizations to better harmonize work, family, and career development.

Work and family career backlash

Career advancement is important to individuals in that it represents economic and personal achievement and it is important to organizations as it signifies developed human resources (HR) (Schwartz, 1994). Does work–family conflict and participation in work–family programs hurt employees' career advancement? One of the reasons often cited regarding why employees do not use so-called family-friendly benefits is because they fear it will have a detrimental impact on their career (Allen, 2001; Anderson, Coffey, & Byerly, 2002; Israeloff, 1995; Levine, 1997; Thompson, Beauvais, & Lyness, 1999). A substantial amount of research suggests these fears are warranted.

Cohen and Single (2001) found that both male and female accounting professionals who used flexible work arrangements (FWA) were judged as less likely to advance to partner, more likely to leave the company, and less likely to be requested on a future assignment than were those not using FWA. Experimental research has shown that women depicted as being on a flexible schedule are rated as less dedicated and as having less advancement motivation than women depicted on a standard work schedule, despite having identical performance (Rogier & Padgett, 2004). Similarly, Almer, Cohen, and Single (2004) found that FWA participants were viewed as less committed and less likely to advance in their careers than were participants without children or participants who had children but were not using an FWA. Research conducted by Catalyst (1993) has also found that flexible work arrangements reduce employees' rate of career advancement. The perceived negative effects of using flexible work arrangements also extend to compensation, with employees believing that salary increases are adversely impacted by their use (Hooks, 1989).

Wiese (2005) found that personnel managers believed there were negative career consequences associated with taking a maternity leave and that managers would advise pregnant professionals to return to work as soon as possible. Such warnings are not surprising given that Judiesch and Lyness (1999) report that managers who took leaves of absence, for illness or for family reasons, subsequently were promoted less often and received smaller salary increases than did employees who did not take a leave. No gender differences were detected, but that could have been because of the small number of men who take such leaves. Other research has demonstrated that career interruptions negatively affect subsequent earnings (Jacobsen & Levin, 1995; Schneer & Reitman, 1997).

In a study of Spanish employees, it was found that employees with high levels of work–family conflict had limited internal occupational mobility in terms of having fewer promotions and lateral transfers within the organization (Carnicer, Perez, Sanchez, & Jimenez, 2003). In a longitudinal field study, Knoke and Ishio (1998) examined gender differences in training program participation. They found evidence that women's greater involvement in part-time work along with marital and childcare obligations decreased their involvement in training opportunities. The authors suggest that employers likely believe that women's familial responsibilities result in transient attachment to the labor force, and thus are less willing to invest company resources in developing women.

Certain family structures alone may negatively impact employee career development. Tharenou (1999) found that family structures (i.e. marital status, parental status, and whether one's spouse is employed outside the home) were associated with managerial career advancement. For example, dads in single-earner marriages advance more than dads in dual-earner marriages. Other research has found that single-earner dads earn more than dads in dual-career marriages (e.g. Schneer & Reitman, 1993, 2002; Stroh & Brett, 1996). Similarly, Eby, Allen, and Douthitt (1999) found that married women and employees in dual-career marriages were less likely to be recommended for a job requiring geographic relocation. These findings were explained by perceptions regarding the applicant's willingness to relocate and perceived family resistance to moving. It appears that decision-makers make assumptions about employees based on their family structure that in turn limit opportunities for relocation.

The detrimental career impact of using family-oriented benefits may be harsher for males than for females. Almer *et al.* (2004) found that male accountants on an FWA were perceived as less likely to stay with the company and to advance to partner than were female accountants on an FWA. Butler and Skattebo (2004) found that men who experienced work–family conflict received lower overall performance ratings and lower reward recommendations than men who did not. Women's ratings were not affected by the experience of work–family conflict. Allen and Russell (1999) found that men who took a parental leave of absence were less likely to be recommended for organizational rewards than were men who did not take a leave. Wayne and Cordeiro (2003) found that males who took a leave of absence for family reasons were rated as less likely to be altruistic at work than were males who did not take a leave or females who did take a leave.

In sum, there is ample evidence that family and using family-supportive benefits may be detrimental to employee career development. Indeed, based on interviews conducted with Fortune 500 executives, DePhillips (2005) reported that pursuing work–life balance gets individuals labeled as "B" players. These findings underscore the need for companies to alter their career management practices, in addition to implementing family-friendly benefits and policies.

Career stages and organizational career systems

The approach to understanding career development from an individual's perspective has long been dominated by the idea that individuals pass through distinct career and life stages. There are different needs and challenges associated with each of these stages (e.g. Levinson, 1986). During young adulthood, individuals are concerned with adjusting to the working world and establishing themselves. This is also the time of peak fertility for women. Concerns regarding career establishment versus family establishment are often at the forefront. Middle adulthood is characterized by reappraisal and concerns regarding career accomplishment. Because childbearing has typically come to a close, this can be a liberating time of career opportunity if earlier focus has been on the family. Older worker issues center on fear of stagnation and planning for retirement. Employers may need to conduct a socio-demographic study of the workforce in order to adapt and prioritize offerings to different age/seniority groups with families in different stages of development. There are important differences between a workforce with a lot of young women at the "fertile" age, like, for instance, in temporary work agencies, and a workforce with mainly mature male engineers with children at the adolescent age, as in more traditional and mature industry sectors. These differences need to be taken into account when designing career systems within the organization.

Organizations are interested in achieving an optimal match between people and jobs. Career development systems refer to the formal structures for evaluating and developing employees within organizations. Clearly management plays an important role in this system as employee evaluation is based on the expectations and implicit standards against which managers judge employees. Successful career management depends on an integrated and comprehensive system of associated practices such as performance appraisal used for career planning, secondment assignments, succession planning, and formal education opportunities. The ideal career system is aligned with organizational objectives and needs.

Recommendations for integrating work and family with employee development

Expand ideas regarding flexibility. Flexibility in terms of the scheduling of work hours (i.e. flextime, compressed workweeks) and in terms of location (i.e. telecommuting) have become relatively common within large corporations. Flextime has been reported as the most commonly offered family-friendly benefit, followed by telework, within the United States and in Canada (Comfort, Johnson, & Wallace, 2003; SHRM Foundation, 2001). However, flexible policies need to extend beyond daily scheduling and the location of work. That is, the flexibility concept can be constructed to encompass the entire career course. As noted by Moen and Roehling (2005) the lockstep arrangements around education, work, family, and retirement are outdated. New work arrangements that allow for *career* flexibility with multiple points for entry and re-entry over the course of an individual's career are required. A career can last forty years. It is often assumed that careers that do not follow a continuous pattern of steady and regular promotion are defective. Taking a few months or even a few years off should not prevent future career advancement prospects. Similarly career progress may vary in pace. For example, an employee may want to continue working, but slow down for a period of time (e.g. reduce travel, reduce long hours) to help care for a dying parent. After a period of time the same employee may be ready to ramp his or her career back up. Organizations that acknowledge and accept the existence of such pace changes over the course of a career can make provisions for employees that avoid permanent career derailment.

It is important for organizations to recognize that career development is still important to those who also place a high value on the family. For example, Ernst & Young has a policy in which women are encouraged to keep in touch during time taken off to care for family and to sign up for part-time projects. The company also offers employees services such as 100 hours of outside help, such as babysitting and elder care, to help ease the transition back into full-time work (Ramachandran, 2005). Ernst & Young has made a commitment to removing the stigma associated with part-time arrangement or telecommuting arrangements, making sure that women stay connected to learning opportunities, development opportunities, and promotions, even while they are using these alternate work options.

Careers researchers have long recognized that the career patterns of women tend to differ from those of men, with the career sequence of women being described as more disorderly than that of men (Mainiero & Sullivan, 2005; Sweet & Moen, 2006). The *Hidden Brain Drain* task force, a group of nineteen global corporations examining reasons why highly qualified women are dropping out of mainstream careers, have more recently been examining the career patterns of women (Hewlett, 2005). The study notes that 37 percent of highly qualified women voluntarily leave their career for a period of time. The vast majority of women (93 percent) who take a break want to return to work. Providing a welcome environment can make it happen. Caroline Waters, director of BT People & Policy, notes, "Supporting the parents in your workforce isn't difficult, disruptive, or expensive, it's just plain business sense." BT has 99 percent of women returning to work at the company following maternity leave. BT offers a generous paid leave program following the birth of a child and the opportunity for both men and women to use flexible work arrangements.

Keep the focus on performance. Employers should let go of assumptions that people in certain family structures will be more or less interested in certain career opportunities. For example, employees with working spouses should not be thought of as less likely to accept job opportunities that involve geographic relocation. Moreover, strong commitment to the family role does not preclude strong commitment to the work role. In many organizations, face time is used as a proxy for performance. Better for both the company and the employee is a focus on measurable objectives tied to company goals. Employee performance should be assessed based on meeting objectives, whether working from inside or outside the office. A collaborative focus between employee and manager on goal setting and providing the employee the freedom to meet those goals in a way that works best for him or her can be both motivating and liberating (Latham, 2004). As long as business objectives are met, employees should not be undervalued simply because they schedule their work at different hours or outside of the workplace.

Implement mentoring programs. Formal mentoring programs are being increasingly incorporated as part of a human resource strategy by organizations seeking a way to increase their competitive advantage through employee learning and development (Allen, Eby, & Lentz, 2006; Allen & O'Brien, 2006; Douglas & McCauley, 1999; Eddy, Tannenbaum, Alliger, D'Abate, & Givens, 2003). Mentoring opportunities are important in that research demonstrates that those who have been mentored reap a vast array of career benefits and increased job satisfaction (Allen, Eby, Poteet, Lentz, & Lima, 2004). Additionally, Nielson, Carlson, and Lankau (2001) found that having a mentor, receiving role modeling and mentor support, and having a mentor who is perceived to have similar work–family values related to less work-to-family conflict. Deutsche Bank, which has been listed among the 100 best companies to work for, uses "mentoring circles" to pair five employees with two senior managers in an effort to help women connect and advance within the organization. Likewise, Burlington Northern Santa Fe Railway Co. uses mentoring circles to bring together mixed-gender groups. Other companies such as Ernst & Young have developed mentoring programs designed to foster employee career development. Programs include those that target minorities (Learning Partnerships) and those that provide mentoring for key women leaders by Executive Board members (PLAN). Specific issues addressed in mentoring partnerships include how to have flexibility between work and non-work activities. Some companies, such as S. C. Johnson include the desire to discuss work–family balance as a topic when determining how to match mentors and protégés. In a new twist on mentoring, several companies have started "reverse mentoring" or "mentor-up" programs in which junior women coach senior executives to increase understanding of women's experiences. One such company is Procter & Gamble. Their mentoring initiatives have been credited with challenging work–family assumptions and with improving the retention of talented female employees. An additional interesting consequence of these mentoring systems is that they can be used to provide a feedback system for finding out how successful career and work–family policies are and why this is or is not the case, allowing further fine-tuning of these systems.

Finkelstein and Poteet (2007) provide a variety of research-based suggestions regarding the design and implementation of formal mentoring programs to enhance their effectiveness. For example, one of the most critical issues for consideration when designing a formal mentoring program is the process used to match mentors and protégés. Random assignment should be avoided. Finkelstein and Poteet recommend basing the matching process on the program's objectives as well as the overall culture of the organization (e.g. if the objective is to provide engineers marketing experience, the organization may proactively pair the engineer with a senior marketing executive).

Employee training and program bundles. Based on research demonstrating a gender gap in training, Knoke and Ishio (1998) recommend that corporations consider integrating job training programs into their bundle of work–family programs to ensure that training and education opportunities are available to all employees. The career management (Eby, Allen, & Brinley, 2005), general human resources (Huselid, 1995), and work–family literature (Perry-Smith & Blum, 2000) has also stressed how companies can bundle benefits and human resource practices into integrated packages that reinforce organizational culture and strategy. Integrated career systems include basic processes such as internal job posting, educational opportunities, and lateral mobility. However, an integrated system will also incorporate other HR systems, such as performance appraisals, as a tool for career planning, formal mentoring and assessment centers as employee development tools, and peer appraisals to provide employees with multidirectional feedback (Baruch, 2002).

One example of an integrated system is Michelin. At Michelin it is recognized that "Just as tires are a complex blend of elements, so too are people." The Michelin career development system is set up to allow a variety of opportunities for career enrichment, education, and training. For example, employees in middle and upper management are assigned to a dedicated career manager. Moreover, each manager is charged with working with employees to establish career directions and objectives. Training opportunities are aligned with specific career paths that employees may choose. Other companies such as Bank of American and United Technologies use assessment centers, multi-source performance appraisals, and individual internal and external career coaches to help employees grow and develop. Often employees are coached on making career decisions that are aligned with their family needs and values.

Supervisor support and training. Research from a variety of areas indicates that supervisors play a key role in how employees experience the workplace (Dormann & Zapf, 1999). For example, previous research has shown that employees who have good relationships with their supervisors are more satisfied, more committed, and perform better (Gerstner & Day, 1997). Not surprising then is that supervisors can also play a critical role in enabling employees to manage their work and family responsibilities (Allen, 2001; Anderson *et al.*, 2002; Thomas & Ganster, 1995; Thompson *et al.*, 1999). Family-supportive supervisors can alleviate work–family conflict by providing flexibility when employees must meet non-work demands such as scheduling doctor and school appointments (Galinsky & Stein 1990). Unsupport-ive supervisors may limit access or make it difficult for employees to use organizational benefits designed to help employees balance work and non-work (Brewer, 2000; Glass & Fugimoto, 1995; Warren & Johnson, 1995). Research shows that the more supervisor support an individual has, the less likely they are to report work–family conflict (Allen, 2001; Frone *et al.*, 1997; Goff, Mount, & Jamison, 1990; Thomas & Ganster, 1995).

Given the importance of supervisor support, researchers have suggested that training supervisors with regard to employee family concerns might promote the use of work–family programs in a way that enhances employee career development and work productivity while also resulting in improved quality of family life (Galinsky & Hughes, 1987; Lobel & Kossek, 1996). For example, Lobel and Kossek (1996) argue that training supervisors in such skills as flexibility, promoting cross-training among employees, communication, coordination, and team-building would encourage the use of family-friendly initiatives. Moreover, in an assessment of the keys to the success of an FWA program, Tombari and Spinks (1999) report that supportive managers were an essential feature.

Sara Lee CEO John Bryan has implemented a policy in which managers' bonuses are tied to the level of their subordinates' satisfaction with such issues as work–life balance (Schwartz, 1999). Bryan has stated, "It's very difficult for a bunch of old white men sitting around in a room to acculturate companies to changing times. You need diversity now, and female diversity is an extremely important element of that." Other organizations such as Quaker Oats have implemented intensive training programs for managers and super-visors. Speaking with regard to why such training is important, Vice-President of Quaker Oats Robert Montgomery has said, "If one has never had to move an older person from a hospital to extended care, one might think it was a matter of two hours off. In fact the process takes weeks, including visits to nursing homes, lawyers, etc." Other companies such as DuPont and Johnson & Johnson have reported employees perceive that their supervisors have become more sup-portive of their work–family issues following the implementation of supervisor training (Schwartz, 1994).

Many aspects of the work environment are under the direct control of supervisors, and training supervisors to be more family-supportive can impact large numbers of employees. This is in contrast to many work–family benefits/policies that benefit only a subset of employees. For example, not all employees have a need for childcare supports and some jobs are not amenable to telecommuting (e.g. nursing). The more supervisors support employee work–life balance efforts, the more that value will be manifested in the overall organizational culture (Allen, 2001; Murphy & Zagorski, 2005).

A 2000 study conducted by the Office of Personnel Management (OPM) demonstrated that the primary reason cited by supervisors and managers for not implementing family-friendly programs, such as flextime and telework, involved anxiety regarding office coverage and problems scheduling meetings. Supervisors and managers also believed that compressed work schedules and telework could negatively impact productivity. The program deemed most problematic by supervisors was telework. Supervisors were concerned about the ability to adequ-ately monitor work done at home. Another issue raised by supervisors was that family-friendly benefits can generate feelings of entitlement among employees that are inconsistent with the needs of the organization. Employees attributed inconsistency in the implementation of family-friendly programs to differences in supervisors' attitudes toward family-friendly programs and to the fact that supervisors often have considerable discretion in terms of deciding whether or not employees can participate in programs. Interestingly, while only 8 percent of the managers interviewed disagreed that employees who have personal or work-related problems are offered help, 21 percent of the employees interviewed disagreed. Clearly, training could go a long way toward alleviating these sorts of concerns. A recommendation that emerged from the OPM study was that supervisors should be trained to understand the beneficial impact of family-friendly programs on attracting and retaining quality employees and on how to use work planning and scheduling tools to assure productivity by employees using family-friendly benefits.

Conclusion

What are the implications for a society of workplace structures that perpetuate the myth of the ideal employee (Williams, 1999)? Organizations that monopolize the time of employees challenge the ability of employees to perform well in other important roles within the family and the community. Cleveland (2005) suggests that organizations should be held accountable for frequently placing demands on their employees that interfere with their ability to function well as spouses, parents, and caregivers. Moreover, Cleveland also advocates that a broader conception of the successful organization is needed that accounts for variables such as the marital health of employees, individual and family stress, children's physical health, educational development, and mental and social well-being. As stated by Xerox Corporation CEO Anne Mulcahy, "Businesses need to be 24/7, individuals don't."

References

Allen, T.D. (2001). Family-supportive work environments: The role of organizational perceptions. *Journal of Vocational Behavior*, 58, 414–435.

Allen, T. D., Eby, L. T., & Lentz, E. (2006). The relationship between formal mentoring program characteristics and perceived program effectiveness. *Personnel Psychology*, 59, 125–153.

Allen, T. D., Eby, L. T., Poteet, M. L., Lentz, E., & Lima, L. (2004). Career benefits associated with mentoring for protégés: A meta-analytic review. *Journal of Applied Psychology*, 89, 127–136.

Allen, T. D. & O'Brien, K. (2006). Formal mentoring programs and organizational attraction. *Human Resource Development Quarterly*, 17, 43–58.

Allen, T. D. & Russell, J. E. A. (1999). Parental leave of absence: Some not so family friendly implications. *Journal of Applied Social Psychology*, 29, 166–191.

Almer, E. D., Cohen, J. R., & Single, L. E. (2004). The incremental effect of families and flexible scheduling on perceived career success. *Journal of Business Ethics*, 54, 51–65.

Anderson, S. E., Coffey, B. S., & Byerly, R. T. (2002). Formal organizational initiatives and informal work practices: Links to work–family conflict and job-related outcomes. *Journal of Management*, 28, 787–810.

Baruch, Y. (2002). Career systems in transition: A normative model for organizational career practices. *Personnel Review*, 32, 231–251.

Butler, A. B. & Skattebo, A. (2004). What is acceptable for women may not be for men: The effect of family conflicts with work on job-performance ratings. *Journal of Occupational and Organizational Psychology*, 77, 553–564.

Brewer, A. M. (2000). Work design for flexible work scheduling: Barriers and gender implications. *Gender, Work, and Organization*, 7, 33–44.

Carlson, L. (2005, December 1). Benefits that meet moms' needs – then and now. *BenefitNews.com*, 19. Available online: www.benefitnews.com/

Carnicer, M. P., Perez, M. P., Sanchez, A. M., & Jimenez, M. J. V. (2003). Human resources mobility management: A study of job related and non-related factors. *International Journal of Human Resources Development and Management*, 3, 308–328.

Carnicer, M. P., Sanchez, A. M., & Perez, M. P. (2004). Work–family conflict in a southern European country: The influence of job-related and non-related factors. *Journal of Managerial Psychology*, 19, 466–489.

Catalyst (1993). *Flexible Work Arrangements II: Succeeding with Part-time Options*. New York: Catalyst.

Cleveland, J. (2005). What is success? Who defines it? Perspectives on the criterion problem as it relates to work and family. In E. E. Kossek & S. Lambert (eds), *Work and Life Integration: Organizational, Cultural, and Individual Perspectives* (pp. 319–346). Mahwah, NJ: Lawrence Erlbaum.

Cohen, J. R. & Single, L. E. (2001). An examination of the perceived impact of flexible work arrangements on professonal opportunities in public accounting. *Journal of Business Ethics*, 32, 317–328.

Comfort, D., Johnson, K., & Wallace, D. (2003). *Part-time Work and Family-friendly Practices in Canadian Workplaces* (The Evolving Workplace Series, No. 71–584–MIE No. 6). Ottawa, Canada: Statistics Canada/Human Resources Development Canada.

Dephillips, S. A. (2005). *Corporate Confidential: Fortune 500 Executives off the Record – What it Really Takes to Get to the Top*. Avon, MA: Platinum Press.

Dormann, C. & Zapf, D. (1999). Social support, social stressor at work, and depressive symptoms: Testing for main and moderating effects with structural equations in a three-wave longitudinal study. *Journal of Applied Psychology*, 84, 874–884.

Douglas, C. A. & McCauley, C. D. (1999). Formal developmental relationships: A survey of organizational practices. *Human Resource Development Quarterly*, 10, 203–224.

Eby, L. T. & Allen, T. D. (2005). A cross-level investigation of the relationship between career management practices and career-related attitudes. *Group & Organization Management*, 30, 565–596.

Eby, L. T., Allen, T. D., & Douthitt, S. S. (1999). The role of nonperformance factors on job-related relocation opportunities: A field study and laboratory experiment. *Organizational Behavior and Human Decision Processes*, 79, 29–55.

Eddy, E., Tannenbaum, S., Alliger, G., D'Abate, C., & Givens, S. (2003). Mentoring in industry: The top 10 issues when building and supporting a mentoring program. Paper presented at the 18th annual meeting of the Society of Industrial and Organizational Psychology, Orlando, Florida.

Finkelstein, L. M. & Poteet, M. L. (2007). Best practices in organizational formal mentoring programs. In T. D. Allen & L. T. Eby (eds), *Blackwell Handbook of Mentoring: A Multiple Perspectives Approach*. Oxford: Blackwell.

Frone, M. R., Yardley, J. K., & Markel, K. S. (1997). Developing and testing an integrative model of the work–family interface. *Journal of Vocational Behavior*, 50, 145–197.

Galinsky, E. & Hughes, D. (1987). *Fortune Magazine Child Care Study*. New York: Bank Street College of Education.

Galinsky, E. & Stein, P. J. (1990). The impact of human resource policies on employees. *Journal of Family Issues*, 11(4), 368–383.

Gerstner, C. R. & Day, D. V. (1997). Meta-analytic review of leader-member exchange theory: Correlates and construct issues. *Journal of Applied Psychology*, 82, 824–844.

Glass, J. L. & Fujimoto, T. (1995). Employer characteristics and the provision of family responsive policies. *Work and Occupations*, 22(4), 380–411.

Goff, S. J., Mount, M. K., & Jamison, R. L. (1990). Employer supported child care, work/family conflict, and absenteeism: A field study. *Personnel Psychology*, 43, 793–809.

Hewlett, S. A. (2005). We can stop the female brain drain. *The Sunday Times Review*, March 6. www.timesonline.co.uk/article/0,,2092-1512330_1,00.html.

Hooks, K. L. (1989). *Alternative Work Schedules and the Woman CPA: A Report on Use, Perceptions, and Career Impact*. Chicago: American Woman's Society of Certified Public Accountants.

Huselid, M. A. (1995). The impact of human resource management practices on turnover, productivity, and corporate financial performance. *Academy of Management Journal*, 38, 635–672.

Israeloff, R. (1995). The truth about paternity leave. *Parents*, 1, 98–100.

Jacobsen, J. P. & Levin, L. M. (1995). Effects of intermittent labor force attachment on women's earnings. *Monthly Labor Review*, 118, 14–19.

Judiesch, M. K. & Lyness, K. S. (1999). Left behind? The impact of leaves of absence on managers' career success. *The Academy of Management Journal*, 42, 641–651.

Knoke, D. & Ishio, Y. (1998). The gender gap in company training. *Work and Occupations*, 25, 141–167.

Latham, G. P. (2004). The motivational benefits of goal-setting. *Academy of Management Executive*, 18, 126–129.

Levine, J. (1997). *Working Fathers: Balancing Work and Families*. Reading, MA: Addison.

Levinson, D. (1986). A conception of adult development. *American Psychologist*, 41(1), 3–13.

Lobel, S. A. & Kossek, E. E. (1996). Human resource strategies to support diversity in work and personal lifestyles: Beyond the "family-friendly" organization. In E. E. Kossek & S. A. Lobel (eds), *Managing Diversity: Human Resource Strategies for Transforming the Work Place* (pp. 221–244). Oxford: Blackwell.

Mainiero, L. A. & Sullivan, S. E. (2005). Kaleidoscope careers: An alternate explanation for the "opt-out" revolution. *Academy of Management Executive*, 19, 106–123.

Miller, J., Miller, M. & Zappone, C. (2005). Get a life: Working 24/7 may seem good for companies, but it often is bad for the talent. *Fortune*, 28 November.

Moen, P. & Roehling, P. (2005). *The Career Mystique: Cracks in the American Dream.* Lanham, MD: Rowman & Littlefield.

Murphy, S. E. & Zagorski, D. A. (2005) Enhancing work/family and work/life interaction: The role of management. In D. Halpern & S. Murphy (eds), *Work Family Balance to Work Family Interaction: Changing the Metaphor.* Mahwah, NJ: Lawrence Erlbaum & Associates.

Nielson, T. R., Carlson, D. A., & Lankau, M. J. (2001). The supportive mentor as a means of reducing work–family conflict. *Journal of Vocational Behavior*, 59, 364–381.

Perry-Smith, J. E. & Blum, T. C. (2000). Work–family human resource bundles and perceived organizational performance. *Academy of Management Journal*, 43, 1107–1117.

Ramachandran, N. (2005). Career spotlight: Mommy track can derail career. *Newsweek.* www.usnews.com/usnews/biztech/articles/050718/18career.htm

Rogier, S. A. & Padgett, M. Y. (2004). The impact of utilizing a flexible work schedule on the perceived career advancement potential of women. *Human Resource Development Quarterly*, 15, 89–106.

Schneer, J. & Reitman, F. (1993). Effects of alternate family structures on managerial career paths. *The Academy of Management Journal*, 36, 830–843.

Schneer, J. A. & Reitman, F. (1997). The interrupted managerial career path: A longitudinal study of MBA's. *Journal of Vocational Behavior*, 51, 411–434.

Schneer, J. & Reitman, F. (2002). Managerial life without a wife: Family structure and managerial career success. *Journal of Business Ethics*, 37, 25–38.

Schwartz, D. B. (1994). *An Examination of the Impact of Family-Friendly Policies on the Glass Ceiling.* New York: Families and Work Institute.

Schwartz, D. B. (1996). The impact of work–family policies on women's career development: Boon or bust? *Women in Management Review*, 11, 5–19.

Schwartz, F. N. (1989), Management, women and the new facts of life. *Harvard Business Review*, 89(1), 65–76.

Schwartz, T. (1999). In my humble opinion: While the balance of power has already begun to shift, most male CEOs still don't fully get it. *FastCompany*, 30, 362. http://pf.fastcompany.com/magazine/30/tschwartz.html

SHRM Foundation. (2001). *SHRM 2001 Benefits Survey.* Society for Human Resource Management.

Stroh, L. K. & Brett, J. M. (1996). The dual-earner dad penalty in salary progression. *Human Resource Management*, 35, 181–201.

Sweet, S. & Moen, P. (2006). Advancing a career focus on work and family: Insights from the life course perspective. In M. Pitt-Catsouphes, E. E. Kossek, & S. Sweet (eds), *Work–Family Handbook: Multi-disciplinary Perspectives and Approaches*. Mahwah, NJ: Erlbaum.

Tharenou, P. (1999). Is there a link between family structures and women's and men's managerial career advancement. *Journal of Organizational Behavior*, 20, 837–863.

Thomas, L. & Ganster, D. C. (1995). Impact of family-supportive work variables on work-family conflict and strain: A control perspective. *Journal of Applied Psychology*, 80, 6–15.

Thompson, C. A., Beauvais, L. L., & Lyness, K. S. (1999). When work–family benefits are not enough: The influence of work–family culture on benefit utilization, organizational attachment, and work–family conflict. *Journal of Vocational Behavior*, 54, 392–415.

Tombari, N. & Spinks, N. (1999). The work/family interface at Royal Bank Financial Group: Successful solutions – a retrospective look at lessons learned. *Women in Management Review*, 14, 186–193.

Wallace, J. E. (2001). The benefits of mentoring for female lawyers. *Journal of Vocational Behavior*, 58, 366–391.

Warren, J. A. & Johnson, P. J. (1995). The impact of workplace support on work–family role strain. *Family Relations*, 44, 163–169.

Wayne, J. H. & Cordeiro, B. L. (2003). Who is a good organizational citizen? Social perception of male and female employees who use family leave. *Sex Roles*, 49, 233–246.

Wiese, B. S. (2005). Negative career consequences of maternity leaves in public and private companies: Personnel managers' risk estimates. *Zeitschrift Personal Psychologie*, 4, 116–122.

William, J. (1999). *Unbending Gender: Why Family and Work Conflict and What to Do about it*. New York: Oxford University Press.

4 | Work–life balance on global assignments

PAULA CALIGIURI
Rutgers University, USA
and
MILA LAZAROVA
Simon Fraser University, Canada

Firms today compete on the effectiveness and competence of their core human talent around the world. Increasingly, both managers and technical experts alike are being required to work effectively across a variety of cultures and in a greater number of cross-national situations. This trend can be seen in firms worldwide and in almost every industry. As an example, typical of many firms, Procter & Gamble (P&G) reinforces the importance of working in cross-national situations. Procter & Gamble asserts, "as we move to truly global businesses, having multicountry experience will be a more common requirement for advancement into mid and upper levels in many functional areas. Separately, leaders in the new, more global company will need some form of geographic flexibility." To capture this experience firms are working to enhance and leverage the experience their employees have cross-nationally. Colgate-Palmolive, for example, has created an expatriate knowledge database that contains information on each manager's experience or awareness of different cultures.

The competitive necessity of working in cross-national situations, as illustrated in the P&G and Colgate-Palmolive examples, has increased the number of employees being sent to host countries, on global assignments, to enhance their cross-cultural competence, fill staffing needs in host national subsidiaries, manage projects, transfer knowledge and corporate culture, and work on global teams. Enhancing cross-cultural competence through these global assignments is one of the leading organization-wide practices affecting firm effectiveness (Stroh & Caligiuri, 1998).

Despite the clear importance of global assignments, they are very challenging for individuals – both personally and professionally.

94

Global assignments permeate both work life (e.g. new job, new colleagues, new organizational norms) and home life (e.g. new house, new friends, new city). Therefore, achieving work–life balance on a stint abroad can be especially difficult. During global assignments, the boundaries between organizational support and personal privacy are increasingly blurred. Most organizations pragmatically understand that in order to manage the risk of a potentially unsuccessful global assignment, they must help their global assignees manage non-work factors, such as establishing social ties, finding social communities, re-establishing hobbies, sports, places of worship, and the like in the host countries.

Many progressive firms have also recognized the powerful influence that accompanying partners and children have on the work–life balance of their global assignees, and in turn, their job performance. As such, these organizations become more involved in the non-work aspects of their assignees and families. Treading carefully to preserve individual privacy, organizations (to varying degrees) have developed programs, policies, and practices designed for global assignees and their family members to help improve their work–life balance. This chapter will highlight some of the key issues for firms managing global assignees' work–life balance. We will also include a brief discussion of the work–life balance challenges faced by international business travelers and employees sent to short-term assignments. This chapter will also provide some examples of the practices organizations have developed to encourage global assignees' work–life balance. The practices include pre-departure decision-making, cross-cultural training, in-country support, career assistance, accompanying partner support, and general work–life assistance.

Global assignments and work–life balance

Global assignments can be exciting for many reasons – an exciting new work position, a larger role in a smaller unit (in the case of a relocation from headquarters to a subsidiary), and often greater professional standing with the firm (often manifest as a professional promotion). The new role, enhanced responsibilities, and increased organizational rank, can make work–life balance a particular challenge for global assignees. Working long hours to get acclimated to new positions in new countries negatively influences the psychological well-being of expatriates (Feldman & Tompson, 1993). Margaret Shaffer, Dave Harrison, and their colleagues (Shaffer, Harrison, Gilley, & Luk, 2001) have detailed the way in which expatriate assignments can negatively influence work–life balance. As an illustration, consider an excerpt from an article in *Workspan* (Pascoe, 2005, p. 40) describing an expatriate's day as follow:

the idea of 24/7 is very real for managers working a "globalized day" that truly does last 24 hours when headquarters is a 12-hour time difference away. A manager in Shanghai is called at midnight because it happens to be noon in Detroit (or constantly e-mailed with an immediate response expected). A 16- or 17-hour working day is not unusual with the assistance of new technologies, and the employee is expected to keep pace for fear of being downsized out of a job compounded by the imperatives of global competition.

Expatriates may need to work longer, socialize more with host national colleagues, and develop culturally consistent behaviors. Any of these may cause a decrease in work–life balance. Another factor which may influence global assignees' psychological well-being and sense of work–life balance is *culture shock*. Culture shock relates to the psychological disorientation experienced by individuals when they find themselves living and working in a culture different than their own. It may result in anxiety caused by the loss of familiar signs, symbols, and cues for interpreting daily life. When new environmental cues are not recognized, customary frames of reference are challenged, calling into question an individual's sense of self (Oberg, 1960).

Research suggests that culture shock involves feelings, such as confusion over expected role behaviors, helplessness at having little, if any, control over the environment, sense of doubt when old values (which had been held as absolute) are brought into question, feelings of being rejected (or at least not accepted) by members of the new culture, and lowered self-esteem due to personal ineffectiveness. Given that the organization was the reason for the move to the host country, culture shock can be detrimental to an individual's sense of work–life balance, as he or she may blame the organization for any negative feelings during the adjustment process.

For most global assignees, culture shock does not last throughout the entire duration of the assignment. Most global assignees will make a gradual adjustment to the host country and most of the negative aspects of culture shock will abate. Some individuals, however, may experience more severe cases of culture shock which could be accompanied by symptoms such as homesickness, psychological withdrawal or isolation, need for excessive amounts of sleep, compulsive eating, alcoholism, substance abuse, and other stress-related physical ailments (Stahl & Caligiuri, 2005). Even in cases of "normal" adjustment, however, individual concerns are still present. Jet lag, physical exhaustion, over-work, and burnout are common complaints among global assignees, especially if their work requires frequent travel and at early stages of their assignments. Thus, even in the best of cases where culture shock is minimal, some negative factors on the global assignee's sense of work–life balance may exist. (See research by Stewart Black, Mark Mendenhall, and their colleagues (Black, Mendenhall, & Oddou, 1991) and Bhaskar-Shrinivas and colleagues (Bhaskar-Shrinivas, Harrison, Shaffer, & Luk, 2005) for reviews of the expatiate adjustment literature).

Families and global assignments

The *Global Relocation Trends 2005 Survey Report* (GMAC, 2005) found that more than 66% of global assignees are between 30 and 49 years old. Most global assignees are married (about 61%), accompanied by a spouse (in about 81% of the cases), and have accompanying children (in about 52% of the cases). About 60% of global assignees' spouses have worked before the assignment, but only 21% of them work during the assignment. Today's global assignees are younger (54% of expatriates are between the ages of 20 and 39). Over 41% have younger (school-age) children and the percent of female partici-pation is at a record high of 23%. While this new generation of global assignees are less likely to be married, those who are married are more likely to have a spouse or partner with a career of his or her own.

In most cases, global assignees' lives are embedded into those of their partners, children, friends, and other loved ones. Partners and children, who often accompany them to the host country, have their lives disrupted for the sake of the assignees' job. Their experiences often have profound influence on the assignee's sense of work–life balance and, subsequently, on the outcome of global assignments. A global relocation can be particularly stressful for all members of a family – both parents and children. Family members may need to learn a new language, adapt to different cultures, food, and schools, make new friends, etc.

These changes associated with the relocation may be even more dramatic for the accompanying partner and children given that the expatriate has the routine and the social network of his or her new position. The cross-cultural adjustment of members of one's family is one of the best predictors of how well the global assignee will ultimately perform while on the assignment (Caligiuri, Hyland, Joshi, & Bross, 1998; Shimoni, Ronen, & Roziner, 2005). Also, family-related problems were ranked first in explaining why expatriates terminated their assignments in the Global Relocation Trends 2005 Survey Report (GMAC, 2005). Given that a large portion of an individual's work–life balance may be related to an individual's family, it is important to understand the ways in which families can be affected by global assignments in order to better develop global work–life balance programs.

The greatest transition problem for accompanying partners arises when both spouses are career professionals and, due to limited available work visas in most countries, the accompanying partner is not able to continue his or her career. While it may seem counterintuitive, *not working* can become an impediment to work–life balance (Harvey 1995, 1996, 1997). This issue may be especially acute when the more traditional roles are reversed and the male is the accompanying partner. Male partners may feel especially isolated in more traditional host countries where many daytime activities are designed for or populated by mostly women. While some men may relish the idea of being in the gender minority, others may experience difficulty coping with the societal norms placing the role on men of working "bread-winner" and may feel isolated, producing an obstacle in achieving work–life balance. Male spouses or accompanying partners who were accustomed to being in a more traditional role in their home countries may need more support to maintain their sense of self-worth (for more on this topic, see Linehan & Scullion, 2001a, 2001b; Linehan, Scullion, & Walsh, 2000, 2001; Selmer & Leung, 2003).

Another work–life balance issue often experienced by accompanying partners is the additional social demands placed on them as a result of their partners' position in the host country. These demands may include, for example, expectations to host social events for the expatriates' colleagues, to participate in organizational functions, and to support the expatriate's career by reducing the expatriate's role in domestic and child-rearing responsibilities. All of these could potentially impede the accompanying partner's sense of work–life balance – and exacerbate the demands on the global assignee's time.

While children may not experience a sense of work–life balance for obvious reasons, they can experience stress during the relocation to a foreign country. Young children may be disoriented by the time zones, different languages, and lack of familiar supports (such as grand-parents). Teenage children, often reliant on their peer group for social support, could experience a sense of loss of control over their lives (McLachlan, 2005; Stuart, 1992). The Counseling Centre in Brussels, which provides counseling services to expatriates and their families, have found that a wide variety of people use the mental health resources available at the centre with the second largest group being children aged up to fourteen years (over 30 percent of the total client base using their services).

In a study of both domestic and international family relocations, 50 percent of children in the 13–18-year-old category were found to experience a variety of social problems attributable to the relocation. These problems included an inability to make new friends, missing old friends, and an inability to adjust to the new school (Brett & Werbel, 1978). Families who have been relocated have a difficult time re-establishing social networks, especially when there are adolescent children in the family (Brett, 1980, 1982; Vernberg, Greenhoot, & Biggs, 2006). These findings suggest that the relocation in a domestic context may be stressful for children, but also for parents trying to contend with their own work–life balance. These problems are typically compounded in instances of international relocation.

In cases where the accompanying partner and children cannot adjust to the host national environment, the relationships within the family may suffer. At the extreme, the anxiety and irritability resulting from culture shock and the ambiguity of the new environment can become a major source of marital conflict, family conflict, and relationship dissatisfaction. When work–life spillover is negative, stress and tension can be generated in the couple due to demands of both the work and the personal life sphere (Harris, 2002). The resulting stress negatively affects the global assignee's sense of work–life balance.

On the positive side, global assignments present all family members with opportunities to experience new surroundings and new cultures together, to make friends from different nationalities, to learn a new language, or pursue new educational opportunities (Elron & Kark, 2000; De Leon & McPartlin, 1995). The transition to another country may, in fact, be beneficial to the couple and family as a unit (Caligiuri *et al.*, 1998). Considering that most families or couples will move to another country knowing only each other, there will be a period of time (before new friendships are made) when they are the sole source of support, friendship, and socialization for each other. For cohesive and adaptive families and couples, global assignments can actually strengthen and deepen their relational bonds as they experience their new environment together (Caligiuri *et al.*, 1998). These positive outcomes of living internationally for couples and families should not be overlooked, especially as they can enhance work–life balance.

"Non-traditional" global assignments and work–life balance

In addition to long-term global assignees, a new category of "assignees" with unique work–life reconciliation challenges has emerged over the last decade. Although a precise label for this category has not yet been agreed upon, the broadly defined term "non-traditional expatriates" is often used. Other common names include "stealth expatriates," "hidden expatriates," or "flexpatriates." Non-traditional expatriates most notably include frequent international business travelers and short-term and "commuter" assignees. International travelers do not have foreign assignments per se but travel incessantly from one company location to another, with trips ranging from a couple of days to several weeks.

Short-term assignees are those who go on assignments stretching over several months but less than a year and whose families typically do not relocate. Similarly, commuter assignees travel to their host country at the beginning of the week and return home at the end of the week and do not establish a domicile at the host country (Harris, Petrovic, & Brewster, 2001; Mayerhofer, Hartmann, Michelitsch-Riedl, & Kollinger; 2004). International business travel or six-month assignments are not really new. Increasingly, however, the pace of globalization coupled with commitment to cost containment and difficulties related to finding employees willing to go on long-term stints abroad, have made these arrangements ever more popular, to a point where now a substantial part of international work is being conducted by people who do not fit in the typical expatriate category. Currently, this is especially true for European multinationals but there are signs that companies originating elsewhere are also adopting this model.

There are positive and negative aspects of this type of work and, interestingly, many of the negatives involve challenges of aligning work and personal life (Mayerhofer *et al.*, 2004; Shellenbarger, 2005; Tahvanianen, Welch, & Worm, 2005). In addition to cost cutting, the obvious benefits of these arrangements are that the family of the expatriate does not have to move; if the spouse has a career, it is not interrupted; children's lives are not disrupted and they can continue to attend their preferred school. In the case of travelers, there are added benefits such as variety, excitement, novelty, the "glamour" associated with business class travel, airline VIP lounges and upscale hotels. Less obvious are the numerous challenges associated with the benefits of business travel and how those affect work–life balance.

Family separation appears to be the biggest concern for employees on flex-assignments. They do not get to establish a "home," except for a temporary one in the host location, although they may practically be living there for months at a time. They have to face all challenges related to living in a foreign location alone and receive no social support from their families. Many end up feeling lonely and isolated. Although the spouse does not have to relocate, his or her cooperation and understanding become invaluable prerequisites for the success of the assignment. The spouse may have to endure various difficulties ranging from inconveniences, such as being left stranded without a car as the employee unexpectedly leaves for the airport directly from work, to more formidable challenges such as having to assume the responsibilities of the absent parent in cases where childcare is involved.

Long and sometimes unpredicted absences due to the "flexpatriate assignments" can strain the relationship between partners. They can be tough on children as well, as their direct contact with the flexpatriate parent may be limited. If a short-term assignment is extended at the last minute or if unexpected travel arises (which, by anecdotal accounts, seem to happen quite frequently), important family events such as birthdays, anniversaries, school recitals, and graduations will have to be missed. This is especially true for frequent business travelers who "must have a bag ready at all times" as the notice for travel is often very short (Mayerhofer *et al.*, 2004). As respondents in a case study of business travelers share, every household develops routines over time. If one remains a flexpatriate for a long stretch, he or she may feel like a stranger in his or her own home. To that end, some suggest that they prefer longer absences with longer times to reconnect rather than multiple short trips that are thought to be too disruptive for family dynamics (Welch & Worm, 2006).

In addition to family separation, flexpatriates, and international business travelers in particular, often have to endure physical ailments related to long flights: lack of sleep, lack of exercise, unhealthy diet, or weight gain. Even though they may be staying in upscale hotels with gyms and swimming pools, late evenings with clients and early morning meetings often preclude them from using these facilities. Female travelers in some locations have the added challenge of finding socially acceptable (by host country standards) options for relaxation, socialization, or entertainment. As one interviewee in Welch and Worm's recent study commented, it was not uncommon that she would spend days without talking to "another human being" (2006, p. 291).

There are challenges on the work front as well. Flexpatriates are often confronted with a backlog of work when they come back from extended travel. The need to take time off to recover from travel is often ignored and they are expected to report to their domestic job responsibilities immediately upon return. Further, some have complained that frequent absences from the office make it difficult to maintain their social contacts and may damage their networks and relationships with mentors and valued colleagues (Welch & Worm, 2006).

In sum, while flexpatriate assignments offer a range of benefits, improved work–life balance for assignees and their families does not appear to be one of these benefits. Quite to the contrary, they bring about a different but equally critical set of challenges. Academic research on flexpatriate issues still lags behind company practice but the little that we do know clearly suggests that these assignments are not a "panacea" (Harris *et al.*, 2001) and need to be carefully managed if the assignee's work and personal lives are to be reconciled successfully.

The organization's role in promoting work–life balance

Global assignments permeate every aspect of an individual's life and the influence of life satisfaction on job performance is particularly acute for global assignees. For this reason, firms will often become more involved in non-work aspects of global assignees and their families (compared to their level of involvement in a domestic context). In this context, there is a delicate balance when organizations intervene to assist global assignees achieve work–life balance. Depending on the organizational culture of the multinational corporation, the type of assignment, and the individual global assignee, a company may handle global assignment work–life balance interventions differently. Treading carefully to preserve individual privacy, organizations (to varying degrees) have developed programs, policies, and practices designed for global assignees and their family members to utilize. These organizational interventions fall into six general categories: pre-departure decision-making, cross-cultural training, in-country support, career assistance, accompanying partner support, and general work–life assistance (Caligiuri & Lazarova, 2005).

Pre-departure decision-making. The first, and perhaps the most critical, step in helping employees maintain work–life balance while on a global assignment happens before the global assignment even begins. As discussed in a previous section, individuals and their partners, if positively predisposed to global experience, will likely accept and enjoy global assignments (Brett & Stroh, 1995; Caligiuri *et al.*, 1998). As such, many organizations have developed methods which will enable future global assignees and their accompanying partners to make a thoroughly realistic and informed decision. There are three common elements in all of these pre-departure decision-making programs. The first is that organizations start early by engaging employees to consider a global assignment (in the context of their career and personal life circumstances) – even before a specific position becomes available. The second element is to involve the family as early as possible in the decision-making process (Caligiuri *et al.*, 1998; Harvey, 1985). The third element is to maintain enough flexibility in the system to allow for deselection at every phase. The best selection decision will be mutual among the employee, his or her organization, and his or her family.

In this pre-departure decision-making phase, future global assignees should understand both the advantages and disadvantages the international move may have on them and their family members (Elron & Kark, 2000). To this end, some multinational corporations offer a visit to the host country prior to accepting the assignment (i.e. a look-see visit); they may offer formal and informal opportunities to discuss their move with former global assignees (i.e. repatriates).

Organizations should consider the fact that all the information they offer an expatriate prior to the assignment will influence his or her expectations – and that the goal for managing those expectations should be *accuracy*.

Cross-cultural training. Cross-cultural training is defined as any planned intervention designed to increase the knowledge and skills of global assignees to live and work effectively and achieve general life satisfaction in an unfamiliar host culture (Kealey & Protheroe, 1996). For more than thirty years, numerous scholars and practitioners have touted the benefits of cross-cultural training as a means of facilitating effective cross-cultural interactions and cross-cultural adjustment (for a review, see Kealey & Protheroe, 1996; Mendenhall *et al.*, 2004).

There has been a positive trajectory of growth with respect to multinational corporations who are offering cross-cultural training. For instance, in the early 1980s, Tung (1981, 1982) found that only 32 percent of multinational corporations offered cross-cultural training, while more than twenty years later, the *Global Relocation Trends 2005 Survey Report* (GMAC, 2005) indicates that 81 percent of multinational corporations surveyed provide a formal cross-cultural program to prepare employees for relocation. While the definitive conclusion on the outcomes of cross-cultural training are mixed, numerous research studies provide support that a well-designed cross-cultural training program can enhance the learning process of the global assignee and thus facilitate effective cross-cultural interactions, cross-cultural adjustment, and work–life balance.

In addition to cross-cultural training, multinational corporations are offering other types of formal training to global assignees and their partners (and children) to help them achieve greater work–life balance. One type of formal training is language-skills training – often offered both pre-departure and within the host country. Another type of training, albeit less common, is stress management training offered to help individuals manage their expectations prior to and their stressors during a global assignment.

In-country support. While much of the cross-cultural training described in the previous section happens prior to departure, many additional programs offered in-country are beginning to become increasingly more popular. Support programs, such as culture coaches, destination services, and on-line support networks are becoming more popular. In some cases, companies are sponsoring these programs in-house – while others are seeking outside vendors. The most formal type of support programs that companies offer is the International Employee Assistance Programs. These programs are available to handle extreme (and even not so extreme) personal concerns and mental and emotional challenges (e.g. depression, anxiety, alcoholism).

In structuring global assignments, there are some additional best practices that companies have tried to help global assignees maintain their work–life balance. For one, organizations can limit additional work-related travel of the global assignee, especially in the beginning of the global assignment, or reduce the number of working hours required at the onset of the assignment. Another policy is to offer frequent home visits for global assignees managing certain non-work situations (e.g. caring for an elderly parent or maintaining a long-distance relationship). In many respects, these are the most sensitive of all practices in helping employees maintain their work–life balance while on assignments. In many cases, organizations offer expatriates a cafeteria-style benefits package, where individuals can select the programs that they need and want – without any questions asked, to preserve individuals' privacy. For example, Crédit Suisse (a Zurich-based global financial-services company) offers possible benefits including social clubs, language or cultural awareness training, etc., and fringe benefits including preferred rates for banking and insurance products, discounts on tickets for major arts, sports, and cultural events, and many other things (Pollitt, 2005).

Career assistance. Organizations offering career-related assistance to their global assignees often do so to prevent the global assignees from leaving their organization upon repatriation. For example, Tesco plc will use assignments to develop broad management skills, and their human resources (HR) team identifies opportunities for the assignees upon repatriation across the business for returning staff. Every year, each expatriate has monthly progress reviews to keep the expatriates "on the radar screen" of their units and they are encouraged to use their eight annual weekly visits home to reacquaint themselves with colleagues and bosses. Tesco plc expatriates will return to their home office six months before the end of their assignment for career planning discussions with their senior decision-makers and Human Resources (Simms, 2004). In combination, these practices have a positive effect on the global assignee and the organization hoping to maintain their human talent.

Accompanying partner support. In many companies, there is a shortfall between the dual-career needs of the accompanying partner and the extent to which they are available in organizations (Suutari & Riusala, 2000). The *Global Relocations Trends 2005 Survey Report* (GMAC, 2005) found that 56% of the companies made provisions for accompanying partners' careers, 73% offered language training, 43% offered education or training assistance, 33% sponsored the partner's work permit, and 31% financed the job-finding fees and search. These percentages are a large increase from even five years ago – reflecting the increased corporate involvement in the non-work aspect of their employees' lives.

Many corporations, such as IBM, 3M, Motorola, and ConocoPhillips, have recognized the influence that partners will have on the success or failure of international assignments. As evidence of this recognition, they provide a wide variety of assistance packages to help spouses, including assistance in obtaining work permits to carry on paid employment, pre-departure and post-arrival training and relocation assistance, and ongoing support, such as financial assistance for a spouse to return to school or return home to attend to aging parents. Thirty multinational companies, including BT, Shell International, Unilever, British Airways, Siemens, and BASF, have joined forces through the Permits Foundation to lobby for lowering or eliminating existing barriers to work abroad for expatriate spouses. The group has been successful in influencing change in the US and France and is anticipating change in the Netherlands (Doke, 2005).

There are other tangible services that companies offer accompanying partners on global assignments. These include monetary policies such as paying fees required by employment agencies in the host countries, offering seed money to start a new business, paying fees to join professional associations, compensation of accompanying partner's lost wages and benefits, or offering financial support to engage in volunteer service (Pellico & Stroh, 1997; Punnett, 1997). Other company-provided tangible services are non-monetary but also considered extremely useful for accompanying partners. These include organization-sponsored support groups for partners, employment networks coordinated with other global firms, and office space in the host location for the purpose of job hunting (Elron & Kark, 2000; Punnett, 1997).

It is interesting to note that Pellico and Stroh (1997) found a surprising lack of awareness among accompanying partners about the types of programs available to them through their partners' organization. In part, this could be due to the fact that firms respect employee privacy and do not contact the accompanying partners directly. The information, therefore, is second-hand through the employees who may, in some cases, have personal reasons for not relaying the information or may not view the information as necessary. Companies should aggressively advertise these services to all employees with families, as a matter of policy, to thwart potential miscommunication or a perceived negative stigma attached to inquiring about these benefits.

General work–life assistance. Every individual, couple, and family will have unique needs that may affect their success and happiness living in another country. As such, most international HR professionals encourage the maximum flexibility and privacy in all global assignment support programs. For example, a global assignee with a special-needs child may require a certain type of educational or medical assistance before the assignment can become viable. Some organizations offer support for global assignees engaging in a commuter marriage as a result of the global position (Harris, 1993). Other organizations, in an effort to solve problems such as the dual-career concern, may encourage a greater use of short-term assignments, generally not involving the relocation of the assignee's partner and children (Harris, 1993).

Support for non-traditional expatriates

Unfortunately, at present there are few "best practices" we can report here. Non-traditional expatriates have not yet fully emerged on the radar of HR departments. Whereas some organizations are more proactive than others, the needs of flexpatriates have largely been ignored. Their assignments are typically managed by their line managers and HR rarely gets involved beyond assisting with administrative details such as visas, travel arrangements, health insurance, immunizations, and the occasional personal safety precaution. Line managers and HR managers alike appear to share the opinion that where there is no relocation, complicated taxation issues, children school fees and the like, then there is no need for HR to play a significant role. By many accounts, line managers prefer that this remains so, with some suggesting that consulting HR will only "create trouble" (Welch & Worm, 2006). Given the relatively short periods of non-traditional assignments, they do not consider training and other preparation programs useful or necessary. Employees generally need to rely on themselves and their personal networks to get prepared and their families' "fate" is not considered to be a part of the assignment agenda. There are no reintegration provisions either, despite the fact that excessive travel may make it difficult to maintain professional and personal relationships and keep in touch with new developments in the organization (Mayerhofer *et al.*, 2004; Welch, Welch, & Worm, 2007).

As organizations continue to expand globally, flexpatriates will play an increasingly important strategic role for sustaining foreign operations. Thus, it is critical that organizations provide support that allows them to maintain a healthy balance between work and personal life. Above all, just as traditional expatriates, they too should be given an accurate description of the job. All who sign up for flexpatriate life can undergo preparation programs similar to those offered to long-term expatriates. All travel contingencies should be taken care of by the company so that employees do not have to rely on personal resources (such as the family car or a personal credit card) to be able to perform their work duties. Care should be taken that travel is scheduled as early as reasonably possible and assignment extensions are kept to a minimum. Trips should be scheduled in ways that allow for some downtime. If an extended stay becomes necessary, flexpatriates can become eligible for additional benefits such as a visit from the spouse on company expense or a short trip home. HR can also educate line managers about the range of physical, social, and psychological demands experienced by flexpatriates and can provide guidelines for initiatives such as additional vacation days based on days of travel or days spent in a foreign location per set period of time.

Improving global assignees' social support to increase work–life balance

Social support and social interaction can create a sense of belonging, enhance psychological security, and improve work–life balance for global assignees. The feeling of having a social network while on assignment will limit the global assignee's feelings of isolation – that they have nothing else to do but work. While seemingly counter-intuitive, organizations should encourage opportunities for non-work social interaction (as opposed to work-related socializing). Attention to improving the global assignees' social network will facilitate global assignees' emotional well-being and cross-cultural adjustment, and, in turn, their performance on the job.

Different types of social support exist – emphasizing different elements of an individual's overall social network. While different in purpose, they will all function to contribute to the global assignees' psychological and physical well-being. According to Caligiuri and Lazarova (2002), three types of support are critical for global assignees' cross-cultural adjustment and feelings of work–life balance. They are *emotional support*, *informational support*, and *instrumental support.*

Emotional support. The first six months of a global assignment are often associated with heightened stress, disorientation, and loneliness. To combat these negative feelings, positive social interactions provide global assignees with the emotional support needed to cope with the transition. Social interaction fulfills the basic human need to affiliate – including the need for contact, companionship, and friendship – and provides global assignees with a mental release from work. Social interactions provide emotional connections that can mitigate the negative psychological effects of isolation over absorption into work and enhance work–life balance.

Social support can improve feelings of anxiety by easing feelings of being socially clumsy and out of place. One example of emotional support is a sympathetic colleague who listens to a new global assignee vent about his or her social discomfort and can help the assignee resolve some of those concerns by providing social guidance. This interaction would provide some psychological comfort and can also compel global assignees to discuss concerns and, once identified, can begin developing solutions.

Informational support. Another type of support which would provide global assignees with a heightened sense of work–life balance is informational support. Informational support is the provision of knowledge – from one person to another – to help make one's daily activities easier. Informational support can be as mundane as where to find desired groceries, the best way to contact the phone company, how to use the subway system, or as critical as how to interpret a host national colleague's behavior, cultural norms for an important meeting, and advice on correct social etiquette. Informational support can help global assignees work through basic challenges and reduce stress and anxiety.

Instrumental support. A type of social support that has a great effect on work–life balance is the instrumental support given to global assignees. Instrumental social support refers to tangible provision of resources that one person can do for another. These resources may include lending money, babysitting, helping with yard work, lending books, or giving free lessons in the host country language. This instrumental support improves work–life balance directly, by freeing time and emotional resources that it would take to seek out this assistance elsewhere.

Organizations can offer a variety of services to enhance expatriates' feelings of emotional, informational, and instrumental support. Emotional support can be provided through employee assistance programs, cultural counselors, mentors, social networks of expatriates, membership of social clubs, and the like. Informational support can be provided through company websites detailing accurate in-country resources and cultural information, assigning a "point person" to answer any resource-related questions, etc. Instrumental support is more tangible and can be provided through the company's relocation service offerings and their international human resources functions. Shell International offers support through a unique program called Global Outpost Services. Shell's Global Outpost Services is a network which offers information and advice on relocation, careers, and development and leverages the vast amount of knowledge and support available through their exceptionally large expatriate population.

Conclusion

When employees achieve balance between their work and personal life, there are positive benefits for the employees, their families, and their organizations. For example, individuals experiencing greater work–life balance have better health and wellness, greater organizational commitment, greater job satisfaction, better goal achievement, and family happiness. At the family level, work–life balance promotes greater marital and family stability, family cohesion, and marital and family happiness. At the organizational level, having employees with greater work–life balance reduces turnover, improves performance, and lowers the incidences of lateness and absenteeism.

For traditional and non-traditional global assignees, work–life balance promotes other important outcomes such as fewer feelings of isolation and loneliness, increases in their career mobility (resulting from assignment success, especially at the executive levels), and greater personal and professional development. For families, work–life balance is experienced along with life satisfaction of the assignees' family members and career satisfaction of the assignees' accompanying partner. For organizations, the benefits of increased assignees' work–life balance include reduced assignment turnover and greater retention among repatriates. With a focus on the future demands for more globally savvy individuals, the ability for firms to help their expatriates improve work–life balance will become increasingly more important.

References

Bhaskar-Shrinivas, P., Harrison, D. A., Shaffer, M. A., & Luk, D. M. (2005). Input-based and time-based models of international adjustment: Meta-analytic evidence and theoretical extensions. *Academy of Management Journal*, 48, 257–81.

Bingham, C., Felin, T. & Black, S. (2000). An interview with John Pepper: What it takes to be a global leader. *Human Resource Management*, 39, 287–295.

Black, J. S. & Gregersen, H. B. (1991). The other half of the picture: Antecedents of spouse cross-cultural adjustment. *Journal of International Business Studies*, 22, 461–477.

Black, J. S., Mendenhall, M., & Oddou, G. (1991). Toward a comprehensive model of international adjustment: An integration of multiple theoretical perspectives. *Academy of Management Review*, 16, 291–317.

Black, J. S. & Stephens, G. K. (1989). The influence of the spouse on American expatriate adjustment and intent to stay in Pacific Rim overseas assignments. *Journal of Management*, 15(4), 529–544.

Brett, J. M. (1980). The effect of job transfer on employees and their families. In C. L. Cooper & R. Payne (eds), *Current Concerns in Occupational Stress*. New York: John Wiley & Sons, Ltd.

Brett, J. M. (1982). Job transfer and well-being. *Journal of Applied Psychology*, 67, 450–463.

Brett, J. M. & Stroh, L. K. (1995). Willingness to relocate internationally. *Human Resource Management*, 34, 405–424.

Brett, J. M. & Werbel, J. D. (1978). *The Effect of Job Transfer on Employees and Their Families*. Washington DC: Employee Relocation Council.

Caligiuri, P. M., Hyland, M. M., Joshi, A., Bross, A. S. (1998). Testing a theoretical model for examining the relationship between family adjustment and expatriates' work adjustment. *Journal of Applied Psychology*, 83, 598–614.

Caligiuri, P. M. & Lazarova, M. (2002). The influence of social interaction and social support on female expatriates' cross-cultural adjustment. *International Journal of Human Resource Management*, 13(5), 1–12.

Caligiuri, P. M. & Lazarova, M. (2005). Work–life balance and the effective management of global assignees. In S. Poelmans (ed.), *Work and Family: An International Research Perspective*. Mahwah, NJ: Lawrence Erlbaum Associates.

Caligiuri, P. M., Phillips, J., Lazarova, M., Tarique, I., & Burgi, P. (2001). Expectations produced in cross-cultural training programs as a predictor of expatriate adjustment. *International Journal of Human Resource Management*, 12(3), 357–372.

de Leon, C. T. & McPartlin, D. (1995). Adjustment of expatriate children. In Selmer, J. (ed.), *Expatriate Management: New Ideas for International Business*. Westport, CT: Quorum Books.

Doke, D. (2005). Global group aims to strike right balance to keep talent. *Personnel Today*. February, 7.

Elron, E. & Kark, R. (2000). Women managers and international assignments: Some recommendations for bridging the gap. In Mendenhall, M. & Oddou, G. (eds), *Readings in International Human Resource Management*. Cincinnati, OH: South-Western College Publishing.

Feldman, D. C. & Tompson, H. B. (1993). Expatriation, repatriation, and domestic geographical relocation: An empirical investigation of adjustment to new job assignments. *Journal of International Business Studies*, 22, 507–529.

GMAC (2005). *Global Relocation Trends 2005 Survey Report*. Woodridge, IL: GMAC Global Relocation Services.

Harris, H. (1993). Women in international management: Opportunity or threat? *Women in Management Review*, 8, 9–14.

Harris, H. (2002). Think international manager, think male: Why are women not selected for international management assignments. *Thunderbird International Business Review*, 44, 175–203.

Harris, H., Petrovic, J., & Brewster, C. (2001). New forms of international working: The panacea to expatriation ills?, Paper presented at the Global HRM Conference, ESADE Barcelona, 20–22 June 2001.

Harvey, M. (1985). The executive family: An overlooked variable in international assignments. *Columbia Journal of World Business*, 20, 84–92.

Harvey, M. (1995). The impact of dual career families on international relocations. *Human Resource Management Review*, 5(3), 223–244.

Harvey, M. (1996). Addressing the dual-career expatriation dilemma. *Human Resource Planning*, 19(4), 18–39.

Harvey, M. (1997). Dual-career expatriates: Expectations, adjustment and satisfaction with international relocation. *Journal of International Business Studies*, 28, 627–658.

Kealy, D. & Protheroe, D. (1996). The effectiveness of cross culture training for expatriates: an assessment of the literature on the issue. *International Journal of Intercultural Relations*, 20, 141–165.

Lazarova, M. B. & Caligiuri, P. (2001). Retaining repatriates: The role of organization support practices. *Journal of World Business*, 36, 389–401.

Linehan, M. & H. Scullion. (2001a). Work–family conflict: The female expatriate perspective. *International Journal of Applied Human Resource Management*, 2(2), 5–13.

Linehan, M. & Scullion, H. (2001b). European female expatriate careers: Critical success factors. *Journal of European Industrial Training*, 25(8), 392–418.

Linehan, M., Scullion, H., & Walsh, J. S. (2000). The growth of female expatriation and male spouses in Europe: The challenges for international human resource management. *The International Journal of Applied Human Resource Management*, 1(1), 37–48.

Linehan, M., Scullion, H., & Walsh, J. S. (2001). Barriers to women's participation in international management. *European Business Review*, 13(1), 10–18.

Mayerhofer, H., Hartmann, L., Michelitsch-Riedl, G., & Kollinger, I. (2004). Flexpatriate assignments: A neglected issue in global staffing, *International Journal of Human Resource Management*, 15, 1371–1389.

McCaughey, D. & Bruning, N. (2005). Enhancing opportunities for expatriate job satisfaction: HR strategies for foreign assignment success. *Human Resource Planning*, 28, 21–30.

McLachlan, A. D. (2005). The impact of globalization on internationally mobile families: A grounded theory analysis. *Journal of Theory Construction & Testing*, 9, 14–20.

Mendenhall, M., Ehnert, I., Kühlmann, T., Oddou, G., Osland, J., & Stahl, G. (2004). Evaluation studies of cross-cultural training programs: A review of literature from 1988–2000. In D. Landis, J. Bennett, and M. Bennett (eds), *Handbook of Intercultural Training*. Thousand Oaks, CA: Sage Publications.

Oberg, K. (1960). Culture shock: Adjustment to new cultural environment. *Practical Anthropologist*, 7, 177–182.

Pascoe, R. (2005). Enriching work and life in the global workplace. *Workspan*, 48, 40–44.

Pellico, M. T. & Stroh, L. (1997). Spousal assistance programs: An integral component of the international assignment. *New Approaches to Employee Management*, 4, 227–243.

Pollitt, D. (2005). How Crédit Suisse competes in the global war for talent. *Human Resource Management International Digest*, 13, 15.

Punnett, B. J. (1997). Towards effective management of expatriate spouses. *Journal of World Business*, 32, 243–257.

Selmer, J. & Leung, A. (2003). International adjustment of female vs. male business expatriates. *International Journal of Human Resource Management*, 14(7), 1117–1131.

Shaffer, M. A. & Harrison, D. (1998). Expatriates' psychological withdrawal from international assignments: Work, non-work, and family influences. *Personnel Psychology*, 51, 87–118.

Shaffer, M. A. & Harrison, D. A. (2001). Forgotten partners of international assignments development and test of a model of spouse adjustment. *Journal of Applied Psychology*, 86, 238–254.

Shaffer, M., Harrison, D., & Gilley, D. M. (1999). Dimensions, determinants, and differences in the expatriate adjustment process. *Journal of International Business Studies*, 30, 557–581.

Shaffer, M. A., Harrison, D. A., Gilley, K. M., & Luk, D. M. (2001). Struggling for balance amid turbulence on international assignments: Work–family conflict, support and commitment. *Journal of Management*, 27, 99–121.

Shellenbarger, S. (2005). Separation anxiety: Short job transfers create problems for families left behind. *Wall Street Journal*, October 27, 2005: D1.

Shimoni, T., Ronen, S., & Roziner, I. (2005). Predicting expatriate adjustment: Israel as a host country. *International Journal of Cross-Cultural Management*, 5, 293–312.

Simms, J. (2004). A leap of faith. *Human Resources*, March 5, 56–59.

Stahl, G. & Caligiuri, P. M. (2005). The relationship between expatriate coping strategies and expatriate adjustment, *Journal of Applied Psychology*, 90(4), 603–616.

Stroh, L. K. & Caligiuri, P. M. (1998). Increasing global competitiveness through effective people management. *Journal of World Business*, 33(1), 1–16.

Stuart, K. D. (1992). Teens play a role in moves overseas. *Personnel Journal*, 71, 71–78.

Suutari, V. & Riusala, K. (2000). Expatriation and careers: Perspectives of expatriates and spouses. *Career Development International*, 5(2), 81–90.

Tahvaniainen, M., Welch, D., & Worm, V. (2005). Implications of short-term international assignments. *European Management Journal*, 23(6), 663–673.

Tung, R. L. (1981). Selection and training of personnel for overseas assignments. *Columbia Journal of World Business*, 16, 68–78.

Tung, R. L. (1982). Selection and training procedures of U.S., European, and Japanese multinationals. *California Management Review*, 25, 57–71.

Vernberg, E. M., Greenhoot, A. F., & Biggs, B. K. (2006). Intercommunity relocation and adolescent friendships: Who struggles and why? *Journal of Consulting and Clinical Psychology*, 74, 511–523.

Welch, D. E., Welch, L. S., & Worm, V. (2007). The international business traveller: A neglected but strategic human resource. *International Journal of Human Resource Management*, 18(2), 173–183.

Welch, D. E. & Worm, V. (2006). International business travellers: A challenge in IHRM. In G. Stahl & I. Björkman (eds), *Handbook of Research in International Human Resource Management* (pp. 283–301). Northampton, MA: Edward Elgar Publishing Ltd.

5 | Case study 2005 – work–life, flexibility, and mobility: ensuring global support of flexibility within IBM's on-demand company

JOAN GENTILESCO-GIUE and OANA PETRESCU
IBM Corporation

Case overview

This case is about change in IBM: not ordinary change, but the most difficult – mindset change. Companies merge, re-engineer, re-strategize, and re-make themselves in order to remain competitive in the market-place. Efforts to "empower" employees in the workplace, and to adapt the workplace to employees' needs of balancing work and life, require new management strategies. Each of these situations brings with it a conflict of values and mindsets between the way we "have always done things" and the way "we're going to do it now." Helping people understand "what" changes occur when a flexible work environment is implemented and how this impacts their roles and responsibilities in the organization is not an easy task. This is exactly what this case will address: the mindset of both managers and employees relative to the acceptance of a flexible work environment at IBM. And last, but not least, is how the company itself changed its mindset, providing tools and support to make change happen.

IBM work–life programs

IBM's attention to work–life issues and flexibility predates any specific strategy. As early as the 1960s, IBM instituted a one-year unpaid leave of absence, and in the early 1980s the company pioneered individual work schedules allowing some day-to-day flexibility.

IBM's more formal focus on work–life issues began in 1984 when the company supported the creation of the first employer-sponsored national resource and referral network for finding childcare across the US. IBM had been conducting work–life issue surveys since 1986 in the United States in an effort to gain a deeper understanding of the issues employees face with regard to balancing their work and personal lives. Initial survey results indicated that "management support" of a flexible work environment was lacking.

Recognizing work–life balance as an industry-wide issue that touched morale, productivity, and retention, in 1998 IBM started a very deliberate, global initiative to help IBMers find more balance between their work and personal lives and to identify the root causes of increasing workload and unnecessary work. Today, IBM recognizes work–life initiatives as a key business imperative to attract and retain younger talent – especially Generation X and Generation Y.

A Global Partnership for Workforce Flexibility was launched to serve as the catalyst for business areas engaged in addressing issues relating to workload and work–life balance and to accelerate changes in the work environment that would enable IBM employees to be more successful. Initially, the Partnership was comprised of thirteen senior executives. To support this initiative, the IBM Global Work–Life & Flexibility Project Office was also formed. The project office immediately launched work–life programs in Latin America; trained all managers in Latin America on the programs and the cultural implications of work–life balance; and conducted significant focus groups across EMEA (Europe, Middle East, and Africa) and for the Americas Manufacturing, Finance, and Human Resource (HR) functions. In 2000, the work was broadened to include Asia Pacific, and extended focus was placed in EMEA to implement a comprehensive technology assessment across eight countries in Europe. In 2002–2003, due to the evolving nature of work–life interest across IBM, the department expanded its mission and role to include global work–life, flexibility, and mobility. Although IBM implemented very aggressive communication and education/training initiatives, in IBM's 2004 global work–life issue survey (conducted in 79 countries; 13 languages; 42k respondents; and 214k write-in comments), management support together with employees' fear of using flexible work options continued to be identified as issues, as well as a desire for more flexibility in where work is done.

Defining a strategy for work life: addressing work/life strategically

To better address work–life issues, IBM formulated a short- and long-term global work–life strategy which linked to its overall business strategy. The work–life strategy consists of three pillars and is simple.

(1) culture – gathering data and using it to address the cultural barriers to productivity and morale that are rooted in work heritage, but are not relevant today;
(2) flexibility – attack flexibility and workload issues to meet the real needs and expectation of current and future employees;
(3) dependent care – increasing the global support offered for dependent care (e.g. childcare, elder care).

Culture – strategic approach
Work–Life Surveys To understand the needs of its employees, IBM initiated, in 1986, the first of its US Work and Life Issues Surveys to obtain demographic data on its population and obtain employee input about current programs and suggestions for future programs. The survey, which has since been repeated with additional questions in 1991 and 1996, provided IBM with findings that have changed its thinking about employees and what is important to them. It was clear, for instance, from the first survey that many employees had dependent care responsibilities and that percentage was steadily growing. Indeed, it has doubled since 1986. Work–life surveys were conducted in Europe and Latin America in 1998 and in Asia Pacific in 1999. In 2001, IBM conducted its first global work–life issue survey in 48 countries and 20 languages, with 59,000 employees being invited to participate. A global five-year work–life strategy covering 18 countries has been implemented based on the results, and quarterly work–life scorecards track the progress worldwide. In the fall of 2004, IBM conducted its most recent and second global work–life issues survey. Over 40,000 employees worldwide participated from 79 countries in 13 languages.

Flexibility – strategic approach
There are two strategies that co-exist to address work–life flexibility and workload issues in IBM. One is to eliminate some of the internal

causes of workload. The other is to give employees more support for meeting responsibilities that emanate from outside of work and contribute to the feeling that there is simply too much to do. IBM has focused on increasing the availability of Flexible Work Options (FWOs), eliminating some of the unnecessary work and inefficient processes by redesigning them, providing employees with more auto-nomy over how, where, and when they work by utilizing leading-edge technology, understanding the variety of workplace environments, and ensuring employees have the equipment and tools that allow them to operate effectively.

The company offers six global flexible work options:

(1) Individualized Work Schedule – employees who vary their work time up to two hours before or two hours after the normal location start and stop times.
(2) Compressed/Flexible Workweek – employees who compress their workweek into fewer than five full days.
(3) Leave of Absence Programs – employees who are on an unpaid leave from work for an extended period of time.
(4) Mobile/Telecommuter – employees who are on the move and have no dedicated IBM workspace
(5) Part-Time Reduced Work Schedule – employees who are under a regular employment option category and have a reduced work schedule.
(6) Work-at-Home – employees who perform their regular work schedule at home without a dedicated IBM workspace.

Dependent care – strategic approach
In 1998 a senior woman attending an IBM conference asked Ted Childs, VP of Global Diversity, if women's babies outside the US were less important to IBM. The issue she was raising was that IBM's current Fund for Dependent Care Initiatives was a US-only fund. Beginning in 1998, IBM began conducting global dependent care needs assessments in 21 countries. The results of these assessments led IBM to create the IBM Global Work–Life Fund which is a $50 million fund to develop and support dependent care programs benefiting working families, which includes childcare, elder care and unique work/life programs. The Global Work–Life Fund serves worldwide communities where IBMers live and work.

Living the work/life strategy: steps IBM took globally

By the end of 2004, IBM introduced flexible work options into all geographies (Asia Pacific; Canada; Europe, Middle East, Africa; Latin America; and the US). Around the world, IBM employees are reacting positively, and workforce flexibility has become a competitive advantage for IBM. It helps make IBM the employer of choice for new hires and enables IBM to retain top talent. IBM finds that in today's competitive work environment, employees are looking for jobs that offer autonomy, learning, and advancement opportunities, and meaning. In addition, a flexible work environment has proven to be a powerful tool for:

- enhancing employee morale, commitment, and loyalty;
- increasing effectiveness, focus, and productivity.

In addition to Flexible Work Options, IBM also launched the Making IBM Feel Small Again initiative in 2003. This was designed to address the isolation and feelings of being disconnected IBMers worldwide were beginning to experience as a result of an increasingly mobile and remote work environment. In focus groups with over 1,000 employees in nine countries, concerns have been identified, and many positive actions have been taken to make IBM feel like a "great place to work" – recapturing the IBM "branch office" feeling of old, where employees knew each other and the business, and where successes were celebrated. The results from this initiative continue to provide valuable insights and have improved employee morale and work–life balance. Business benefits of this initiative include:

- A better understanding of many of the causes of unnecessary/ unproductive work, which have been addressed.
- Management teams at all levels engaged in actions suggested by employees. For example, in Australia and New Zealand, activities have included morning teas, barbeques, "Great Place to Walk," tennis lessons, baby photo guessing competition, golf club, and movie nights. In India, employees participate in tsunami relief and holiday decorations. In the United States, Santa visits at all offices and employees are provided with useful holiday information like lists of concerts and other activities.

- Insights gained relative to the challenges technology presents to employees which allow IBM to deliver technology tools and help desk emergency services operate more effectively.

To address the issue of time spent on low-value work, IBM implemented a process that helped employees and managers reduce unnecessary work, relieving some of the time pressure employees feel. Employees were feeling that heavy workloads prevented them from taking advantage of flexible work options, and that high levels of work were a root cause of high workload. This anecdotal input was confirmed with the results of the 2001 global work–life issues survey where 33 percent of IBM global employees reported spending 15 percent or more of their time on unnecessary work. With a steering committee that had global representation, IBM developed a work reduction process and tested it worldwide to ensure cultural applicability. The process begins with management training and an on-line workload assessment tool, introduced at a group meeting where the program is explained, and the objective is discussed. The survey is short and simple, designed to "dig out" the root causes of inefficiency and identify the low-value work. Derived from the survey results, managers generate a "solution design worksheet," and begin implementing solutions. The tool offers employees, managers, and work groups an easy, replicable way to improve work.

In order to promote and encourage greater flexibility, IBM developed extensive resources for employees and managers. These resources inform, educate, and underscore the company's commitment to providing employees with maximum control over where and when they work. Some of the primary tools include IBM's *Flexibility@Work* website which receives on the order of a million plus hits per year. *QuickCase* and *QuickView* Web-based tools include work–life scenarios that illustrate the use of IBM flexibility programs and policies. Web-based multimedia e-learning segments define how flexibility and mobility are transforming how, when, and where people do their work to get better business results. IBM provides web-based education and training on working remotely titled *Going Mobile* and a CD tool providing tips and strategies for staying connected is titled *TeleWork: Making it Work for You*. The "Global Guide to Mobile Work" (available in both hard and soft copy formats) helps mobile employees and managers "stay connected," perform effectively in their mobile environments, and respond quickly and effectively to the changing needs of both customers and the company. IBM's *Flexibility Brochure* – available in both hard copy and electronic formats – describes the range of IBM flexible work options and provides success stories of IBM employees working on the whole array of flexible work options.

By listening to the global employee population, IBM continues to address issues that have a direct positive effect on the business and on employees' careers. This makes employees more effective at their jobs, provides additional free time for more creative and innovative work, and improves employee satisfaction and retention. It has also allowed IBM to understand and focus on the critical few action items – those that can have the most positive effect on employees' work lives.

Assessing the strategy and the success – measuring results

Measurement is key to IBM's business case for work–life flexibility. Two types of analysis are used in IBM to collect data from employees and managers:

(1) Qualitative analysis – Qualitative analysis helps to gather in-depth information about a particular program, practices, or initiative utilizing employees' opinions, feelings, and attitudes. Some examples of the ways qualitative data are collected include small groups, employee interviews, focus groups, and benchmarking what other organizations are doing. Qualitative data provides valuable information relative to values and perceptions; this structured communication provides valuable information to IBM's flexibility programs and can help identify the strengths and weaknesses of the flexibility strategy.

(2) Quantitative analysis – Quantitative measures are extremely helpful in summarizing large quantities of information quickly. IBM uses data from employee surveys as well as feedback questionnaires to help better understand the organization. Using statistics, IBM can assess its flexibility programs and practices, evaluate trends, and easily compare itself against other companies. This type of data provides valuable information for validation of the flexibility strategy. It is important to collect quantitative data

from an internal and external viewpoint. Internal data helps IBM measure the employee's perceived availability and the relative importance of flexibility in a person's decision to stay with the company. External data provides IBM benchmarking data on best practices and key learnings from other organizations.

Some of the work–life strategy measurable results have been:

- Over forty-two countries have the minimum required flexibility options (three) deployed.
- IBM has received external recognition for its leadership in the area of work–life, flexibility, and mobility in Asia Pacific, Canada, Europe, Middle East, and Africa, and in Latin America.
- Work reduction activities continue to yield positive results, and 100 percent of the managers who use the IBM work reduction/ elimination process said that they would use it again as well as recommend it to other managers.
- New dependent care programs around the world continue to grow in numbers and to diversify.

Key global issues

The traditional walls that used to house IBM no longer exist. In 2005, on an average day, more than 42 percent of IBMers are working outside traditional office environments. They are working on-site with customers, telecommuting, working from home, or are working mobile. For many, changing the space and time boundaries of the workplace increases time spent with customers, decreases commuting, and gives employees more options for balancing their personal and work lives. Being able to work "anywhere" and "anytime" is both enabled by and accelerating the development of IBM's own technical products and services. However, along with this dramatic shift in the business landscape is the management acceptance and support of a quickly changing work environment.

Along with the internal environmental challenges are culture shifts. The demographics are changing rapidly. In 2005, approximately 56 percent of IBM employees had less than five years with the company, and the people who are assuming management positions are changing constantly. Consequently, from a management point of view, having flexible and mobile employees creates some interesting challenges.

Some of those challenges lie in the start-up and maintenance of remote work assignments. One can't make the assumption that each and every employee is equally adaptable. Managers need to help them. And just because someone is a top performer doesn't necessarily mean he or she automatically has a high capacity for change. Managers need to help clarify some realistic expectations for employees as they face their flexible work assignment.

For some managers, the challenges occur at a deeper, personal level. There are very real issues of trust and control to deal with. Plus, the very role of the manager is challenged, as the manager makes the transformation from *director* to *facilitator*.

Then, there are day-to-day areas of concern for new managers which can include:

- Any degree of flexibility can be associated with some risk especially in a difficult business environment where profitability and customer satisfaction are key elements to the success of the business.
- Workforce flexibility and/or employee mobility may diminish the camaraderie of a team or department. Some managers bemoan the loss of informal contacts.
- Mobility requires learning new styles of communicating.
- Ad hoc "management by wandering around" is dead:
  - Some employees are not adequately using the tools that are at hand.
  - Without disciplined communication, some employees may struggle.
- Flexibility and mobility blur work and family boundaries:
  - It's "difficult" to leave work if working from home.
  - Some employees may feel like they are working all the time (during vacations, holidays, etc.).
  - Some employees may not fully optimize the new mix of venues offered by a flexible work environment.

From an employee perspective, there are issues as well. Employees may be reluctant to utilize FWOs because they fear it will somehow negatively impact their promotional opportunities and/or advancement within the company. Employees are also insecure about having some of their colleagues sitting in an office environment alongside their manager, when they are working from a remote setting, such as from home or at a client location. Lastly, what happens if one IBM manager allows his or her employee to work a compressed work week, yet another manager from a peer department does not exercise the same flexibility. Employees could be confused if flexibility is not administered consistently across the enterprise. And, lastly, are flexible work options an employee entitlement? Are they something that is bestowed upon top performers only? Questions continue to remain in employees' minds.

Workload issues

Workload escalation is a real, not perceived, threat to the retention of IBM talent. Internal surveys document that it is among the strongest factors causing both men and women to think about leaving and contributes to an undesirable level of turnover in the first year(s) of employment. Work–life and workload issues are inextricably linked. Employees cannot be autonomous if heavy workload and an overwhelming feeling of "low-value" work tasks continue to exist; it has become increasingly obvious that work–life and workload issues are grounded in business, not as exclusive Human Resources challenges. Consequently, enterprise-wide support is required to take appropriate actions that will have the highest potential of removing obstacles that impede a high-performing work culture, one that enables employees to deliver high value and quality, timely services and solutions to customers and prospects. IBM needed to take very specific actions to accelerate changes in the workplace to enable employees to team, executive, perform at high levels, and win new business. Leaders need to chart the way.

Technology issues

Technology also plays a key role relative to effect on work–life balance. Significant technological advancements within the last ten years or so have simultaneously displaced and empowered employees, and technology has proven to alter the way we live. However, at IBM, although technology has enabled us to work faster and smarter, it challenges us with the temptation and/or expectation to work anyplace at any time (and at all times). Internal IBM studies have indicated that 76 percent of employees believe that technological advancements have improved their ability to balance work and personal obligations.

However, 62 percent of employees also have growing concerns about technology's impact on the length of the workday. Employees feel compelled to check email and/or voicemail messages after traditional work hours end, on the weekend, and during vacations, and say technology is intrusive. Even though employees recognize that self-discipline is needed to maintain balance, the onus is often on the employee's ability to set those boundaries.

Key EMEA issues

EMEA key issues mirror the global issues. Survey results show the same problems: employees are asking for more management support in balancing their work and life, are fearing damaging their careers if taking advantage of the flexibility work options, and are missing interaction with colleagues if using one of the flexible work options. On the other hand, managers still want to see their employees in the office and have problems changing their management styles from control to trust (i.e. focusing their employees' performance assessments on business results/objectives rather than "face" time or time in the office). Although steps have been taken to develop work–life programs or policies – daycare, resource and referral website, seminars, flex policies, camps – managers continue to overlook the critical importance of reshaping the underlying organizational culture and the opportunities that arise from linking work–life strategies to core business strategies.

It has been observed that, far too often, the reality in business is a practice of accommodating a few individuals rather than engaging all workers through clear and well-communicated work–life strategies.

Europe, the Middle East, and Africa are very diverse territories which include hundreds of countries, nations, languages, and cultures. Changing the culture is an extremely significant factor in actualizing work–life. This means aligning the values, attitudes, and behaviors of managers at all levels to support employees and last but not least changing the cultural mindset of a certain country, changing the unspoken rules that govern behavior there. It also means asking if the day-to-day activity is directly related to achieving results and it means asking if there are alternative ways of getting the job done that improve the end product and benefit the lives of employees. Successful change agents pay careful attention to the barriers that stand in the way of new ideas.

Employees fear that taking advantage of work–life initiatives will damage their careers. Such fears are justified and must be addressed with clear communication, support, and coaching. All managers and all employees need to understand the purpose of work–life policies and how work–life benefits the business. It calls for top leadership's commitment, clear statements of values, modifications to incentives, training for supervisors, real evidence of daily commitment, and practical evaluation feedback. This shift links the work–life message to key business drivers.

Employees across the European, Middle Eastern, and African territories are diverse, and they face a complex range of personal issues and responsibilities. Another important issue in the work–life arena is the broad array of legislation. Some countries are offering protection and support to employees, some are not. Institutional support for families and work varies greatly between countries and so do social policy outcomes in terms of child welfare, women's labor market attachment, and gender equality more broadly. There is a huge difference between Europe and most of the Muslim countries included in this territory. European parents are supported by a variety of subsidies and legislative provisions.

The levels of public care also influence cultural flexibility. In Germany and particularly in the Netherlands part-time working has risen dramatically and is the norm for working mothers, not least because of low levels of public care. In Europe "flexibility" seems to be defined as an accommodation between employers and employees, while in the US it is seen primarily as a strategy to drive down labor costs.

The decisive factor in increasing employee work–life balance is not a reduction of hours as such but consultation or co-determination in the process. Current economic climate also plays a significant role because when recruitment and retention pressures slacken (like in most of the big European countries), managers are less willing to implement work–life programs.

Nevertheless, IBM is focused on ensuring management and employee support and acceptance of a flexible work environment.

Steps IBM took in EMEA

In Europe, Middle East, and Africa, specific steps were taken to address each pillar of the work–life strategy.

Culture – considering the diverse territory EMEA comprises, analyzing and interpreting survey results was not an easy task. Although regional reports were produced, when digging into data and comparing region with countries, big discrepancies were observed. The conclusion was very simple: each country should be treated separately and specific actions should be defined. This has been done with the help of the regional coordinator and the person with country responsibility for work–life (where this function exists) or country HR manager. A thorough follow-up is requested to see if something really happened or the plan remained only on paper.

Flexibility – Flexible Work Options are made available in all countries, their implementation depending very much on local country legislation and culture. At least one or two options are implemented in each country but there is a long way until all of them could be used everywhere. Significant resistance has been observed in eastern Europe (former Communist countries where a coercive management style is prevalent) and in some of the Middle East and African countries where local culture and religion play a big role in acceptance of FWO.

Dependent care – as more and more employees are reported to have dependent care responsibilities, the Global Work–Life fund in EMEA focused on addressing these increased demands. Based on a strategic business analysis thirteen countries were selected to be eligible to receive funds. The decision has been made considering also the IBM population in a certain country because, without a certain critical mass, these programs can't have the required utilization rates.

Programs were customized by country and included childcare centers, vacation camps all through the year, international camps, resource and referral services, seminars on topics pertaining to dependent care, building in-home care networks, priority slots in centers and schools for IBM employees, after-school programs, etc.

One of the latest findings in the 2004 survey was the high demand in back-up care. Employees all over the territory were asking for support in case of emergency, either due to urgent business requests or due to an unpredictable situation in their normal dependent care arrangement. To address this need it has been decided to pilot different back-up care programs in four countries (two big and two small) and based on results to evaluate if a general implementation is feasible or not, cost being one of the major issues. The pilot started running in 2005 and the evaluation was done at the end of 2006. Also, new countries will be added to the Global Work–Life Fund list (eight in the next two years), priorities being established according to business performance, population size, and IBM strategic investments in some territories.

Next steps for IBM

Although progress has been made, the challenge of integrating work and family life is part of everyday reality for the majority of IBM workers around the world. While the specifics may vary depending on job responsibility, income level, stage in life/career, this challenge cuts across all socioeconomic levels and is felt directly by both women and men.

IBM understands that it needs to play a significant ongoing role to:

- communicate to employees and reinforce organizational commitment (and not "just" communicate, but ensure that messages are sincere. The concepts of "achieving business results and enhancing work–life balance" are inconsistent to employees – the message needs to be very clear and straightforward);
- address organizational issues and obstacles;
- provide clear guidelines, training, and resources.

The company also understands that mindset is that constant daily programming people receive, and that determines their eventual level of achievement in everything they do. Changing this programming is not an easy task, it takes time and sustained efforts which finally might prove to be worthwhile (or not). People mindset might be equated to a garden (James Allen). If you leave the garden uncultivated, whatever the wind blows in – plants, weeds, or whatever – will grow there. If you consciously plant it, and cultivate it and keep it weeded, you will grow the flowers, fruits, or vegetables you desire.

Then and now – questions for discussion

The challenge:

(1) Globally, what could IBM have done differently at the beginning of the process to help managers accept this change more readily?
(2) What can IBM do now, globally, to encourage employees to be more "flexible"?

(3) What can IBM do now, specifically in EMEA, to encourage employees to be more "flexible"?
(4) What can IBM do now to encourage managers to support work–life balance?
(5) How can companies develop a cultural mindset favorable to work–life balance?
(6) What is the return-on-investment of work–life policy? How can it be measured?

PART II

Policy design, implementation, and deployment

6 | Stages in the implementation of work–life policies

STEVEN A. Y. POELMANS
IESE Business School, Spain
SHILPA PATEL
MTL Instruments Group, UK
and
BARBARA BEHAM
University of Hamburg, Germany

"There is nothing more difficult and dangerous, or more doubtful of success, than an attempt to introduce a new order of things in any state. For the innovator has for enemies all those who derived advantages from the old order of things while those who expect to be benefited by the new institutions will be but lukewarm defenders."

Niccolò Machiavelli – *The Prince*

Managers in firms that decide to develop work–life programs are confronted with four major decisions: the adoption decision, the design decision, the organizational implementation decision, and the individual allowance decision (Poelmans & Sahibzada, 2004). In Chapter 2 we addressed the adoption and design decision. This chapter seeks to consider the *how*, not the what or why, of developing a work–life program in the firm. We will focus on to what extent and how work–life programs are implemented and apply in general (implementation), and in specific cases (allowance), in order to have a real impact on the reduction of conflicts between responsibilities at work, in the family, and on personal life, while improving the bottom line. Questions we will address are: how to identify a realistic path for development; where to begin when introducing initiatives; and what factors to take into account in order to optimize the efficiency of the implementation and allowance decision processes in the firm.

There is no one "right" solution or path to improvement: the route to achieving excellence in work–life harmony must be appropriate to an organization's current standing. Policies and practices adopted should complement an overall strategy to shift the cultural climate of the

133

organization, if the benefits of family-responsible initiatives are to be realized and sustained in the long run. The introduction of policies is certainly an improvement, but it is really only the first step in a continuous process of development to become an organization that truly supports and advocates work–life harmony. The change towards becoming such a firm is a slow and steady process, and requires commitment, motivation, and staying power. Like any fundamental shift in organizational practices, the successful implementation of work–life harmony initiatives is shrouded in the careful management of change – and like any change process, it requires a "change" approach. With conscientious planning, prudent project management, tenacious communication, and carefully considered implementation, a company can confidently take the critical first steps to becoming what the officially announced, formal policies pretend.

The specific development path a company can take will depend on a number of internal and external business parameters. These include: the organization's current position in relation to work–life harmony; its size and organizational complexity; its previous competitive and strategic choices; the sector in which it operates; the nature of the current labor market; country-level government-supported policies; and the broad cultural and socioeconomic environment (for a systematic review, see Poelmans & Sahibzada, 2004).

Later on in this chapter we will introduce the four-stage "Family Responsible Company Development Model," developed by the International Center of Work and Family at IESE Business School, based on five consecutive national surveys of work–life policies in organizations. The model describes the existing *stages of implementation* of work–family policies in a specific organization and the path of improvement. Four main parameters are present to assess the current stage of development, or "phase," the organization is in: *policies*, *practices*, *culture*, and *enablers*. The model, as an instrument of change, is complemented by a suite of evaluation and diagnostic tools designed to assess the needs and priorities of an organization in relation to these four parameters. For a short version of the diagnostic tool, see (www.iesedti.com/ifrei2006/ifrei.htm). Underlying this methodology is the overall objective to create a workplace that is both effective in achieving economic results and respectful of every individual's choice to harmonize his or her work, family, and personal life. This "dual agenda" lies at the heart of the business case in support of work–life initiatives (Rapoport, Bailyn, Fletcher, & Pruitt, 2002) and provides a powerful argument in favor of this work. It should therefore be emphasized when soliciting support from an organization's policy-makers and stakeholders.

To describe the *allowance decision* we present a theoretical framework that distinguishes various factors which have an influence on the allowance decision, and thus offer a useful checklist of elements managers should take into account when confronted with the request for a work–life benefit by an employee. We also present a variety of behavioral outcomes with which employees and co-workers may respond to a manager's allowance decisions.

The implementation decision

The changes associated with the goal of harmonizing work, family, and personal life are development activities that require the close collaboration of all people within *all* levels of the organization to work. If the changes are to be sustainable, they should not merely be imposed upon employees from on high. Every person within an organization has something to contribute – and gain – from the successful implementation of work–life initiatives. In the words of Peter Senge,[1] "People don't resist change. They resist being changed!"

In order to guarantee successful change of work–family attitudes and practices, organizational change agents need a clear structure and process to realize this change. In this chapter we will describe the process to implement policies in the firm with the four-stage "Family Responsible Company Development Model." At each stage of the developmental process, change agents need to evaluate and improve the status of the four basic elements of a work–life program – policies, practices, culture, and enablers – in order to implement and further develop them.

Policies

In Chapter 2 we described in detail the various work–life policies companies may choose to adopt. Policies are formally designed and formally communicated rules which are applied within the organization. They

---

[1] Dr Peter M. Senge is a senior lecturer at the Massachusetts Institute of Technology, and author of *The Fifth Discipline: The Art and Practice of the Learning Organization.*

set the general, company-wide ground rules for adapting work to personal responsibilities. Basically, family-responsible policies can be broadly classified into five categories – flexibility policies, leave arrangements, care provisions, supportive arrangements, and conventional provisions for job quality and compensations benefits (see Chapter 2 for more details on the different types of policies).

Practices

The second element used to describe a company's positioning in terms of development concerns work practices. These refer to the actual *use* of the policies described above, or to non-policy-driven habits and practices that are prevalent within the organization (García, 2006). Every organization has its unique habits and practices which have formed over months or years as a result of the way work is organized within the company and the roles that people within the organization have traditionally played. Whilst such practices may originally stem from the actions of one or two individuals – for example a president who insisted on holding his management review meetings on a Saturday morning – they can easily become deeply engrained within the corporate culture of the organization, and as such become difficult to break. Some of these practices are positive and contribute to the creation of a supportive organizational culture. They support or inherently encourage individuals to develop a harmonic relationship between their work, family, and personal lives. Some examples of such constructive practices are:

- *Individuals are encouraged to go home by a certain hour each day, establishing a "lights out" time.* At Caja Madrid, Spain, lights are switched off at 8.00 p.m. and an obligatory notification is required if employees plan to work over the weekend. The same technique is also used in other companies in Spain, like at Sanitas and Randstad, at 6.00 p.m. and at MRW at 7.00 p.m. (Chinchilla, Poelmans, León, & Tarrés, 2004).
- *Employees are encouraged to set limits between their work and family lives, and these limits are generally respected by their colleagues, bosses, and subordinates.* For instance, Intel provides courses for employees on how to tell their bosses that they should not be called at home late in the night. A subsidiary of Nestlé in the US forbids its employees to plan any meetings after 10.00 a.m. on

Fridays in order to reduce the pressure from the work that gets accumulated over the weekend. When meetings were held on Fridays after 10.00 a.m., employees tended to stay at work longer or took work home (Chinchilla *et al.*, 2004).

- *Personal reviews/evaluations and professional career paths that take into consideration the personal life of the individual in a supportive way.* More and more professional services firms are leaving behind the "up or out" rule to implement career plateaus that allow collaborators to stay at a certain level in their career to meet caring needs, without jeopardizing possible future promotions.

- *A general acceptance and approval to talk about the family or personal issues at work.* In Happy Ltd, an award-winning training company in the UK, during the school holidays, parents can bring children into the office if there is an urgent need. Moreover the company adopted the "we can do" attitude and tries to find ways for accommodating the needs of its employees (BusinessLink, 2006).

- *A positive effort is made to reintegrate staff back into the workplace and into their working roles upon return from extended leave (maternity, paternity, sabbatical).* Deutsche Bank in Germany has developed a special program to keep in touch with and reintegrate employees who took parental leave.

Other work practices can exacerbate the conflict experienced by employees in managing their personal and professional responsibilities. Such practices are destructive by nature and can compromise the successful implementation and overall effectiveness of policies and programs, and thus hinder progress towards developing a supportive organizational culture. One example of such "bad" practices that manifests itself on a day-to-day basis is the notion that working longer hours implies more output and increases the chance to get a promotion. Working late each day or regularly taking work home at weekends is viewed as a positive demonstration of hard work and commitment. Managers often personally set such an example for their staff who, in turn, feel compelled to follow suit. Another example of a destructive practice is the regular scheduling of meetings outside of normal working hours, with the expectation that all people involved will adjust their personal schedule accordingly. In doing so, a manager forces his staff to choose between spending more time in the workplace or leaving work to be with their family or salient social groups. While some employees may not be concerned with this choice – they may be quite happy to attend such meetings that extend their normal working day – others may want to leave work at their contracted time, and even resent their manager for holding meetings at "unsociable" times. Such destructive practices do nothing to foster goodwill among employees. Instead, they provide an additional source of conflict and stress for at least those employees with family responsibilities.

Some additional examples of negative behaviors and practices are:

- Turning down a promotion in order to seek harmony between work, family, and personal life (reaching a so-called "career plateau") carries along the stigma of poor commitment and amounts to professional suicide.
- Employees that are allowed a work–life benefit – especially those associated with flexible working – are seen as less committed to the company and their careers, and as a result have fewer opportunities for promotion.
- Employees covertly resent colleagues taking extended leave to care for small babies or personally develop themselves, either because of the extra workload that is imposed upon them as a result, or because they dislike the idea of a colleague "getting more time off." This applies to both men and women.
- Practices like a generalized "open-door-policy" or strong unwritten rules like "customer is king" may lead to multiple interruptions at work, which amount to the fact that in order to get things done, employees have to work overtime.
- Human resource (HR) managers consider the personal life of their staff to be "none of their concern," and therefore do not promote any actions to help employees reconcile their work and personal lives. Any private concern is banned from the workplace.

Culture

A third element to evaluate at each stage of the developmental process is the organizational culture. Cathy Busani, managing director of Happy Ltd, UK, states, "achieving a better work–life balance is a cultural mindset, not just a set of policies." If organizational change is to be effective and sustainable, it is necessary that informal culture and behavior, as well as formal policies and practices, are changed. It is therefore essential to take into consideration culture as one of the four parameters that define the current status of an organization with respect to work–life harmony.

In a general business sense, "work culture" can be defined in terms of the implicit assumptions, social norms, and expectations that govern the working atmosphere of an organization. Collectively, these three behavioral elements dictate what is acceptable and what is not, and imply a set of values and beliefs against which each employee is expected to act. In the context of family-responsible initiatives, these elements define the extent to which an organization supports and values the integration of employees' work and family lives (Allen, 2001; Thompson, Beauvais, & Lyness, 1999). Unlike policies and practices, the culture of an organization is more difficult to capture. Research suggests that a family-supportive culture can be measured by assessing three dimensions of culture: managerial support for work–life harmony, career consequences associated with utilizing work–life benefits, and organizational time expectations that could interfere with family responsibilities (Thompson *et al.*, 1999). Perceptions of a supportive organizational culture were found to be reflected in a healthy take-up of work–life benefits. The presence of a supportive culture was a better indicator of work behaviors and attitudes than the availability of work–life benefits per se.

An organizational culture also has a significant impact on how, and how quickly, a firm can make a positive and conscious change towards a more supportive environment. This idea reinforces the need to assess the culture of the organization in a first step before making plans for improvement. A company that is taking steps to change its organizational culture is likely to be at a more advanced stage in its evolution towards the creation of a supportive workplace. In TYF Group, an adventure, education, and leisure business, Andy Middleton, managing director, shares his reading of this topic: "Over the years, we've learnt that it's less about enforcing rules and more about instilling values and principles" (BusinessLink, 2006). In Chapters 8 and 9 we will explore culture in more depth.

Enablers

Under the term "enablers" we have brought together a set of factors that drive each phase of development – indeed any process of organizational change: strategy and resources, leadership/attitude, communication, and accountability. The experiences of many companies, both large and small, support the view that a breakdown in any one of these enablers, at any stage of the developmental process, is likely to lead to frustration, disappointment, and unsatisfactory results. Such responses may sap the energy, momentum, and drive from change processes and can even result in the withdrawal of the resources and support needed to achieve the change projects' goals. The four factors presented, and discussed in more detail in the following paragraphs, provide a firm foundation upon which organizations can build a strong framework of supportive policies, promote positive practices and behavior, and translate values into norms that encourage work–life harmony and a supportive organizational culture.

Strategy and resources

The strategic choice of an organization to create a culture that not only supports, but also actively encourages and promotes, harmony between work, family, and personal responsibilities is fundamental to achieve long-term and sustained success. This commitment should be reflected in the corporate mission of the organization, in its vision and values. Time, people, and financial resources need to be allocated to the change process in the short, medium, and long term.

In companies with a strong supportive culture, the development of solutions that are aimed at helping employees to harmonize work and personal life is perceived as an integrative, strategic part of doing business (Galinsky, Friedman, & Hernandez, 1991). Such organizations no longer rely upon a corporate mission to guide their decision-making. Work–life harmony naturally permeates all day-to-day working practices at all levels of the corporation. At Procter & Gamble (P&G), for example, each employee designs his or her own working schedule that includes the possibility of starting and finishing work earlier or later. The only requirement is that the person works eight hours daily and that a sufficient number of hours coincide with the general schedule of the company (Poelmans & de Waal-Andrews, 2005).

Leadership/attitude

Family-responsible companies count on strong leaders at all levels of management who establish and communicate a consistent and clear family-responsible direction for the company as a whole. These leaders openly recognize and fully support the belief that work–life harmony is fundamental to the long-term success of the business, and act on this belief by integrating work–life issues in their decision-making and engaging in regular communication and discussion with colleagues. They serve as role models and motivate others around them to "walk the talk." Thus, they lead by example to create a truly supportive work environment.

For example, in Happy Ltd, UK, the managing director works a four-day week and the CEO takes Wednesday mornings off to go to a reading class with his daughter (BusinessLink, 2006). The head of the sales department of P&G in Spain works 100 percent flexible. He testifies that working this way contributes a lot to spending time with his two sons, six and eight years old. Being a divorced father, his flexible working schedule allows him to pick them up from school, help with classes, play with them, and spend more time with them overall. Moreover, his supervisor is satisfied with the results he achieves at work and he feels much happier with his personal and professional life (Chinchilla *et al.*, 2004). In this way he sets an example to other employees that working flexible is possible and productive.

Communication
The need to communicate the aims, objectives, and benefits of a family-responsible program to both internal and external audiences is of paramount importance if such an initiative is to achieve long-term success. Strong and effective channels of communication provide an organization with a valuable tool with which to minimize fear, uncertainty, and misunderstandings amongst the workforce over the changes that will inevitably take place. The use of a variety of channels – for example, discussion sessions, speakers, leaflets, and the company intranet – can help to convey information more convincingly and memorably.

For example, when the flexibility program was planned to be introduced at Procter & Gamble, the national general managers were the ones to communicate the policies to the employees, in order to give more credibility to the program. A three-month period was allocated to the communication, during which the employees were shown a video and provided with a folder containing detailed information on the policies and where to obtain more information (Poelmans & de Waal-Andrews, 2005). IBM has a program entitled "Work–life" which is aimed at promoting harmony between private and professional life. The company culture is thoroughly explained on the intranet, which gives the employee more confidence when asking for accommodations (Chinchilla *et al.*, 2004).

In all companies, communication should be formal and informal, and also both internal and external to the organization. The outside voice not only publicly acknowledges the initiatives or the organization but also helps to transmit the message that it fully believes in its family-responsible mission within the organization. It should be emphasized that it is not sufficient to occasionally pass on a little information to staff with regard to what is going on in terms of work–life initiatives. Both quality and quantity in terms of communication should be maintained throughout all stages of development. In Happy Ltd, UK, information on available work–life policies is explained at induction and the twice-yearly appraisals that are held, including questions on work–life balance. The company has won several national awards and its good image as an employer attracts a big workforce and makes them save on recruitment advertising. The TYF Group policies are clearly communicated during the interview and induction, making employees feel comfortable to use part-time working, flexible hours, home working, shift swapping, and sabbaticals. For example, a staff member recently took a two-month sabbatical in Mexico and arranged her coverage, which worked out well (BusinessLink, 2006).

Accountability

In order for an organization to change its culture, it is critical that all employees at all levels assume a degree of personal responsibility for creating the new environment. Peer pressure can be very powerful during times of gradual change, and fundamental to the success of responsible initiatives is the underlying notion that both the organization and its employees not only support improved working practices, but also take ownership for their implementation.

An important aspect of accountability is whether the company, in addition to policies for the use of benefits, has policies for rewarding its use and adoption in managers, or ways of penalizing disrespect for work–life balance. Sun Microsystems, for example, includes "respect for diversity" in its yearly 360° feedback system, and does not tolerate low scores on this criterion. In this way they clearly make their managers accountable for respecting employees of different races and sex.

Ideally though, accountability is pushed down to the employees themselves and translated into a shared understanding in the firm that keeping an eye on productivity and flexibility at the same time is the responsibility of each employee. Productivity and flexibility should go hand in hand by designing work processes and providing resources that allow employees to assume responsibility themselves.

The employees of Cloisters Barristers' chambers, London, have developed an outline Service Charter. A schedule is completed weekly by all the members and it accounts for the working time of the employees (BusinessLink, 2006). The scheme is flexible, since employees may adjust the proposed times, but only with the agreement of their colleagues and if an appropriate cover is ensured. This commitment and accountability is only won through strong and consistent leadership, effective communication, and a well-defined strategic direction, in such a way that each and every individual understands the importance of harmony and assumes personal responsibility for promoting and supporting policies and practices. Vodafone UK applied its strategy of a mobile, flexible environment in all parts of its work. All employees are provided with mobile handsets, equipped with a mini intranet, which allow them to move around the company campus and access the necessary information. This also facilitates casual, part-time, and full-time home working as well as the mobility of personal assistants who do not have to be bound to the chair to receive phone calls. Salford City Council, UK, promotes working from home among its employees and creates the necessary environment for making work productive through a special system, ADSL connection, and the appropriate telephone (BusinessLink, 2006). These three examples illustrate that the accountability for work–life harmony can be shared with the employees, rather than assumed entirely by management. This creates "ownership" in employees for their own work–life needs and takes away part of the burden from management.

The Family-Responsible Company Development Model[2]

In the following section we will describe each stage of the model of development, particularly emphasizing what these stages represent in

[2] In order to make a quick assessment of the company status in terms of development in developing a family-responsible firm, see www.iesedti.com/ ifrei2006/ifrei.htm.

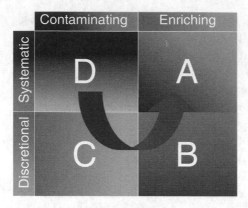

Figure 6.1 Four development stages in becoming a "family responsible" firm.

terms of transition. Company culture takes time to evolve, as policies translate in practices, practices become habits, habits become norms, and these norms, in turn, define and promote the culture. The four-stage model of change perfectly complements this process of evolution, and draws upon the environmental metaphors of systematic contamination and enrichment to describe the management of human capital – or human ecology – in today's business environment. Figure 6.1. shows the four main stages of development.

Some decades ago, there were hardly any policies or formal procedures in place within companies to either protect the environment or to prevent its abuse. Rather than willful destruction, this situation arose more as a result of a lack of consciousness that certain business practices were contaminating the environment, and companies were so used to following these old practices that they were not aware or mindful of the damage that was being done. Functioning in this way, these organizations were "systematically" or "structurally" contaminating their working environment. In the same way, a company in the first stage "D" of the model, does not assume any responsibility for the human ecology within its social environment, and such a firm is not conscious of the damage it is causing to its employees, its employees' families, and the community at large as a result of the destructive practices prevalent in the organization. Thus, a stage D company can be described as being "systematically contaminating."

Stage D: "Systematic contamination"

The first stage of development is marked with stage D. A company in this initial stage pays little attention to the social impact of working conditions and practices on employees. There are no policies in place to support work–life harmony and, to compound the situation, prevalent in the company are certain policies, practices, or habits that actually hinder employees from integrating their day-to-day work and personal responsibilities (e.g. regular scheduling of meetings outside of normal office hours). The "system," or the organization as a whole, does not recognize the damaging impact of such practices or simply ignores it, thus allowing habits to contaminate a potentially healthy and harmonious working environment.

Within the overall strategy or mission of a stage D organization, there is no reference to the topic of work–family or work–life balance, and therefore no resources, neither time nor money, have formally been allocated to the change process. In addition, there is no championing of the topic at senior levels, and hence little or no communication is associated with the topic. There appears to be no distinct ownership of this issue, and not surprisingly, no responsibilities towards improvements have been assigned at any level.

To start the transition process of a company from stage D to stage C, first awareness of the damaging impact of day-to-day work methods needs to be created among managers and employees equally. In a second step, policies, practices, culture, and enablers as described earlier in this chapter need to be assessed. Table 6.1 presents a series of questions designed to assess the current status within the company, and provides answers typically given by an organization in this early step of development. In the next step policies and practices that help employees to reconcile their work and family responsibilities are identified and implemented. Senior management is required to promote these within the organization.

In the second stage C, there may still linger practices that hinder work–life harmony, but in principle they are not systematically present in the day-to-day operations on the business. Each manager applies his or her own discretion and judgment in supporting employees with caring responsibilities. In this stage the company is still contaminating the working environment, but in a "discretional" way.

Table 6.1. *Assessment of company's location in the model of development. Answers of a stage D company*

---

(1) **How aware are the company's managers of work–family issues?**
 (a) Hardly any managers consider work–family balance to be a problem.
(2) **Do the company's managers set a good example as far as meeting family responsibilities is concerned (for example, by seeking a work–family balance in their own lives, and by taking advantage of family-friendly policies and practices in an exemplary fashion)?**
 (a) No, most of the company's managers do not practice such a culture; on the contrary, often they set a bad example.
(3) **What stage is your company at in the process of designing and implementing family-friendly policies?**
 (a) The possibility of developing family-friendly policies is not on the company's agenda.
(4) **Does the company allocate a budget for the development of these policies/ practices?**
 (a) No budget is allocated.
(5) **How are employees informed about the various family-friendly initiatives?**
 (a) No special information procedure is used.
(6) **To what extent has the issue of work–family balance been incorporated into the company's external communication?**
 (a) Not at all; in fact, it is something of a weak point for the company.
(7) **What would be the consequences for a manager or supervisor who went against the company's program of family-friendly policies?**
 (a) None. On the contrary, the manager would probably benefit.
(8) **Who is responsible for the "family-friendly company" project?**
 (a) Nobody.

Stage C: "The implementation of policies and commitment at senior levels"

The key distinction between stage D and stage C companies is the existence of few formal policies to help employees to establish a better harmony between their work and private responsibilities. Policies may introduce a degree of flexibility in working hours in the short or medium term (to allow an individual the opportunity to better integrate their professional and personal commitments), or enable an employee to free up more "quality" personal time, for example, through virtual office facilities. However, take-up is still limited within the eligible population of the workforce and some contaminating practices are still quite common at most levels of the organization.

Research revealed that companies operating in tight labor markets with low unemployment adopt family-responsible policies as a means of attracting high-caliber, highly motivated individuals to their doors (Goodstein, 1994; Ingram & Simons, 1995). Such policies can also be considered a rational attempt to increase the commitment and loyalty of employees and to reduce staff turnover (Osterman, 1995; Poelmans, Chinchilla, & Cardona, 2003). Highly committed employees can be expected to be more productive, more creative, and engage in organizational citizenship behavior that goes beyond the strict legal or psychological contract (Lambert, 2000). While the benefits of adopting such policies appear to be clear, the implementation of any of these policies may present significant challenges. One of the most fundamental pitfalls associated with this early stage of development is the creation of a *perception gap* between what was intended by the organization with the implementation of such policies and what an employee perceives as the result (Poelmans *et al.*, 2003). If cross sections of the workforce are unaware of the availability of work–life policies, or if there is a misperception of who is eligible to take up these policies, then the very presence of such programs can create more resentment and hostility than if they did not exist at all. This problem can be avoided through conscientious and rigorous communication throughout the whole implementation process.

Another main distinction we see between stage D and stage C organizations is the commitment of senior management to work–life harmony. In stage C the concept of work–life harmony is supported at the highest levels within the company and appears on the agenda of senior management and/or board-level meetings. However, there is still no formal inclusion of this initiative in the overall strategy or mission of the company. Some resources have been officially allocated to evaluate opportunities and develop the company further in this area, but middle managers put policies into practice at their own discretion, which means that whilst some champion the policies and encourage their staff and peers to use them, others, often the majority, are reluctant to introduce them into their departments. Managers who do not promote the use of family-responsible initiatives may feel that it is culturally unacceptable within the organization to do so, or may act according to their personal beliefs and values. In addition, their decision-making is likely to be influenced by their past personal experiences as both managers and subordinates, as well as the behavior of their own line manager. In many companies, supervisors' and middle managers' offices resonate with the beat of a familiar drum: "Well, I had to do it the old way, so my staff can, too!"

To conclude, the introduction of certain work–life policies alone is not sufficient to create a supportive environment, and the transition from stage C to stage B will be marked by steps towards changing the culture of the organization. Table 6.2 presents the profile of a C-stage company.

A stage B organization openly recognizes that employees have important responsibilities outside of their professional environment, and that it is the responsibility of the organization to help individuals reconcile their duties and aspirations at work, in their family, and in personal life. Destructive work norms have been replaced by practices that help employees in their desire to strike a healthy work–life harmony, and whilst decision-making still depends on the varying willingness of individual managers, the behavior of the organization moves from being "contaminating" to "enriching," as the majority of managers have favorable attitudes towards seeking optimal work–life harmony in their collaborators.

Stage B: "Broader buy-in, healthier practices, and a supportive culture"

Culture does not change because we desire to change it. Culture changes when the organization is transformed; the culture reflects the realities of people working together every day. Frances Hesselbein, The key to cultural transformation, *Leader to Leader* (Spring, 1999)

As indicated in the quote, this stage is about changing people's fundamental assumptions about how work should be organized, how dominant it should be in people's lives, and how success is defined (Rapoport *et al.*, 2002). The transition from stage C to stage B is characterized by a deepening and generalization of beliefs that investing in work–life harmony is not merely a cost to the firm but a requirement for sustainable employee productivity. The elements that need to be considered in this transition are described in depth in Chapter 9 of this book.

Table 6.2. *Assessment of company's location in the model of development. Answers of a stage C company.*

---

(1) **How aware are the company's managers of work–family issues?**
   (a) Some managers acknowledge the importance of balancing work and family, but they do not consider it necessary to design specific policies.
(2) **Do the company's managers set a good example as far as meeting family responsibilities is concerned (for example, by seeking a work–family balance in their own lives, and by taking advantage of family-friendly policies and practices in an exemplary fashion)?**
   (a) Only a minority of managers set a decent example, the rest do not share this mentality.
(3) **What stage is your company at in the process of designing and implementing family-friendly policies?**
   (a) The issue is on the agenda, but so far only a few policies have been implemented.
(4) **Does the company allocate a budget for the development of these policies/ practices?**
   (a) Resources are allocated to studying and designing work–family reconciliation policies.
(5) **How are employees informed about the various family-friendly initiatives?**
   (a) By official notification from top management, through some internal channel (notice board, intranet, email, etc.).
(6) **To what extent has the issue of work–family balance been incorporated into the company's external communication?**
   (a) Only a few managers speak freely about the issue with people from outside the company.
(7) **What would be the consequences for a manager or supervisor who went against the company's program of family-friendly policies?**
   (a) It may be that the manager does not agree with the formal policies; he/ she would be advised to adhere to them.
(8) **Who is responsible for the "family-friendly company" project?**
   (a) A manager or employee (e.g. in Human Resources) devotes a certain amount of time to the issue.

While in earlier stages support for work–life harmony was not deeply entrenched in the culture of the organization, Stage B companies have certainly succeeded in taking positive steps towards a more family-responsible corporate environment. The most appropriate programs are in place and available for most staff, and employees actually make use of the policies and benefits offered. Only very few informal practices which jeopardize an individual's free choice to establish his or her own harmony are still present. The implemented policies demonstrate a tangible commitment to development in the area of managing work–life conflicts.

There is a strong belief at most levels that a healthy balance between work and family responsibilities will result in a more satisfied, productive workforce overall, even though it is challenging to quantify increased levels of satisfaction and productivity as direct results of family-responsible initiatives. A willingness to improve the situation exists at most levels within the organization. Managers take ownership of the issue with more conviction, and actively encourage practices that enable staff to better harmonize their work and family lives. Discussions on this theme often take place during the employee review and evaluation process, at the discretion of the people involved. While decision-making is still discretionary in nature, it is supportive of work–life issues and is intended to enrich the organization in terms of work–life equilibrium. Rather than "allowing" employees to harmonize work and personal life, they are actively encouraged to do so. Overall, there is little misperception of the eligibility and availability of supportive policies.

However, there may still exist pockets within the organization in which work–life harmony is perceived as an alternative, not a complement, to increased satisfaction, productivity, and long-term improved bottom-line performance. While communication channels are generally open and feedback is constructive, negative feelings may still run privately through discontented employees, and their personal views and beliefs are reflected in their work practices. All of this is well reflected in the answers given in Table 6.3 by a company currently in stage B.

The fourth and final stage A, represents a state in which the protection and support of the human ecology form an integral part of company culture and permeate all day-to-day work practices of the organization. In stage A, both the company and its employees recognize the contribution work–life harmony makes to the lives and well-being of staff and their "significant others," as well as the positive impact it has on the company's bottom line through improved productivity and employee satisfaction. Through its policies, practices, and overall culture, a stage A company can be described as "systematically enriching" and also family-responsible.

Table 6.3. *Assessment of company's location in the model of development. Answers of a stage B company.*

(1) **How aware are the company's managers of work–family issues?**
  (a) Some managers acknowledge the importance of balancing work and family, and believe it necessary to design specific policies.
(2) **Do the company's managers set a good example as far as meeting family responsibilities is concerned (for example, by seeking a work–family balance in their own lives, and by taking advantage of family-friendly policies and practices in an exemplary fashion)?**
  (a) Most managers set a good example for the rest of the organization, using the various policies and practices, such as flexible working hours, leave, and so on.
(3) **What stage is your company at in the process of designing and implementing family-friendly policies?**
  (a) Several company policies have been drawn up and implemented, but they are not widely used by employees.
(4) **Does the company allocate a budget for the development of these policies/ practices?**
  (a) A specific budget is allocated to work–family reconciliation.
(5) **How are employees informed about the various family-friendly initiatives?**
  (a) Information sessions on work–family issues are held for managers/ supervisors.
(6) **To what extent has the issue of work–family balance been incorporated into the company's external communication?**
  (a) Most managers feel comfortable informing the world outside that the company promotes work–family reconciliation.
(7) **What would be the consequences for a manager or supervisor who went against the company's program of family-friendly policies?**
  (a) The manager would be told clearly and firmly that s/he must change his/ her behavior if s/he does not want to jeopardize his/her future in the company.
(8) **Who is responsible for the "family-friendly company" project?**
  (a) The task of coordinating work–family reconciliation initiatives has been assigned to a specific employee or team.

Stage A: *"Managing with conviction for sustained improvement"*

Stage A organizations not only have successfully implemented a suite of consistent policies and practices, but have also instilled in their workforce a culture fully supportive of work and family integration. The day-to-day implementation of policies and practices is systematically enriching and meets the actual needs of the whole workforce.

The topic of work–family–life balance is fully integrated into the overall mission of the company, and has been implemented as part of the corporate strategy at all organizational levels. Evidence of this supportive corporate culture is clearly visible in day-to-day business, and increased levels of employee satisfaction and commitment as a result of relieving work–family conflicts are viewed as a distinct competitive advantage. Such organizations have in place strong channels of communication and regularly engage in open and constructive discussion on the topic, in the spirit of continuous improvement. Examples of such organizations are Iberdrola, Sanitas, Banesto, MRW, Ferrovial, Cintra, and Schering in Spain. At Procter & Gamble a so-called women's business network was created to maintain the existing orientation towards work–life harmony. The network is getting together on a regular basis to discuss various issues and ideas that were communicated to the diversity managers of the company and provided them with important insights on the situation of women in P&G (Poelmans & de Waal-Andrews, 2005). This type of initiative shows that work–life harmony is a legitimate concern of an organization and employees are directly involved in monitoring that policies and practices remain relevant.

In this stage, almost all managers embrace the evolving needs of their staff at all levels with respect to work–life harmony. The discussion of how an individual could benefit from certain work–life policies is woven into the formal review process for each employee. Resources are dedicated to ongoing, company-wide improvements. All employees – those with family responsibilities and those without – take on the responsibility to promote changes, thus creating a supportive working environment for all. Employees are encouraged to identify and participate in ongoing improvements with respect to balancing work and family commitments, and are reprimanded for working in a way that could jeopardize the work–life equilibrium of their colleagues. The workforce genuinely respects each individual's choice and is offered equitable opportunities.

The strength of a stage A company's culture with respect to work–life harmony is evident from the commentaries and references of top

Table 6.4. *Assessment of company's location in the model of development. Answers of a stage A company*

---

(1) **How aware are the company's managers of work–family issues?**
   (a) Most of the company's managers believe it necessary to design specific work–family policies.

(2) **Do the company's managers set a good example as far as meeting family responsibilities is concerned (for example, by seeking a work–family balance in their own lives, and by taking advantage of family-friendly policies and practices in an exemplary fashion)?**
   (a) Most managers and supervisors embody in their own lives a respect for the family as a value inherent in the company's culture, and encourage employees to do the same.

(3) **What stage is your company at in the process of designing and implementing family-friendly policies?**
   (a) Several company policies have been drawn up and implemented, and possible new initiatives are constantly being considered. They are widely used by employees.

(4) **Does the company allocate a budget for the development of these policies/ practices?**
   (a) Every year, the budget provides sufficient resources to promote new family-friendly policies/practices.

(5) **How are employees informed about the various family-friendly initiatives?**
   (a) Information sessions on work–family issues are held for all employees.

(6) **To what extent has the issue of work–family balance been incorporated into the company's external communication?**
   (a) The reconciliation of personal, family, and professional life is so important that it is often included in external communications as one of the company's strong points.

(7) **What would be the consequences for a manager or supervisor who went against the company's program of family-friendly policies?**
   (a) Besides being given a warning, the manager would be disciplined for his/her behavior.

(8) **Who is responsible for the "family-friendly company" project?**
   (a) Besides formal responsibilities, there are spontaneous, informal initiatives by employees to drive the project forward.

---

managers in the press and official documents like the company Internet and annual reports. Formal inclusion in the personal review process, and external communications on the topic, as well as day-to-day dialogue within the organization itself is part of the company's practices.

The strength and quality of this culture is considered to be a tangible competitive advantage to attract and retain skilled and motivated personnel. Illustrative examples of answers given by a company in stage A of the developmental model are presented in Table 6.4.

The transition from stage B to stage A is perhaps the shortest of the three processes of development described in the previous paragraphs, but it is undoubtedly the most challenging one. Before taking this final step, it is vital that a company creates a firm foundation of policies and practices upon which to build its supportive and systematically enriching culture.

To conclude, in order to reach the final stage, the company goes through a complex process: from denying the existence of practices contaminating the environment to the support of human ecology as a part of the company's culture.

The allowance decision

According to the theoretical model as proposed by Poelmans & Sahibzada (2004) the allowance decision is the last decision an organization needs to take into account when implementing work–life programs. With the allowance decision, the organization actually decides whether and when to approve the request of a certain work–family benefit to an employee. The mere decision of a company to implement and offer work–life programs to its employees does not guarantee actual utilization of these programs. We argue that the allowance decision is an important determinant of the success of a work–life program. Only when employees actually can make use of work–family policies and their real needs and expectations are met, can we talk about a successful implementation of the program.

The allowance decision is often the responsibility of the direct supervisor of the employee who applies for a certain policy or program. Only if the employee and the manager do not come to a satisfying result, the HR department may get involved. Inconsistency in the approval of employees' requests may lead to feelings of unequal treatment and resentment among employees. To avoid such negative behavioral outcomes, objective decision-making criteria and a consistent application process need to be promoted within the organization. One approach to increase consistency of allowance decisions is to centralize this decision process, for example in the HR department. The disadvantage of this approach is that by removing the responsibility for these decisions from first-line managers, the supervisor's perspective gets lost. The direct supervisor is the person closest to the employee and the working team, and therefore knows best about how to reschedule tasks and responsibilities within the team or department. In order to minimize the risk of inequities in decision-making these managers need to be educated regarding legitimate factors and decision criteria (Powell & Mainiero, 1999).

Research on managerial decision-making in the work–family context has mainly been based on two theoretical frameworks. According to work disruption theory (Powell & Mainiero, 1999), managers do consider the potential for a requested work arrangement to disrupt the conduct of work in the department. More disruptive arrangements such as long leaves of absence were found to receive less favorable decisions by managers then less disruptive arrangements such as working certain days a week from home. Dependency theory (Bartol & Martin, 1990) argues that managers depend in various ways upon their subordinates, and therefore they want to retain and motivate valuable employees since those individuals also contribute most to the performance of the department or work group. High-performing, difficult-to-replace, and/or well-connected employees were found to receive the most favorable outcomes (Klein, Berman, & Dickson, 2000). Furthermore, if these respondents threatened to quit in the case that their request was rejected, their requests were significantly more likely to be approved.

In a recent study, den Dulk and de Ruijter (2005) investigated managers' attitudes towards the use of work–life policies by testing hypotheses based on both dependency and disruption theory. They mainly found evidence for the disruption argument. The performance of the department or work group was found to be the major interest of managers. Work–family policies are often seen as disruptive, making it difficult to achieve the department's targets. Other factors, such as the type of work–life policies requested, the education level of the workforce in the department, and whether the employee has a supervisory position were also found to influence the decision.

To summarize, recent empirical work on managerial decision-making in the work–family context has mainly focused on the type of work–family policy requested, employee characteristics (e.g. gender,

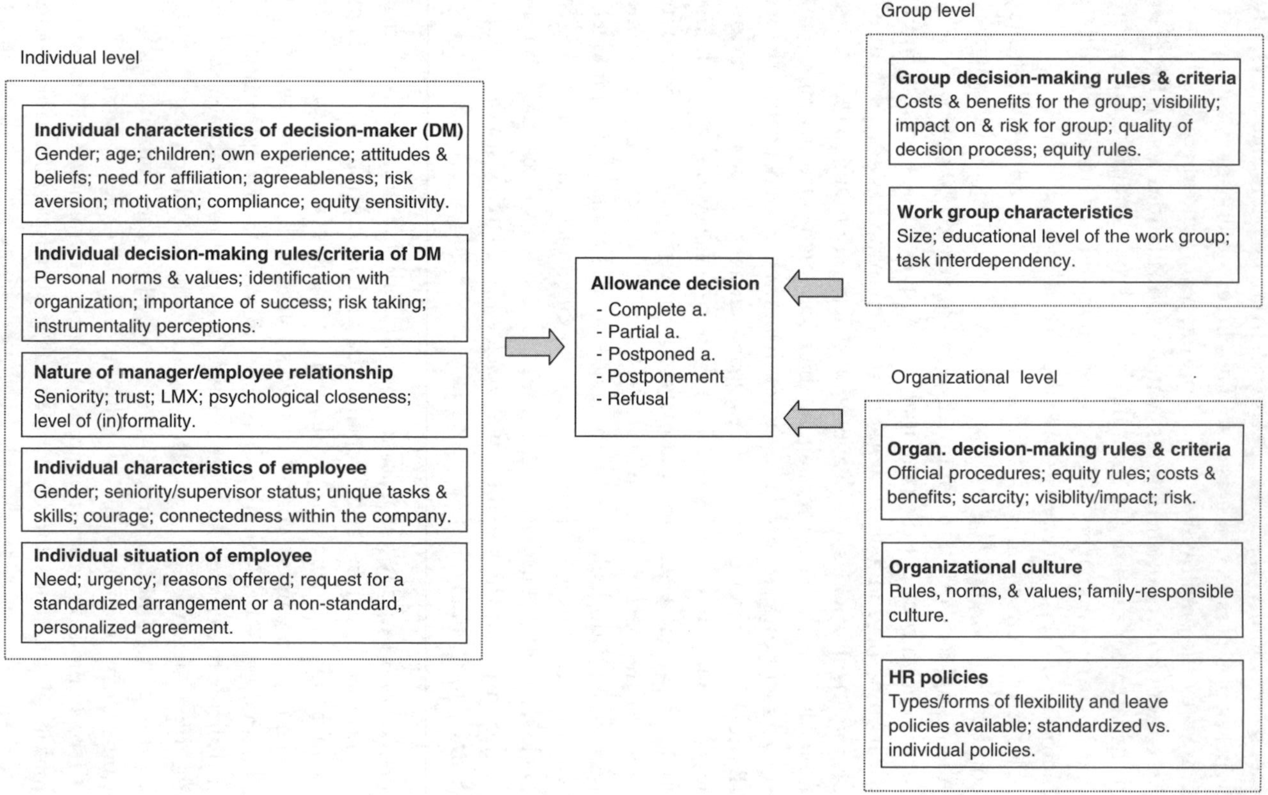

Figure 6.2 Factors influencing the supervisor's allowance decision.

Individual level

Individual characteristics of decision-maker (DM)
Gender; age; children; own experience; attitudes & beliefs; need for affiliation; agreeableness; risk aversion; motivation; compliance; equity sensitivity.

Individual decision-making rules/criteria of DM
Personal norms & values; identification with organization; importance of success; risk taking; instrumentality perceptions.

Nature of manager/employee relationship
Seniority; trust; LMX; psychological closeness; level of (in)formality.

Individual characteristics of employee
Gender; seniority/supervisor status; unique tasks & skills; courage; connectedness within the company.

Individual situation of employee
Need; urgency; reasons offered; request for a standardized arrangement or a non-standard, personalized agreement.

Allowance decision
- Complete a.
- Partial a.
- Postponed a.
- Postponement
- Refusal

Group level

Group decision-making rules & criteria
Costs & benefits for the group; visibility; impact on & risk for group; quality of decision process; equity rules.

Work group characteristics
Size; educational level of the work group; task interdependency.

Organizational level

Organ. decision-making rules & criteria
Official procedures; equity rules; costs & benefits; scarcity; visiblity/impact; risk.

Organizational culture
Rules, norms, & values; family-responsible culture.

HR policies
Types/forms of flexibility and leave policies available; standardized vs. individual policies.

skills, educational level, responsibilities), and situational factors (e.g. department size, labor market situation) (den Dulk & De Ruijter, 2005; Klein *et al.*, 2000; Powell & Mainiero, 1999). In addition, program awareness, instrumentality perceptions, and supportive attitudes of the decision-maker were found to predict the frequency of supervisors' referrals to work–family programs (Casper, Fox, Sitzmann, & Landy, 2004). However, other individual characteristics of the decision-maker (e.g. agreeableness, equity sensitivity, own experience), individual/group and organizational decision-making criteria and rules, the nature of the relationship between the decision-maker and the applicant, and the organizational culture may play an equally important role in the decision process. Figure 6.2 presents a more inclusive conceptual model of within-company factors that influence managers' allowance decisions for work–life programs.

At the core of the model is the allowance decision of the line manager/supervisor. The manager may either completely or partially approve the request for a family-friendly arrangement of the employee depending on the various factors he or she takes into consideration when making a decision. If the situation is currently not considered as very favorable (e.g. the workload of co-workers does not allow the take-over of additional work from the employee requesting reduced working hours, and there is no budget to hire an additional employee to take on the additional tasks) the supervisor may either postpone the allowance decision, or approve the request but postpone actual take-up until a critical project deadline has passed by. In the worst case scenario, the supervisor comes to the conclusion that it is impossible to approve a certain employee request at any point of time, and rejects the request.

Factors that influence the allowance decision

Individual level

At the individual level, personality and individual characteristics of the decision-maker and the employee requesting a certain program have a major impact on the decision process. Powell & Mainiero (1999), for example, found that the sex of the decision-maker did matter in allowance decisions. Females were more likely to grant requests for alternative work arrangements than males. Den Dulk and de Ruijter

(2005) reported that requests from women were judged more positively than requests from men. In addition, highly skilled employees
and employees with unique qualifications were also more likely to be
granted a work–family program, thus providing evidence that individual characteristics of the applicant do matter in the decision process.

Age, own life experience, values, beliefs, and attitudes regarding
gender stereotypes, family, religion, etc. of the decision-maker can have
an important impact on how to deal with work–life requests of
employees. For example, a senior manager with a wife full-time at
home taking care of family and children will have different views on
this issue than a younger junior manager with a career-oriented wife.
Personality traits and predispositions such as a strong need for
affiliation (McClelland, 1961, 1965) or a manager's level of consci-
entiousness, agreeableness, openness, compliance with department
and organizational rules or risk aversion may also influence the
decision. Furthermore, equity perceptions of the supervisor play an
important role. Individuals differ significantly in how they perceive
equity and inequity (equity sensitivity) depending on individual
cognitive abilities, personality, values, and moral reasoning (Huseman,
Hatfield, & Miles, 1987). Consequently, managers may respond
differently to employees' requests depending on whether inequity
(e.g. in comparison with the labor market, policy specifications, or
other team members) is perceived or not.

Within the organizational context, managers develop their own
norms regarding work and collaboration with subordinates. While for
some managers daily interaction and a high level of face time is
important, others have no problems with employees working from
abroad and autonomously on well-defined tasks. Managers who
require more face-to-face contact with their employees may be more
negative towards employees' requests for flexibility arrangements
(e.g. telework).

According to expectancy theory (Vroom, 1964), individuals behave
in ways that are self-serving. Instrumentality refers to the belief that a
change in behavior will lead to a certain outcome. If supervisors believe
that the use of a work–family policy will result in a positive outcome
for them, their department, or the organization in general, it is more
likely that they will come to a positive decision. On the other hand, if
a manager perceives organizational policies as not contributing to a

positive outcome or even presenting a risk to personal success, he or she may respond negatively to an employee's request. High importance of individual and organizational success and strong identification with the organization may additionally foster such negative decisions. In general, supervisors need to have full information of the different types of work–family policies offered by the organization, and need to be aware of the corporate benefits that can be achieved with such programs (Powell & Mainiero, 1999).

In addition to characteristics of the supervisor and the applicant, also the actual situation of the individual applying for a program or benefit may play an important role. The more urgent the request, and the more severe the actual needs and/or conflicts of the employee, the more likely the manager may come to a positive decision. Also the type of arrangement requested (e.g. standard vs. non-standard arrangement; short-term vs. long-term solution) will have an impact on the decision.

A last group of factors influencing supervisors' allowance decisions on the individual levels include factors characterizing the manager–employee relationship. High-quality supervisor–subordinate (leader–member) exchange relationships are based on trust, respect, loyalty, interaction, and interpersonal support (Wayne, Shore, & Liden, 1997). Managers who have a long, high-quality relationship with an employee requesting a work–life policy can be expected to be more favorable in their allowance decision. "Psychological closeness" between supervisor and employee also may have a certain impact on the decision process. Psychological closeness refers to a process through which supervisors strive to learn and understand employees' personal and work problems, and psychologically support their performance (Hopkins, 2005). The closer the supervisor to his or her employee, the more favorable decisions can be expected.

Group level
Managers need to carefully evaluate the consequences for the team or the department when allowing a member of the team to make use of a certain program. An employee's request for a part-time schedule, for example, may cause the need to split the remaining tasks among other team members. Depending on the current workload, the team members may be able to take over the additional task. If not, a new employee needs to be hired and additional costs are generated. If there is no

budget for hiring additional staff, a rejection or a postponement of the decision can be the consequence in this case. However, if the manager comes to a favorable evaluation for the team, he or she may approve the request. In addition to costs and benefits, the manager also needs to assess the risk potential of the decision for the team – whether the decision presents a threat to the success and performance of the team. If the manager, for example, comes to the conclusion that approving a telework request presents a threat to the work of the team, he or she may not give an OK. Furthermore, the visibility of the decision within the team or department, together with perceptions of equity and eligibility of all team members, need to be considered.

Organizational level

At the organizational level, official company rules relevant to the benefit (e.g. universality of work–life policies), as well as implicit company norms and values regarding the importance of face time, working extra hours as part of supervisor evaluations, or signs of commitment, definitions of career, etc. will influence the decision of the supervisor.

Table 6.5. *What should companies do to ensure a sound allowance decision?*

✓ Analyze the potential of the specific programs to disrupt the conduct of work in the various departments and working teams.

✓ Assess the costs and benefits of the allowance of a specific policy for the team or the department.

✓ Assess the costs of a negative decision in case the request is refused (e.g. potential turnover and substitution costs, decrease in productivity due to reduced motivation of the employee, etc.).

✓ Design a transparent and consistent application and decision process for all policies offered in your organization.

✓ Communicate the application procedure and decision criteria within the organization.

✓ Create awareness of the various factors that may influence the allowance decision among managers in charge of such decision.

✓ Create awareness of the various individual-level outcomes of employees and co-workers and their impact on work relations.

✓ Provide guidelines for the communication of decisions and results among employees.

The overall organisational culture is a crucial variable contributing to the allowance decision of managers, as well as to individual outcomes of such decisions. Similar to the group level, also at the organizational level costs associated with a positive as well as a negative decision (e.g. potential turnover and substitution costs, decrease in productivity due to reduced motivation of the employee, etc.) and benefits for the company need to be taken into account. Again, the manager needs to assess the risk potential and visibility of the decision, this time for the whole organization (see Table 6.5).

Reactions to managers' allowance decisions

Employees will respond differently to the allowance decision, depending on the decision outcome presented by the manager and the employee's perception of the fairness/justice of the decision. Both positive or negative behavior may be the consequence. Examples of positive behavioral responses are increased commitment and loyalty, higher levels of job satisfaction, performance of behavior that is not formally required by the organization and exceeds contractual agreements (referred to as organizational citizenship behaviors in the literature). Employees may respond to the negative decisions of their supervisors with negative emotions targeted at the supervisor directly or co-workers, lower levels of satisfaction, withdrawal behaviors (absenteeism, turnover, neglect), or even counter-productive behaviors (e.g. avoiding work, doing tasks incorrectly, physical aggression, verbal hostility (insults), and sabotage) which are intended to hurt the organization or other members of the organization. Diminishing trust in the supervisor may further decrease the quality of the employee–manager relation.

Work–life programs are meant to facilitate work and personal life integration, and to ultimately decrease the work–family conflict experienced by employee. Individuals who are confronted with a rejection or postponement of the allowance may experience increased levels of conflict at least until they can make use of a certain benefit or policy. The negative outcomes of work–family conflict on job performance, satisfaction, commitment, etc. are well documented in work–family literature (see Allen, Herst, Bruck, & Sutton, 2000, for an overview). In addition to the employee who requested a work–life benefit, also co-workers and team members may respond in different ways to such a decision as they can be affected by the re-scheduling of agendas or additional tasks and responsibilities they have to take over when a co-worker switches to a part-time schedule, for example. Furthermore, co-workers who cannot use such programs (e.g. they do not have any family responsibilities) may display negative reactions towards co-workers and supervisors or the organization as a whole. This phenomena is referred to a as "backlash" (Rothausen, Gonzalez, Clarke, & O'Dell, 1998) and can harm the relationships with colleagues and supervisors.

Conclusion

One of the most important paradoxes in creating work–life harmony in firms consists in the contradictory, pivotal roles managers play in the implementation process, as both victims of work–family conflict and stress, primary sources of resistance or support for these policies and practices, and necessary change agents in the implementation (Poelmans, 2003). Managers responsible for implementing work–life programs in organizations and for allowing benefits have often been acculturated to work long hours and sacrifice their family lives in order to advance in their profession. Now they suddenly have to deal with their own demons when motivating employees to work hard while at the same time maintain a healthy balance between work and personal life. From this chapter it has become clear though that the organizational culture, and more specifically, managers and colleagues, are crucial to policy utilization (Allen, 2001). Our conclusion is clear: assuming and spreading the basic philosophy of human ecology is a crucial task for any board of directors that truly wants to build a competitive advantage through work–life harmony.

In order to build a competitive advantage in the labor market, companies need to be aware of the Red Queen phenomenon. The biologist Van Valen (1973) coined the term Red Queen evolution, referring to Lewis Carroll's *Through the Looking Glass*, in which Alice observes that she appears to be standing still even as she is running a race and the Red Queen replies that in a fast world one must run just to stay still. Barnett and Hansen (1996) have introduced this image in strategic management, indicating that an organization exposed to competition is likely to learn as a consequence. Assuming that learning is adaptive, the organization becomes a stronger competitor, triggering search and learning in its rivals. This response, in turn, strengthens competition from rivals felt by the first organization, starting the whole process over again (Barnett & Burgelman, 1996, p. 13). Even if each incremental adjustment is minor, over time this mutual incrementalism could conceivably add up to a very large difference.

Therefore we strongly recommend that an organization embarks upon a progressive and tenacious journey through all four stages or levels of development and plans the change process, the necessary budget for it, and people who will be at the lead. Organizations may differ dramatically in the pace at which they move from one stage to another. A small-to-medium-sized enterprise, for example, may run through the whole process much faster than a larger and more complex organization because of its more direct impact on staff, low power distance, and shorter communication procedures, resulting in a much faster adaptation of its corporate culture. It is also possible that companies recede and repeat stages or come to a halt before coming to the final stage. What counts though is staying power, continuous learning, and relentless responsiveness to changing needs in the internal and external workforce. Only then can a firm build a *sustainable* competitive advantage.

References

Allen, T. D. (2001). Family-supportive work environments: The role of organizational perceptions. *Journal of Vocational Behavior*, 58, 414–435.

Allen, T. D., Herst, D. E. L., Bruck, C. S., & Sutton, M. (2000). Consequences associated with work-to-family conflict: A review and agenda for future research. *Journal of Occupational Health Psychology*, 5, 278–308.

Barnett, W. P. & Burgelman, R. A. (1996). Evolutionary perspectives on strategy. *Strategic Management Journal*, 17, 5–19.

Barnett, W. P. & Hansen, M. T. (1996). The red queen in organizational evolution. *Strategic Management Journal*, 17, 139–157.

Bartol, K. M. & Martin, D. C. (1990). When politics pays: Factors influencing managerial compensation decisions. *Personnel Psychology*, 43, 599–614.

BusinessLink. (2006). *Practical Advice for Business*. Retrieved May, 2006, from www.businesslink.gov.uk.

Casper, W. J., Fox, K. E., Sitzmann, T. M., & Landy, A. L. (2004). Supervisor referrals to work–family programs. *Journal of Occupational Health Psychology*, 9(2), 136–151.

Chinchilla, M. N., Poelmans, S., León, C., & Tarrés, J. (2004). *Guía de buenas prácticas de la empresa flexible. Hacia la conciliación de la vida laboral, familiar y personal.* Barcelona: IESE Business School.

den Dulk, L., & de Ruijter, J. (2005). Explaining managerial attitudes towards the use of work–life policies in the UK and the Netherlands. Paper presented at the International Community, Work and Family Conference, Manchester.

Galinsky, E., Friedman, D. E., & Hernandez, C. A. (1991). *The Corporate Reference Guide to Work–Family Programs.* New York: Families and Work Institute.

García, M. (2006). *Estado de la relación Trabajo/Familia en el Perú a tres niveles: directivo, organizativo y de toma de decisiones. Reflexión a partir de una Teoría Antropológica de la Organización y de la Dirección.* Barcelona: IESE Business School.

Goodstein, J. D. (1994). Institutional pressures and strategic responsiveness: Employer involvement in work–family issues. *Academy of Management Journal*, 37(2), 350–382.

Hopkins, K. (2005). Supervisor support and work–life integration: A social identity perspective. In E. E. Kossek & S. J. Lambert (eds), *Work and Life Integration: Organizational, Cultural, and Individual Perspectives.* Mahwah, NJ: Lawrence Erlbaum Associates.

Huseman, R. C., Hatfield, J. D., & Miles, E. W. (1987). A new perspective on equity theory: The equity sensitivity construct. *Academy of Management Review*, 12(2), 222–234.

Ingram, P. & Simons, T. (1995). Institutional and resource dependence determinants of responsiveness to work–family issues. *Academy of Management Journal*, 38(5), 1466–1482.

Klein, K. J., Berman, L. M., & Dickson, M. W. (2000). May I work part-time? An exploration of predicted employer responses to employee requests for part-time work. *Journal of Vocational Behavior*, 57, 85–101.

Lambert, S. J. (2000). Added benefits: The link between work–life benefits and organizational citizenship behavior. *Academy of Management Journal*, 43(5), 801–815.

McClelland, D. C. (1961). *The Achieving Society.* Princeton, NJ: Van Nostrand.

McClelland, D. C. (1965). Toward a theory of motive acquisition. *American Psychologist*, 20, 321–333.

Osterman, P. (1995). Work–family programs and the employment relationship. *Administrative Science Quarterly*, 40, 681–700.

Poelmans, S. (2003). The multi-level "fit" model of work and family. *International Journal of Cross Cultural Management*, 3(3), 267–274.

Poelmans, S., Chinchilla, M. N., & Cardona, P. (2003). The adoption of family-friendly HRM policies. *International Journal of Manpower*, 24, 128–147.

Poelmans, S. & de Waal-Andrews, W. (2005). Launching flexible work arrangements within Procter & Gamble EMEA. In S. Poelmans (ed.), *Work and Family: An International Research Perspective*. Mahwah, NJ: Lawrence Erlbaum Associates.

Poelmans, S. & Sahibzada, K. (2004). A multi-level model for studying the context and impact of work–family policies and culture in organizations. *Human Resource Management Review*, 14, 409–431.

Powell, G. N. & Mainiero, L. A. (1999). Managerial decision making regarding alternative work arrangements. *Journal of Occupational and Organizational Psychology*, 72, 41–56.

Rapoport, R., Bailyn, L., Fletcher, J. K., & Pruitt, B. H. (2002). *Beyond Work–Family–Personal Life Harmony: Advancing Gender Equity and Workplace Performance*. San Francisco: Jossey-Bass.

Rothausen, T. J., Gonzalez, J. A., Clarke, N. E., & O'Dell, L. L. (1998). Family-friendly backlash – Fact or fiction? The case of organizations' on-site child care centers. *Personnel Psychology*, 51, 685–705.

Thompson, C. A., Beauvais, L. L., & Lyness, K. S. (1999). When work–family benefits are not enough: The influence of work–family culture on benefit utilization, organizational attachment, and work–family conflict. *Journal of Vocational Behavior*, 54, 392–415.

van Valen, L. (1973). A new evolutionary law. *Evolutionary Theory*, 1, 1–30.

Vroom, V. (1964). *Work and Motivation*. New York: Wiley.

Wayne, S., Shore, L., & Liden, R. C. (1997). Perceived organizational support and leader–member exchange: A social exchange perspective. *Academy of Management Journal*, 40, 82–111.

7 | Policy deployment across borders: a framework for work–life initiatives in multinational enterprises

ANNE BARDOEL and HELEN DE CIERI
Monash University, Australia

The difficulties of balancing work and family life are experienced all over the world. For managers in multinational enterprises (MNEs), it is imperative to define a global work–life strategy that establishes shared principles and guidelines and also allows for local initiatives and differences. Although there are a number of common issues faced by working women and men and their families, a global work–life strategy needs to balance shared concerns with a course of action that is appropriate to each local environment. Global work–life needs assessments conducted by leading work–life consultants Shapiro and Noble (2001) have identified three surprisingly consistent themes in what employees from around the world identify as being important barriers to reconciling their work and personal lives. The three issues identified included a lack of flexible work policies and practices, the availability and affordability of dependent care, and the negative impact of work overload and long working hours.

Although such issues are increasingly recognized as important for employers and employees in the global context, there has been very little research focused on this area. The aims of this chapter are, first, to develop a framework that can be used to guide managers' decision-making to build a global work–life strategy, and second, to illustrate how this framework can be applied, by analyzing approaches to work–life strategy in several MNEs. We compare an MNE that is at an early stage of developing a work–life strategy with other firms that are well-advanced in this area. The contrasts serve to highlight the challenges that managers may face, and provide examples of ways in which such challenges may be dealt with.

166

Michaels (1995) noted that, although many US corporations have been leaders in developing work–family programs, there is much to be gained by comparing how other countries' values, policies, and programs address work–family issues; in particular the role of additional change agents such as unions, agencies, and governments (see Table 7.3 for a review of categories of work–family practices). Korabik, Lero, and Ayman (2003) distinguish two different approaches to work–family research that has been carried out globally: micro- and macro-level approaches. First, the micro-level approach emanating mostly from North America has focused mainly on workplaces and the business case for developing more effective management approaches to reducing work–family conflict. Second, the macro-level approach has derived mainly from Europe and has identified the critical importance of public policies in relation to expectations about men's and women's roles and employment-supportive policies such as paid parental leave and benefits. We suggest that, for researchers and managers, it is important to consider the potential interactions between micro- and macro- level approaches to work–family issues, and so we seek to integrate these two approaches. Hence, we draw on both micro-and macro-level work–family approaches, to develop a comprehensive framework of work–life issues from a global perspective.

Before focusing on work–life issues, it is appropriate to consider the context of human resource management (HRM) research and practice. Perry-Smith and Blum (2000) concluded that the HRM literature, which is largely dominated by US-focused research, has included the presentation of numerous models or frameworks of HRM practices, yet all of the models have noticeably excluded work–family policies from the list of individual HRM practices.

Leading scholars in HRM have raised awareness of the constraints and challenges for HRM in a global context (Brewster & Suutari, 2005: Ferris, Hall, Royle, & Martocchio, 2004; also see Dowling & Welch (2004) for a comprehensive overview of the development of the field of international HRM). However, there has been little discussion amongst researchers of work–life balance as a concern for HRM in a global context. Most of the attention to matters that might be viewed as related to work–life issues has been limited to expatriate management matters (e.g. see Lazarova & Caligiuri, 2001). Even when expatriate management researchers have taken a more strategic approach to

HRM in a global context, work–family policies remain noticeably excluded (e.g. see Stroh & Caligiuri, 1998). Similarly, researchers discussing the transferability of HR practices across national borders have not included work–life strategies (Aycan, 2005), and researchers focused on diversity initiatives in MNEs have not included work–life issues (Egan & Bendick, 2003).

Early research on HRM in MNEs was principally concerned with expatriate selection and training, usually for expatriate management assignments (Dowling & Welch, 2004). While expatriates remain an important aspect of transnational staffing strategies, recent research has broadened the focus, to reflect the broader concerns of HR practitioners in MNEs, and to recognize the increasing diversity of international work assignments, moving away from long-term expatriation towards more flexible forms of international work, such as transnational project teams, short-term assignments, and virtual assignments. Such assignments are increasingly being undertaken by employees outside the senior levels of management (Harris & Brewster, 2003). Recent issues identified for HRM in MNEs include concerns such as HRM initiatives for host country nationals (Bartlett, Lawler, Bae, Chen, and Wan, 2002) and the extent to which transnational firms may seek to localize their HRM practices (Aycan, 2005). Much of the activity amongst MNEs has been driven by large Western firms, those headquartered in the US or Europe. However, there is growing activity amongst organizations operating in non-Western regions, and in emerging and transition economies (Ramamurti, 2004). There is also increasing activity amongst firms that are headquartered in developing economies and expanding into operations across global markets. For example, over the last decade, China has become one of the world's leading foreign investors; Chinese MNEs such as Haier and Lenovo have become important global players in their industries (Deng, 2004). Such developments in international business present many important challenges, demands, and opportunities for HR practitioners in MNEs (Losey, Meisinger, & Ulrich, 2005; Roehling *et al.*, 2005).

However, recently work–life researchers have called for future research to incorporate a focus on how global organizations can be inclusive of work–life issues in multiple cultural contexts (Gelfand & Knight, 2005; Poelmans, 2005; Poster & Prasad, 2005). As Poelmans (2005) concludes, there is a need for more qualitative research that involves case studies of international companies to explore the impact of globalization on work–family policy development in companies. Globalization of business requires managers to face many complex HR issues and sometimes conflicting pressures for global integration and local differentiation (Schuler, Dowling, & De Cieri, 1993). Managers in MNEs need to balance the often conflicting needs of global efficiencies and coordination (integration) with responsiveness to factors such as political pressures in each local market (differentiation) (Doz & Prahalad, 1991; Edwards & Kuruvilla, 2005). To manage this global/local dilemma, there are several important areas for HR managers' attention, including work–life initiatives. In the globalized economy, organizations increasingly derive value from human resources, or "human capital." Mehra, Kilduff, and Brass (1998) refer to human capital as the knowledge and skills of the workforce. Human capital is the broad term that includes all resources contained within the workforce. For MNEs, there are specific and unique challenges related to the development of human capital, as part of a strategic approach to HR, as attracting and retaining the human capital required to implement a global strategy is of critical importance to the organization's long-term survival (Stroh & Caligiuri, 1998).

Welbourne (2005) argues that the support of top management for HRM initiatives is critical for success; further, HRM should be recognized as a priority for all managers. Pfeffer (2005, p. 128) similarly puts forward a case for the need to develop a shared philosophy or mindset for the successful uptake of HR, and particularly work–life strategies, arguing that "what we do comes from what and how we think." This is most effective when it is led by senior leaders and is supported and understood throughout the organization. An implication of these ideas is that HR professionals may have to proactively assist the organization in understanding and adjusting its mindset, so that human resource practices become a source of competitive advantage. Part of the strategy to achieve this is to attract and retain individuals who possess higher-quality human capital. Research conducted by the Boston College Center for Work and Family found that there is a link between family-friendly work policies and programs promoting corporate community involvement and becoming an "employer of choice." McWilliams, van Fleet, & Wright (2001) also identify the need for managers to develop transnational human resource systems that take advantage of the recruiting and utilization opportunities that arise from having access to multiple human resource pools.

Haas, Hwang, and Russell (2000) have conducted analyses in a broad range of cultural contexts and summarize the broad commonality in arguments supporting the potential benefits that can accrue to organizations implementing work–life practices and policies. First, work–life practices can provide an incentive to increase motivation and commitment and thus achieve higher levels of productivity from the current labor pool. Second, these practices can be part of a strategy that supports attracting and retaining the best-quality people. Third, an effective work–life strategy can enable the best-quality people to advance in the organization. For example, it has been recognized that barriers to women include having to take time out for dependent care responsibilities and a lack of flexibility in career structures. Finally, companies can obtain community recognition by being seen as a "good" corporate citizen or caring organization.

Thompson and Richter (1998) refer to global HR strategies as those that accommodate national cultural differences while preserving work culture principles that encourage people to effectively execute the global strategy. The paradox of "think globally, act locally" is a dilemma facing HR professionals working in MNEs facing unprecedented levels of global mergers, acquisitions, and international growth. When a business becomes global it means that the more complex set of business strategies also require new HR strategies to be implemented across a broad range of cultures. The aim of this chapter is to fill this gap by proposing a framework for companies to use when developing a global work–life strategy that balances global integration and local responsiveness.

We propose that the development of a sound global work–life strategy can enable an organization to retain higher levels of human capital relative to its competitors by becoming an "employer of choice." This is consistent with Shapiro and Noble's (2001) contention that a focus on work–life issues can be used as an effective avenue for understanding and managing a globally diverse workforce and also assist HR professionals to develop cultural sensitivity in local contexts.

Challenges for a global work–life strategy

Dowling (1988) has argued that the complexity of global HRM can be attributed to six factors which differentiate international from domestic (single-country) HRM. Two of these factors are particularly applicable to work–life strategies. The first factor concerns the problem of designing and administering programs for more than one national group of employees and the need to adapt and change in light of new responsibilities as the organization matures.

For example, the global compensation policies will need to incorporate sensitivity to national differences in compensation levels, expectations about work–life strategies and benefits, and taxation conditions. In addition, the types of international assignments may also vary across global operations, to include not only expatriation but also global team projects, and short-term and virtual assignments (Roberts, Kossek, & Ozeki, 1998). Hence, employees' needs and demands for various work–life strategies will vary.

The second factor is that several major external variables influence HRM and thus work–life strategies in a global context, such as the type of government, the state of the economy, and the generally accepted practices of doing business and living in each of the various host countries in which an organization operates. For example, an HR manager in a foreign subsidiary may become involved in administering work–life strategies and other benefits either provided or financed by the organization, such as housing, education, and other facilities not readily available in the local economy (see, for example, Zhu, 1997).

Local influences on work–life strategies

It is important to recognize that, just as HRM strategies will have local variations depending on the laws and customs of different countries, so will work–life strategies. Developing a global work–life strategy can positively contribute to organizational outcomes. An understanding of the organizational outcomes associated with developing effective work–life strategies in a transnational company is imperative in order to direct the focus of work–life initiatives.

Vincola (1998) argues that in order to offer benefits and programs that are meaningful to a global workforce, companies must assess work–life issues from the perspective of their employees' social, cultural, and national context. Hence, the building of an effective global work–life strategy requires an organization to be cognizant of a number of local factors that influence their work and personal lives. Local factors, or differences across national contexts, are predominantly attributed to a "country of origin effect," generally assumed to be produced by the interaction of local culture and institutional factors (Aycan, 2005). According to Spinks (2003), these factors include the culture and tradition, the role of key stakeholders, public policies, community resources and infrastructure, and workplace practices and demographics.

Culture and traditions. Meyerson and Martin (1987) identified the differentiation perspective of cultural change and argued that organizations are reflections and amalgamations of surrounding cultures, including national, occupational, and ethnic cultures. In developing a global work–life strategy there are particular cultural factors that are critical to the development of a culturally sensitive work–life strategy. These include the role of women in society, the role of religion and the faith community, traditional family structures and support, and gender roles.

Global organizations operate in countries where there are vast variations in cultural characteristics (e.g. social values such as individualism/collectivism, masculinity/femininity, and gender egalitarianism) (Hofstede, 1980). Research has shown that national culture has an impact on a variety of organizational activities, and national cultural diversity continues to be an important issue for transnational firms (see Earley & Gibson, 2002). However, national cultures are not easily reduced to similarities across a small number of dimensions and differences may be more important than similarities. Landmark cross-cultural studies such as Hofstede's research have made valuable contributions to our understanding of cultural diversity, but several researchers have queried the emphasis that has been placed on national culture. Husted (2003, p. 428) points out that national cultures "usually represent the values and practices of the dominant groups in society, and not of the marginalized." Also, it is important to be aware of the perils of attribution errors with regard to cultural diversity; such errors can lead to misunderstandings and problems in the workplace when applied in areas such as HR practices (Leung, Bhagat, Buchan,

Erez, & Gibson, 2005). In particular, substantial debate surrounds the work and several theoretical and methodological criticisms have been directed at Hofstede's work (Gerhart & Fang, 2005). Overall, it is suggested that there needs to be better understanding of the complex effects of culture when developing work–life policies (Gerhart & Fang, 2005; Leung *et al.*, 2005).

The role of key stakeholders. Societies vary in relation to the legitimate role given to key stakeholders such as the state and organized labour. The term "stakeholder" has been defined as "those groups without whose support the organization would cease to exist" and originally included shareowners, employees, customers, lenders, and society (Freeman, 1984, pp. 31–32). The stakeholder concept has become widely used in recent years, due to factors such as increased public interest and concern about corporate governance. The role of the state in family factors, the role of the state in employment, and the role of unions in determining desirable benefits all influence a society's approach to work–life balance issues.

Public policies. Public policy has been defined as actions which employ government authority to support preferred community values. Public policies involve the exercise of power and are a central way that societies respond to major social, economic, environmental, and political issues. In particular, employment legislation that covers conditions related to hours of work, vacation, minimum wages, and maternity and parental leave conditions have particular ramifications for a global work–life strategy.

Community resources and infrastructure. Countries also vary in terms of the community resources and infrastructure that are available to support employed persons' ability to manage their work and personal life effectively. Factors such as healthcare, homecare, childcare, and parenting supports, elder care and care-giving supports, supports for persons with special needs, education, and employment and training will influence the necessity for organizational involvement in some areas (Sheridan & Conway, 2001).

Workplace practices and demographics. Finally, issues concerning workplace characteristics such as workplace demographics and practices covering working hours, vacation days, sick days, leaves, and return to work supports will also influence work–life practices for employees in organizations (Eaton, 2003; Patrickson & Hartmann, 2001).

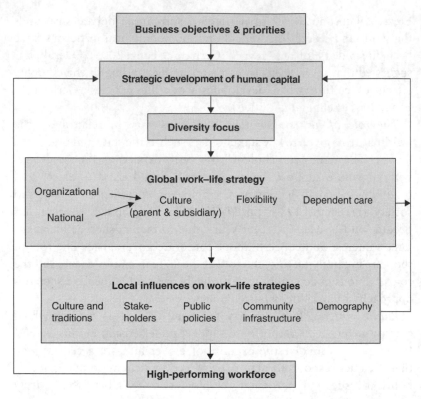

Figure 7.1 A framework for building a global work–life strategy.

A framework for building a global work–life strategy

The Canadian Workplaces website provides a common definition that "Work–life balance is about creating supportive, healthy work environments for employees who are striving to better integrate their work and personal responsibilities" (Human Resources Development Canada, 2002). Consistent with this objective, global work–life efforts need to be strategically connected to diversity, performance management, and other business objectives.

Lobel and Faught (1996) identified four basic approaches to evaluating work–life initiatives: (1) the *human cost approach*, which focuses on savings associated with reduced labor costs; (2) the *human investment approach*, which attempts to document the long-term financial benefits related to work–life initiatives (e.g. recruitment, retention, morale, productivity); (3) the *stakeholder approach*, that considers the benefits gained by members of stakeholder groups including not only employers and employees but other stakeholders such as customers and unions; and (4) the *strategy approach*, which assesses the extent that work–life initiatives facilitate the achieving of the organization's business strategies. The *strategy approach* is the most relevant framework to apply to developing a global perspective of work–life strategy because it focuses on how work–life supports can strengthen and support broad business strategies such as globalization.

Drawing from the literature reviewed above, Figure 7.1 attempts to summarize the key relationships between the HRM objectives of an organization and the link to building a strategic approach to global work–life issues. We test this framework in a case study conducted in a large MNE, by examining the roles of corporate policy and local influences on work–life balance issues in each of three geographic locations. Further, we draw upon evidence reported of other MNEs to further test our framework.

Research method

As this is a new area of research, an exploratory case-study methodology was chosen as the means of guiding the researchers "to understand specific phenomena and develop theory" (Alvesson 2003). Given that the central research objective is exploratory in nature, and that this research project focuses exclusively on organizations, the research was suited to a case-study approach (Patton, 2002; Yin, 2003; Zikmund, 2000). We conducted primary data collection, using interviews and document analysis, with one MNE and secondary data collection, using published material, for several other MNEs.

For the primary case, a large MNE associated with the port management industry was approached to assist with this study. Access to the organization was organized through personal contact with the global (corporate) human resources director. The global HR director of ABC Ports[1] was requested to nominate several members of the organization from different parts of the world who could speak about the organization's approach to work–life balance issues. Semi-structured interviews were conducted with the global HR manager and

---

[1] The name of the organization has been changed.

HR managers in Australia and North America who are responsible for work–life management and HRM in their respective territories. All interviews were taped, transcribed, and returned to the interviewee for perusal.

The interview questions addressed:

- The organization's business objectives and priorities related to strategic development of human capital, how these objectives were described in policies and how they were monitored; whether diversity, flexibility, and dependent care were addressed in policy.
- How work–life policies were determined; which stakeholders influenced the policies; did the policies derive from the corporate office or were they developed locally; were the policies adjusted due to local influences and if so, by whom?
- Times when the organizational culture and the national culture come into conflict concerning work–life issues.
- National or government policies which are different from organizational policy; how these differences are resolved.
- Availability of community infrastructure to support the work–life policies.

The responses were analyzed by grouping common themes from each participant and by comparing these with information obtained from company documents.

Background and contextual information about the company was also obtained from company documents that detailed human resource management standards.

For comparisons between different organizations, we have also reviewed case material, reports, and documentation for IBM and several other MNEs that are regarded as leading organizations with respect to work–life strategies. Evidence from these firms is used to supplement the findings from our primary case analysis.

Research findings

Context: the organization

ABC Ports is a leading global cargo handling and port management organisation with operations in eighteen countries. It was founded in Australia in the early 1990s, growing out of its parent company, ABC

Australia, which had a long involvement in conventional port operations in Australia. Using their experience in the development of specialized terminals when Australia–Europe cargo liner trades were containerized at the end of the 1960s, ABC Australia became the major service provider in most ports in Australia. In the mid-1980s developing economies looked to the private sector for partners and ABC Australia expanded overseas. Now, as ABC Ports, a wholly owned subsidiary of ABC Australia, it operates twenty-seven container terminals and logistics operations in over one hundred ports in eighteen countries. ABC Ports has experienced approximately 29 percent growth year on year for the last five years through acquisition and increased terminal activity. New acquisitions have consisted of full or partial ownership of new terminal facilities, full, partial, or minority ownership of existing businesses and facilities, or joint ventures to operate container terminals. These businesses may or may not directly employ the stevedore workforce. The globalization of this organization reflects in many ways the globalization of the shipping and ports industries (Juhel, 2001; Turnbull, 2000).

Because the organization derives its heritage from shipping and stevedoring, ABC Ports has a male-dominated workforce; across the globe only approximately 8 percent of the employees are female. The organisation also has a culture of working long hours, with 70-hour weeks not an uncommon experience.

While ABC Ports is at an early stage in the development of work–life strategies, the other MNEs analyzed are at more advanced stages of development in this area, and are viewed as leading this field. These provide a useful contrast to an MNE that is facing numerous challenges in this area.

Business objectives and priorities

When asked about business objectives and priorities related to work–life balance, the interview participants admitted that they were limited. There were a few oblique references to providing people with opportunities to contribute in work in a manner that respects lifestyle choices, respecting the human rights, dignity, and needs of all employees, promoting a diverse workforce, and committing to social responsibility by ethical, environmental, and social accountability. ABC Ports HR Management Standards documentation is very oriented to training and development and to providing a discrimination- and harassment-free workplace.

Reporting on issues that may be construed as work–life balance was limited to those reports required by various governments such as equal opportunity reports and reports on family and medical leave taken. Reports to corporate headquarters were primarily oriented to training and development and to understanding the demographics of the workforce.

ABC Ports is making some progress with regard to work–life initiatives, but, in contrast, firms that are leading the way on global work–life strategies have built this into their business objectives. IBM has a short- and long-term global work–life strategy that is integrated with the firm's overall business strategy (Giue & Petrescu, 2005).

Strategic development of human capital

The ABC Ports' corporate HR director indicated that their primary concern with strategic development of human capital was oriented to training and to treating people fairly. Respondents from all three geographic areas for ABC Ports identified that the company was renowned for its commitment to training and this was construed as a competitive advantage when attracting staff. Work–life balance policies were not used as a method to develop or retain human capital.

In contrast, IBM has recognized that work–life balance is an issue related to employee morale, productivity, and retention and in 1998 introduced a global initiative to help IBM employees balance their work and personal lives. According to Giue and Petrescu (2005), at IBM, work–life initiatives are recognized as a key business imperative to attract and retain employees, particularly younger talent. It is acknowledged that younger employees, those in Generation X or Y, place higher value on work–life balance than those in older generations may have done.

Diversity focus

Because of its business structure, ABC Ports as a whole has a huge level of diversity. With operations in eighteen countries and with many possible business structures, it has individuals and organizations of many national cultures that must become one organizational culture.

This has been the focus of attention by the corporate HR director. Because of the high growth rate and relatively short history of the organization, the main focus of corporate HR has been to establish an organizational culture through the performance management system, by the training of managers, and through dissemination of their primary operational process, their port planning systems. In short, the corporate HR focus has been to remove diversity of culture and to find some commonality.

However, on a national level, it has been recognized that, historically, the maritime and stevedoring industries have been male-dominated industries. Despite attempts to get female stevedores brought into the Australian workforce, the percentage of female stevedores is still in single digits, primarily due to the slow progression of any new stevedore through the casual employee ranks into permanent employment. In North America, where ABC Ports employs only port management personnel (no stevedores), the personnel are overwhelmingly male, primarily due to the tendency for longevity and promotion from within the industry. In short, ABC Ports has considerable ethnic and cultural diversity, globally and locally, but has little gender diversity.

Other firms have developed strategies specifically to deal with gender diversity. For example, financial and banking firms such as Citigroup and Deutsche Bank have made strong progress in developing women for managerial positions. In the US operations in 2004, Citigroup provided management and leadership training to 2,600 female employees; Citigroup holds annual Women's Councils, which focus on identifying ways to attract and retain women in management. Deutsche Bank has initiatives such as women's networking and mentoring programs, flexible work schedules and telecommuting, and a range of leave options (*Working Mother Magazine*, www.workingmother. com). While such initiatives are commendable, we note that some contexts (e.g. cultural, industry, or occupational factors) present greater barriers than others to the development of work–life strategies focused on diversity.

Global work–life strategy

Strategic implementation requires a comprehensive approach, not a piecemeal approach. In pursuing a work–life strategy that is both strategic at a global level and adaptive to local needs, MNEs have to align and learn to balance not just their business objectives and corporate values but also take into consideration societal norms, values, and the ever-changing aspects of operating in foreign markets. For example, the IBM work–life strategy comprises three pillars: culture, flexibility, and dependent care (see Giue & Petrescu, 2005, for detail).

Organizational culture. The operational activity of ABC Ports is one of twenty-four hours per day and seven days per week as ships arrive at any time and need to be offloaded in order to reduce turnaround time, which is the key measure of the productivity of a port. In North America, it is not uncommon for junior port managers to work 70-hour weeks, sometimes for three weeks in a row. The corporate HR director and regional HR managers indicated that long working hours are very common in ABC Ports. In fact, long working hours seems to be a predominant element of the ABC Ports' organizational culture.

National cultures. As indicated above, ABC Ports has many national cultures. However, according to the global HR director the predominant culture which influenced the organizational culture is that of the founding country, Australia. The scope of this case study did not include enough examples of ABC Ports' organizational culture to determine if this Australian influence is a feature of the overall organizational culture.

Each interviewee at ABC Ports was asked if the organizational policies established with respect to work–life balance in their region came in conflict with the national culture. Uniformly, the interviewees indicated that there had never been a conflict, and if there was any apparent disagreement, the local culture, rather that the corporate one, would be predominant. It was firmly stated that local culture should determine the requirements and policy to address work–life balance issues.

While ABC Ports are making some progress, IBM provides an example of an MNE at a much more advanced stage of development with respect to global work–life strategy. IBM has had a long-standing commitment to work–life strategy. Although their work–life initiatives began in the US, they have been expanded across global operations (Giue & Petrescu, 2005). IBM conducted its first global employee work–life survey in 2001, with 59,000 employees across forty-eight countries invited to participate. The survey was provided in twenty languages. Utilizing the results of this survey, IBM has implemented a global five-year work–life strategy. They also use quarterly work–life scorecards to track the firm's progress on work–life issues globally (Giue & Petrescu, 2005). IBM's experience demonstrates how an MNE can develop a global strategy but respect local diversity.

Work–life programs should be reflective of what employees want in a particular national context. For example, for an MNE operating in Singapore, such as Agilent Technologies, dependent care services may involve the setting up of childcare facilities within the organization itself but this may not be as well suited for its operations in China because childcare services are cheaper to access, and moreover, children are often cared for by family members (Ministry of Manpower Singapore, 2005; Yang, 2005).

Flexibility. Discussions concerning flexibility and how it was applied in the various areas of ABC Ports focused very much on individual applications of flexibility. Each participant was able to relate anecdotes of individuals who had established flexible work arrangements, such as working from home, job sharing or part-time work. All participants stated that these arrangements were usually derived after discussion between the individuals and their own managers; occasionally these became models for similar arrangements within other parts of the organization.

Flexibility in ABC Ports appears to be more focused on allowing individuals to exercise control over their daily work schedule, rather than about flexible career structures or an overall corporate commitment to organizational flexibility. It seems that if the individual is sufficiently talented, then the organization will accommodate the individual's needs for flexibility.

In contrast, at IBM, flexible work options are made available in all countries, although their implementation depends very much on local country legislation and culture. Admittedly, not all options are available in all countries, and it is unlikely that they will be. According to Giue and Petrescu (2005), IBM has experienced significant resistance in eastern European countries (given the history of a command society) and in some of the Middle East and Africa countries, where local culture and religious values are important considerations that influence attitudes to flexible work options.

Dependent care. ABC Ports focuses its attention concerning dependent care on maternity and parental leave. Maternity and parental leave provisions correspond with the local legal requirements which are occasionally extended to meet community expectations. For example, in Australia, ABC Ports currently meets the legal requirements for maternity leave, but extends it to both sexes by the provision of parental leave where a parent may take up to six weeks paid leave and up to twelve months unpaid leave as the primary caregiver of the child. In addition, all its policies are under review to determine if more generous entitlements are appropriate.

While each interviewee indicated that dependent care was occasionally an issue and options had been examined in their part of the organization, no corporate or regional commitment was specifically made to assist employees with dependent care. In contrast, at IBM, strategies to introduce dependent care are in progress, largely in response to recognition of employee needs. Based on a strategic business analysis, thirteen countries were selected to be eligible to receive funds to support dependent care initiatives, and this is planned to increase in future. Programs were customized by country and included initiatives such as childcare centers, resource and referral services, seminars, and after-school programs (Giue & Petrescu, 2005).

Local influences on work–life strategies

Culture and traditions. National culture and traditions were not a differentiating characteristic among the participants and the portions of the organisation which they represented. All participants came from Western, developed countries of similar cultural heritage. The participants were similar in areas of culture which particularly impinge on work–life balance, notably participation of women in the paid workforce, family structures, and access to extended family supports. In addition, the nature of the multicultural community in Australia, the UK, and North America defies one description of "culture" and "tradition."

Giue and Petrescu (2005) discuss the diversity of cultures across IBM territories, such as Europe, the Middle East, and Africa. The diversity in these contexts presents a complex array of work–life issues. IBM have plans to address each of the three pillars in their work–life strategy, in ways that are appropriate in each of these local contexts.

Stakeholders. ABC Ports has a mixed group of stakeholders, with varying perspectives and concerns. Corporate headquarters was clearly concerned about shareholders and the view of the UK government, particularly with reference to their commitment to social responsibility. The Australian respondent indicated that, because ABC Ports Australia had a largely unionized workforce, the unions were major stakeholders in any issues concerning work–life balance, particularly those affecting leave entitlements and hours worked. However, in North America, because it does not employ stevedores and is not a unionized workforce, the individual employees tended to negotiate on their own behalf and were the stakeholders expressing the highest level of concerns.

Many MNEs seek to involve their stakeholders in the broader community through volunteer programs to help the local community, fund-raising events, and sponsorship of local community activities, schools, or sporting associations (Anonymous, 2005).

Public policies and infrastructure. As would be expected, the public policies affecting work–life balance are different in the UK, North America, and Australia. Particularly with reference to maternity leave, each organization had established its own leave entitlements starting from the baseline of the local legal requirements.

Availability of community infrastructure also reflected the local regulatory environment. For example, in the ABC Ports US operations, where maternity leave entitlements were paid for six weeks, childcare facilities have developed for very young children to support the women who return to work with a very young baby. In Australia, where statutory maternity leave entitlements are unpaid leave for twelve months, there are very few childcare places available for very small babies. With respect to ABC Ports, the Australian company was very proud of their high return rate from maternity leave.

All MNEs face the challenge of meeting the different requirements of local legislation; some nations provide high levels of protection and support for employees, while others do not. The infrastructure available for working parents, such as childcare, might be limited. In Indonesia, approximately 40 percent of working women care for their children while working, so without workplace childcare support many women who cannot afford domestic help have little choice but to bring their children to the workplace or not work (Hein, 2005). It is for these reasons that some employers might find it in their interests to facilitate childcare by either providing on-site crèches or subsidising childcare costs. For example, in Malaysia the banking sector provides a childcare subsidy to women with a child under seven years of age (Hein, 2005).

Demography. As indicated above, ABC Ports is in a very male-dominated industry; worldwide only 8 percent of their employees are female, with even fewer working in operational areas as stevedores.

However, there are other aspects of workforce demography that can influence an employee's ability to combine family and paid work. ILO (International Labor Organization) estimates have indicated that the social burden on families of HIV/AIDS will have devastating effects on families in large parts of sub-Saharan Africa. This includes workers taking leave to care for an infected family member, deaths from the illness, and the increasing number of single-parent families. Even where community hospices and home services are provided the ILO recommends that the most useful form of support for workers in these situations will be flexibility or special leave provided by the employer (Hein, 2005).

As noted earlier, workforce demography is an important factor in the development of work–life strategies. Many MNEs have introduced work–life strategies in response to pressure from employees, or in recognition of employee needs. A diverse workforce may be more likely to voice concerns for a diverse array of work–life issues. However, even in homogeneous workforces, the need for work–life strategies should be considered.

Discussion

Work–life balance in MNEs

Our primary case study incorporates information from a small sample of representatives of a major ports management organization, ABC Ports. Despite the study's small size, some interesting observations can be made about how work–life balance issues are addressed in this large MNE. Further, these observations can be compared with examples from MNEs leading in the field of work–life management.

First, the history of a firm influences its demography and its organizational culture, which in turn clearly influence its approach to work–life balance issues. ABC Ports by history is a marine organization, where employees worked on ships and at ports. These employees traditionally have been male and continue to be male; less than 10 percent of its workforce is female. In addition, mariners/sailors tended to leave home for extended periods of time while they sailed the seven seas; they continue to do so. When a ship is in port, it has a finite period of time for it to offload its cargo and move on; as the saying goes, "time and tide wait for no man." The history and development of ABC Ports has led to a very male, very committed, very long working hours organizational culture.

In addition to this history, in more recent times ABC Ports has undergone rapid growth through acquisition of ports in many areas of the world. From a corporate view, the variety of national cultures and business structures has caused a need to remove diversity and develop some commonality of purpose and culture, which is being pursued through the performance management system and training processes. The organization has not developed a level of maturity where work–life strategies are foremost in its approach to employee attraction and retention.

It is worth noting that those organizations that have made most progress with regard to work–life strategies tend to have a history that is quite different from ABC Ports. These organizations tend to have greater representation of women, and tend to be in industries with occupations where flexibility is perhaps easier to introduce. Where historical factors have presented barriers to work–life strategies, organizations perhaps need a "burning platform" for change; there needs to be a shared mindset that supports work–life strategies, driven and supported by HR professionals, alongside the CEO and senior management (Pfeffer, 2005).

With respect to the framework, ABC Ports does not have business objectives and priorities related to work–life balance. While they do have a strategic commitment to development of human capital, the commitment focuses on training and performance management, not on work–life balance issues. While their commitment to diversity is very strong, it is national and ethnic diversity, not gender diversity. The global work–life strategy that derives from this corporate orientation uses flexibility as a means to achieve the culturally expected long working hours, and dependent care supports are related to removing the need for the worker to be away from work. In short, there is not much corporate or global policy on work–life strategies; indeed, the corporate HR director suggested that global policy evolves from the input from the regions, rather than emanating from the center. The global policies are derived from the best of the local policies and each region is encouraged to develop their own work–life balance approach responsive to local conditions.

In contrast, IBM and other MNEs that are at a more advanced stage of developing a global work–life strategy have developed more comprehensive, less piecemeal approaches. Even in organizations that have placed work–life strategies as a business priority, it is evident that there remain areas to be addressed in the development of their work–life initiatives. This is important to note: the journey towards a global work–life strategy is complex, challenging, and lengthy.

A major aspect to be dealt with in global work–life strategies is the responsiveness to local demands. For ABC Ports, the local organization addresses work–life strategies as appropriate and as demanded by their local regulations, community expectations, and the demographics of their local organization. They use work–life balance policies to be seen as an employer of choice and as a good corporate citizen. Local influence on the work–life strategies is much stronger than global influence. Locally, the organization is attempting to derive the benefits ascribed to work–life balance programs (Haas *et al.*, 2000).

Interestingly, Edwards and Kuruvilla (2005) question the common assumption that MNEs should possess some degree of uniformity to ensure that their work–life programs across countries are consistent with the global HR strategy. They argue that this uniformity creates a legacy effect, spreading the values based on the MNE's country of origin to ensure that the local branches conform and contribute. Subsequently adaptation to local context becomes questionable.

However, a focus on local needs in determining work–life strategy is consistent with the findings of Poelmans, Chinchilla, and Cardona (2003) who found that, when examining family-friendly work practices in Spain, the size of the organization, the percentage of female employees, and the tightness of the labor market greatly influenced the implementation of a work–family program. With ABC Ports, the percentage of female employees is very low and labor is readily available in the stevedoring industry as a result of the high wages paid. These two features would predict against having well-developed work–family programs. In addition, ABC Ports is in a strong growth phase. Dowling and Welch (2004) would suggest that, as the organization moves into a more mature phase, it would or could focus more on using work–life strategies to retain its highly valued employees. This appears to have been the case for those MNEs that are more advanced with regard to global work–life strategies.

Applying the framework

We have proposed a framework (see Figure 7.1) to identify the main factors that managers would need to understand and address when developing global work–life strategies. To accompany the framework, we have developed a checklist of questions that HR managers in MNEs could use to guide their decisions with regard to their global work–life strategy (see Appendix). From our analyses we also propose a list of steps (see Table 7.1) and a checklist and questions (see Table 7.2) for building and implementing a global work–life strategy (adapted from Spinks, 2005).

This study is the preliminary testing of a framework that describes the development of commitment to work–life strategy in an MNE. Clearly, the framework needs to be tested in more MNEs, preferably some known to have strong global commitment to work–life strategy as well as some others with lesser global focus. In addition, different regions should be examined, particularly those with a non-Western approach to these issues. However, this preliminary study has been useful in identifying and examining the concepts and ideas of how the local influences of the local macro-environment affect the local organization and how this is incorporated into the global strategy. The development of a set of global work–life principles enables MNEs to take into account trends in globalization and in doing so create a framework for local policies.

Table 7.1. *Steps for building and implementing a global work–life strategy*

Step 1: Share experiences and learning across regions
This involves not just sharing information about specific work–life programs
  (e.g. childcare) but more importantly how needs were identified, and the
  process of developing programs and identifying solutions.
Step 2: Focus on commonalities
This includes the need for flexibility, challenges to find balance when working
  hours are increasing, aging populations, dropping flexibility rates, increased
  number of women in the workforce with children under two years of age.
Step 3: Adapt work–life initiatives to local cultures and expectations
Recognise and respect local culture experience perspectives and knowledge as
  well as local organizational culture.
Step 4: Resource and support local management and leadership
Step 5: Find local work–life champions
Step 6: Partner with local experts
Step 7: Adapt to local socioeconomic and political climate
Step 8: Celebrate local achievements

Table 7.2. *Checklist and questions for global work–life strategies*

(1) Does our organization have business objectives and priorities related to strategic development of human capital? If so, what areas do they address and how are they measured and/or monitored? Are there written policies related to these areas? For example:
   - Diversity.
   - Flexibility concerning work hours, holidays, etc.
   - Dependent care.
   - Other policies related to work–life.
(2) How are the global work–life policies determined? Does the head office work–life policy ever need to be adjusted for local conditions? Which types of issues come up? If there is adjustment, how does this take place? Who is responsible for the modifications? What communication takes place concerning the need for change and about the changes that are made?
(3) What impact does local culture have on global work–life policies? Which takes precedence?
(4) Do we have times when the organizational culture and the national culture come into conflict concerning work–life issues? How do we accommodate this?
(5) Are there national or governmental public policies, such as sick leave, maternity leave, hours of work, etc. that are different from the corporate policy? How are these taken into consideration; which takes precedence?
(6) Does the local community have the infrastructure to support the global corporate work–life policies, e.g. childcare facilities?
(7) How important is it to our organization to develop a high-performing workforce? How is this related to work–life balance?
(8) What other issues in our organization related to work–life balance do we need to understand and address?
(9) With regard to the following list:
   - Does our organization have a global policy for each of these areas?
   - In what ways does local policy/practice differ from the global policy?

Table 7.3. *Categories of work–family practices*

Child and dependent care benefits
(1) On-site or near site company-provided day childcare center.
(2) Company resource/referral systems for childcare.
(3) Company resource/referral systems for elder care.
(4) Tax-exempt care programs.

Table 7.3. *(cont.)*

---

(5) Fully paid or reimbursed benefits for dependent care assistance.
(6) Partial costs for childcare or elder care.
(7) Contribution to community childcare, elder care, after-school programs or summer programs.
(8) Program for emergency care of mildly ill children or dependents.
(9) Purchase of childcare spaces.
(10) Home care networks.
(11) School-age day-care programs.
(12) Summer and weekend programs for dependents.

Flexible working conditions
(13) Flexitime.
(14) Job sharing.
(15) Part-time work.
(16) Compressed work week.
(17) Shorter work days for parents.
(18) Work at home programs.
(19) Home telecommuting.

Leave options
(20) Paid maternity leave.
(21) Paternity leave.
(22) Parental leave or leave for other family emergencies.
(23) Bereavement leave.
(24) Sabbatical leave tied to key family events.
(25) Re-entry scheme.
(26) Phased retirement.

Information services and personnel policies
(27) Life skill educational programs or counseling (e.g. parenting skills, health issues, financial management, retirement).
(28) Professional and personal counselling.
(29) Work and family resource kit or library.
(30) Exercise or subsidized fitness center.
(31) Cafeteria benefits plan ("family" benefits based on needs/preferences up to a dollar amount).
(32) Relocation assistance (e.g. career options for spouses).
(33) Other policies not listed.

Organizational cultural issues
(34) Family-sensitive supervisors.
(35) Social support from co-workers and supervisors for family issues.
(36) Organizational culture that is supportive of family issues.

Appendix: ACREW key performance indicators (KPI) checklist of work–life best practice©[2]

Developed by

Anne Bardoel, Helen De Cieri, Susan Mayson, Siusan MacKenzie, and Marie Crozier-Durham.

There is a need to develop a measurement tool that provides some structure and definition for work–life effectiveness in organizations. Researchers at the Australian Centre for Research in Employment and Work (ACREW) have developed a detailed checklist to measure the value and impact of work–life initiatives in organizations. The measurement instrument is the result of collaboration between academics and experienced work–life consultants. The ACREW key performance indicators (KPI) checklist of work–life best practice has four sections which provide information about four dimensions of work–life practice in organizations:

- *Section 1 – Planning and alignment* i.e. extent to which comprehensive planning processes are used to establish the business case and align the work–life strategy with the organization's priorities;
- *Section 2 – Customization* i.e. extent to which the work–life program has been appropriately customized and developed to deliver outcomes for the specific organization and individuals;
- *Section 3 – Supportive culture and leadership support* i.e. extent to which steps have been taken to build a culture to support a work–life balance program and demonstrate leadership commitment; and
- *Section 4 – Demonstrated value* i.e. extent to which the work–life program is monitored to demonstrate value to all stakeholders and evaluated to identify opportunities for improvement.

The Checklist is intended for use by managers responsible for work–life and diversity issues in organizations to assist them comprehensively report outcomes of work–life initiatives. In addition, the results can be used to demonstrate to senior-level management the value and impact of work–life initiatives at the organization and individual levels.

[2] Reproduced by kind permission of the Australian Centre for Research – Employment and Work (ACREW).

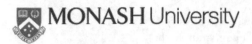 **MONASH** University

AUSTRALIAN CENTRE
FOR RESEARCH IN
EMPLOYMENT AND
WORK (ACREW)

Throughout this survey the terms work/life program, action plan, initiative and actions are used. In the context of this survey they mean:

- Work/life program refers to a documented set of strategic actions and initiatives to meet defined business objectives
- Work/life action plan is a documented strategy to achieve program objectives
- A work/life initiative is a single component of the work/life program (e.g. a flexible work arrangement or a particular leave policy)
- Work/life actions are activities involved with implementing the work/life program

Please indicate whether there is no evidence, some evidence or strong evidence by circling the appropriate point on the scale provided. If there is no evidence, circle number 1, if there is some evidence, circle 2 and if there is strong evidence, circle 3. There are **no right or wrong answers** – choose the number that truly reflects the evidence.	No evidence	Some evidence	Strong evidence

1. HAS STRATEGIC ALIGNMENT BEEN MADE?
Key actions required to strategically align the work/life program

1.1 External environmental analysis conducted			
• The external environment reviewed to identify potential work/life program drivers, e.g. things like what competitors are doing, labour market trends, customer analysis	1	2	3
• Evidence to support a business case gathered	1	2	3
1.2 Initial internal environmental analysis conducted			
• The internal environment reviewed to identify potential work/life program drivers, e.g. things like corporate/ business plan objectives, corporate values, workforce demographics, turnover and absenteeism data, existing work/life initiatives	1	2	3
• Evidence to support a business case gathered	1	2	3
1.3 Work/Life drivers determined			
• External information evaluated to identify work/life drivers	1	2	3

- Internal information evaluated to identify   1   2   3
  work/life drivers
- External information evaluated to identify   1   2   3
  potential value of a work/life program to the
  organisation
- Internal information evaluated to identify   1   2   3
  potential value of a work/life program to the
  organisation
- External information evaluated to identify   1   2   3
  potential value of a work/life program to staff
- Internal information evaluated to identify   1   2   3
  potential value of a work/life program to staff

**1.4 Cultural work/life barriers and enablers
identified**

- The internal environment reviewed to identify   1   2   3
  potential work/life program enablers, e.g.
  experience of other successful culture change
  programs, links to OHS, known champions
- The internal environment reviewed to identify   1   2   3
  potential work/life program barriers, e.g.
  known sceptics, resistance to change,
  unwillingness to seek staff opinion, poor
  communication processes

**1.5 Work/life program aligned to the business
strategy**

- A work/life business case developed   1   2   3
- The work/life business case is directly linked to 1   2   3
  business objectives/priorities
- The work/life business case documented   1   2   3
- The work/life business case received executive   1   2   3
  endorsement
- The work/life business case widely promoted   1   2   3
  throughout the organisation
- The work/life business case is frequently spoken   1   2   3
  about by organisational leaders
- The work/life program is subject to the same   1   2   3
  risk assessment processes as other business
  decisions

1.6 Work/life program objectives established

- Work/life program objectives are aligned to a   1   2   3
  business objective in relation to cost saving for
  example turnover, real estate, WorkCover, or
  legal costs

- Work/life program objectives are aligned to a   1   2   3
  business objective in relation to talent
  management for example attraction, retention,
  turnover
- Work/life program objectives are aligned to a   1   2   3
  business objective in relation to reputation for
  example employer of choice/best employer
  status, recognition through awards,
  recruitment capacity or shareholder interests
- Work/life program objectives are aligned to a   1   2   3
  business objective in relation to productivity
  for example lateness, absenteeism, time spent
  on personal issues, sick leave or job redesign
- Work/life program objectives are aligned to a   1   2   3
  business objective in relation to customer
  service for example extending hours or mode of
  operation, staff attitudes or repeat business.

1.7 Has any additional action been taken in order to plan and align the work/
life program with your organisational priorities?

_____

_____

_____

_____

_____

_____

_____

_____

Totals for each column

SO WHERE DO YOU SIT IN RELATION TO STRATEGIC ALIGNMENT?
If you mainly ticked 1s
Our approach to work/life is based largely on assumptions rather than a business case
If you mainly ticked 2s
Our approach to work/life makes some links to evidence and business objectives
If you mainly ticked 3s
Our approach to work/life is based on a business case which makes use of internal and external evidence and aligns work/life efforts to business objectives

	No evidence	Some evidence	Strong evidence

2. HAS THE WORK/LIFE PROGRAM BEEN APPROPRIATELY CUSTOMISED AND DEVELOPED TO DELIVER OUTCOMES FOR THE ORGANISATION AND INDIVIDUALS?

Key elements of an effective work/life program

2.1 Employee needs determined

	No evidence	Some evidence	Strong evidence
• Employees work/life needs identified	1	2	3
• Work/life needs of different employee groups identified	1	2	3
• Work/life needs of employees' partners & families identified	1	2	3

2.2 Opportunities for business improvement identified

• Business opportunities in relation to flexibility identified	1	2	3
• Business opportunities in relation to work redesign identified	1	2	3
• Business opportunities in relation to work/life benefits identified	1	2	3

2.3 Work/life actions balance business and employee need

• The business context is the key determinant of work/life actions	1	2	3
• Employees needs are considered in light of business needs in negotiating work/life actions	1	2	3

2.4 Range of work/life initiatives on offer

• Work/life initiatives are designed to meet diverse needs of the workforce e.g. different life cycle stage needs	1	2	3
• Work/life program offers 'something for everyone' for example flexible work arrangements, carer support, wellbeing initiatives and leave options	1	2	3

2.5 Work/life action plan

• A work/life action plan is documented	1	2	3
• The work/life action plan includes action to address known cultural barriers and enablers	1	2	3
• The work/life action plan identifies areas of accountability across the organisation	1	2	3
• Guidelines are available to encourage consistent interpretation and application of work/life initiatives across the organization	1	2	3
• The work/life action plan includes a process to review initiatives	1	2	3
• Work/life action plan has executive endorsement	1	2	3

2.6 Has any additional action been taken in order to customise the work/life program at your organisation?

_____

_____

_____

_____

_____

_____

_____

Totals for each column

SO WHERE DO YOU SIT IN RELATION TO PROGRAM CUSTOMISATION?

If you mainly ticked 1s

Our approach to work/life program development is to provide the common range of options without clear understanding of individual needs

If you mainly ticked 2s

Our approach to work/life program development is at the stage of progressing our understanding of staff and business needs and developing a customized approach

If you mainly ticked 3s

Our approach to work/life program development is an action plan customized to suit our staff and our business needs

	No evidence	Some evidence	Strong evidence

3. WHAT STEPS HAVE BEEN TAKEN TO BUILD A CULTURE TO SUPPORT THE WORK/LIFE PROGRAM?
Key cultural elements required to support implementation of a work/life programs

3.1 Leadership support

	No evidence	Some evidence	Strong evidence
• Leaders actively demonstrate support for work/life, e.g. by modelling work/life balance in their own lives, participating in the work/life team, seeking regular program reports, often speaking about work/life program to staff	1	2	3

3.2 Managers positioned to support

	No evidence	Some evidence	Strong evidence
• Specific work/life training programs exist for managers	1	2	3
• Managers have access to tools and resources to help them support work/life program implementation	1	2	3
• Managers are recognised and rewarded for effective work/life implementation efforts	1	2	3

3.3 Staff involvement in developing initiatives

	No evidence	Some evidence	Strong evidence
• A staff work/life team/group/committee exists to guide program implementation	1	2	3
• Development of work/life initiatives is a team effort	1	2	3

3.4 Effective work/life program communication

	No evidence	Some evidence	Strong evidence
• Introduction of new work/life initiatives is accompanied by a comprehensive communication plan	1	2	3
• System in place to encourage feedback on initiatives	1	2	3
• Work/life program information is included in recruitment documents	1	2	3
• Work/life program information is included in induction programs	1	2	3

• Work/life program information is regularly included in internal newsletters/intranet updates/noticeboards	1	2	3
• Work/life issues are regularly on the agenda at Team meetings	1	2	3
• Work/life program information is on the company website	1	2	3
• Work/life progress is celebrated	1	2	3

3.5 Work/life accountability process

• Statement of work/life responsibilities exists	1	2	3
• Work/life accountabilities are regularly monitored	1	2	3

3.6 Adequate budget and resource allocation

• Each new work/life initiative is provided with appropriate budget/resource allocation	1	2	3

3.7 Has any additional action been taken to build a culture to support the work/life program at your organisation?

_____

_____

_____

_____

_____

_____

_____

_____

Totals for each column

SO WHERE DO YOU SIT IN RELATION TO BUILDING A CULTURE TO SUPPORT WORK/LIFE?

If you mainly ticked 1s

To date our work/life program has not placed any emphasis on building cultural support

If you mainly ticked 2s

Our approach to building cultural support for work/life is limited to some of the elements listed above

If you mainly ticked 3s

Our approach to building cultural support for work/life is that it is integral to our program

	No evidence	Some evidence	Strong evidence

4. CAN THE VALUE OF THE WORK/LIFE PROGRAM BE DEMONSTRATED?

Key elements of measurement required to demonstrate the value to all stakeholders of a work/life program linked to Balanced Scorecard perspectives (People, Culture, Financial and Business Performance)

4.1 Measurement of program objectives

	No evidence	Some evidence	Strong evidence
• Work/life program objectives are individually evaluated at regular intervals to determine impact on business, and or financial performance	1	2	3
• Work/life program performance is reported to executive at regular intervals	1	2	3
• Work/life program performance reports are used to inform the organisation's strategic decision making and work/life program improvement	1	2	3

4.2 Measurement of employee satisfaction

	No evidence	Some evidence	Strong evidence
• Staff asked if the work/life initiatives offered meet their need	1	2	3
• Staff asked to assess the organisation's work/life culture	1	2	3
• Staff are asked for ways of improving the work/life program	1	2	3

4.3 Measurement of program impact

	No evidence	Some evidence	Strong evidence
• Staff are asked to indicate how work/life initiatives affect their personal work/life balance	1	2	3
• Staff are asked to indicate how work/life initiatives affect their job satisfaction	1	2	3
• Staff are asked to indicate how work/life initiatives affect their intention to remain with the organization	1	2	3
• Staff are asked to indicate how work/life programs affect their family	1	2	3
• Staff are asked to indicate how work/life initiatives affect their community involvement	1	2	3
• New recruits are asked how knowledge of the work/life program affected their decision to join the organisation	1	2	3

4.4 Has any additional action been taken to demonstrate the value of the work/
   life program at your organisation?

_____
_____
_____
_____
_____
_____
_____
_____

4.5 Does the work/life program have a separate financial allocation?

_____
_____
_____
_____
_____
_____
_____

4.6 Does the work/life program have a separate staffing allocation?

_____
_____
_____
_____
_____
_____
_____

Totals for each column

SO WHERE DO YOU SIT IN RELATION TO DEMONSTRATING THE VALUE OF THE WORK/LIFE PROGRAM?

If you mainly ticked 1s
We are not currently in a position to demonstrate the value and impact of our work/life program
If you mainly ticked 2s
Our approach to work/life program measurement is limited to reporting on only some of the elements listed above
If you mainly ticked 3s
Our approach to work/life program measurement is to ensure we are in a position to demonstrate the value and impact of the program on the business and other stakeholders

Strategy Map Summary

To create a visual representation of your work/life performance transfer your results from the end of each of the four sections. What pattern emerges?

1. Alignment

Our approach to work/life is based largely on assumptions rather than a business case	Our approach to work/life makes some links to evidence and business objectives	Our approach to work/life is based on a business case which makes use of internal and external evidence and aligns work/life efforts to business objectives

2. Customisation

Our approach to work/life program development is to provide the common range of options without clear understanding of individual needs	Our approach to work/life program development is at the stage of progressing our understanding of staff and business needs and developing a customized approach	Our approach to work/life program development is an action plan customized to suit our staff and our business needs

3. Culture

To date our work/life program has not placed any emphasis on building cultural support	Our approach to building cultural support for work/life is limited to some of the elements listed above	Our approach to building cultural support for work/life is that it is integral to our program

4. Value

We are not currently in a position to demonstrate the value and impact of our work/life program	Our approach to work/life program measurement is limited to reporting on only some of the elements listed above	Our approach to work/life program measurement is to ensure we are in a position to demonstrate the value and impact of the program on the business and other stakeholders

Revisit the responses in relation to the individual items in each section to determine where action is required to improve work/life performance.

_____

_____

_____

_____

_____

_____

_____

_____

_____

References

Alvesson, M. (2003). Beyond neopositivists, romantics and localists: A reflexive approach to interviews in organisational research. *Academy of Management Review*, 28, 13–33.

Anonymous (2005). Juggling work with life. *graphicartsmonthly.com*, February, S14–S15.

Aycan, Z. (2005). The interplay between cultural and institutional/structural contingencies in human resource management practices. *International Journal of Human Resource Management*, 16, 1083–1119.

Bartlett, K.R., Lawler, J.J., Bae, J., Chen, S.-J., & Wan, D. (2002). Differences in international human resource development among indigenous firms and multinational affiliates in East and South East Asia. *Human Resource Development Quarterly*, 13, 383–405.

Brewster, C. & Suutari, V. (2005). Global HRM: Aspects of a research agenda. *Personnel Review*, 34(1), 5–21.

Deng, P. (2004). Outward investment by Chinese MNCs: Motivations and implications. *Business Horizons*, 47(3), 8–16.

Dowling, P.J. (1988). International and domestic personnel/human resource management: Similarities and differences. In R.S. Schuler, R.S. Youngblood, & V.L. Huber (eds), *Readings in Personnel and Human Resource Management*. St. Paul, MI: West.

Dowling, P.J. & Welch, D.E. (2004). *International Human Resource Management: Managing People in a Multinational Context* (4th ed.). London: Thomson Learning.

Doz, Y. & Prahalad C.K. (1991). Managing DMNCs: A search for a new paradigm. *Strategic Management Journal*, 12, 145–164.

Earley, P.C. & Gibson, C. (2002). *Multinational Teams: A New Perspective*. Mahwah, NJ: Lawrence Erlbaum and Associates.

Eaton, S. C. (2003). If you can use them: Flexibility policies, organizational commitment, and perceived performance. *Industrial Relations*, 42(2), 145–167.

Edwards, T. & Kuruvilla, S. (2005). International HRM: National business systems, organizational politics and the international division of labour in MNCS. *International Journal of Human Resource Management*, 16(1), 1–21.

Egan, M. L. & Bendick, M., Jr. (2003). Workforce diversity initiatives of U. S. multinational corporations in Europe. *Thunderbird International Business Review*, 45, 701–727.

Ferris, G. R., Hall, A. T., Royle, M. T., & Martocchio, J. J. (2004). Theoretical developments in the field of human resource management: Issues and challenges for the future. *Organizational Analysis*, 12, 231–254.

Freeman, R. E. (1984). *Strategic Management: A Stakeholder Approach*. Boston, MA: Pitman.

Gelfand, M. J. & Knight, A. P. (2005). Cross-cultural perspectives on work–family conflict. In S. A. Y. Poelmans (ed.), *Work and Family: An International Research Perspective*. Mahwah, NJ: Lawrence Erlbaum Associates.

Gerhart, B. & Fang, M. (2005). National culture and human resource management: assumptions and evidence. *International Journal of Human Resource Management*, 16, 971–986.

Giue, J. & Petrescu, O. (2005). *Case Study 2005 – Work–life, Flexibility & Mobility: Ensuring Global Support of Flexibility within IBM's On-Demand Company* (Chapter 5, in this volume).

Haas, L. L., Hwang, P., & Russell, G. (2000). *Organizational Change and Gender Equity*. Thousand Oaks, CA: Sage.

Harris, H. & Brewster, C. (2003). Alternatives to traditional international assignments. In W. Mayrhofer, G. Stahl & T. Kuhlmann (eds), *Innovative Ansatze im Internationalen Personalmanagement* (Innovating HRM). München/Mering: Hampp Verlag.

Hein, C. (2005). *Reconciling Work and Family Responsibilities: Practical Ideas from Global Experience*. Geneva, Switzerland: International Labour Organization.

Hofstede, G. (1980). *Cultures' Consequences: International Differences in Work-Related Values*. Beverly Hills, CA: Sage.

Human Resources Development Canada. (2002). Work–life balance in Canadian workplaces (http://labour-travail.hrdc-drhc.gc.ca/worklife/welcome-en.cfm).

Husted, B. W. (2003). Globalization and cultural change in international business research. *Journal of International Management*, 9, 427–433.

Juhel, M. H. (2001). Globalization, privatization and restructuring of ports. *International Journal of Maritime Economics*, 3(2), 139–174.

Korabik, K., Lero, D., & Ayman, R. (2003). A micro–macro approach to cross-cultural work–family research. Paper presented at the European Academy of Management, Milan, Italy.

Lazarova, M. & Caligiuri, P. (2001). Retaining repatriates: The role of organizational support practices. *Journal of World Business*, 36, 389–401.

Leung, K., Bhagat, R. S., Buchan, N. R., Erez, M., & Gibson, C. S. (2005). Culture and international business: recent advances and their implications for future research. *Journal of International Business Studies*, 36, 357–378.

Lobel, S. & Faught, F. (1996). Four methods for proving the value of work-life initiatives. *Compensation and Benefits Review*, 28(6), 50–57.

Losey, M., Meisinger, S. R., & Ulrich, D. (2005). Conclusion: reality, impact and professionalism. Human Resource Management, 44, 201–206.

McWilliams, A., van Fleet, D. D., & Wright, P. M. (2001). Strategic management of human resources for global competitive advantage. *Journal of Business Strategies*, 18(1), 1–24.

Mehra, A., Kilduff, M., & Brass, D. J. (1998). At the margins: A distinctiveness approach to the social identity and social networks of underrepresented groups. *Academy of Management Journal*, 41, 441–452.

Meyerson, D. & Martin, J. (1987). Cultural change: An integration of three different views. *Journal of Management Studies*, 24, 623–647.

Michaels, B. (1995). A global glance at work and family. *Personnel Journal*, 74(4), 85–93.

Ministry of Manpower Singapore. (2005). *Work–Life Harmony Report: Findings and Recommendations for Employers on how to use Work–Life Strategies to Optimise Business Performance*. Singapore: Ministry of Manpower.

Patrickson, M. & Hartmann, L. (2001). Human resource management in Australia. Prospects for the twenty-first century. *International Journal of Manpower*, 22(3), 198–206.

Patton, M. (2002). *Qualitative Research and Evaluation Methods*. Thousand Oaks, CA: Sage.

Perry-Smith, J. E. & Blum, T. C. (2000). Work–family human resource bundles and perceived organizational performance. *Academy of Management Journal*, 43, 1107–1117.

Pfeffer, J. (2005). Changing mental models: HR's most important task. *Human Resource Management*, 44, 123–128.

Poelmans, S. (2005). Organizational research on work and family: Recommendations for future research. In S. Poelmans (ed.), *Work and*

Family: An International Research Perspective. Mahwah, NJ: Lawrence Erlbaum Associates.

Poelmans, S., Chinchilla, N. & Cardona, P. (2003). The adoption of family-friendly HRM policies: Competing for scarce resources in the labour market. *International Journal of Manpower*, 24(2), 128–147.

Poster, W. R. & Prasad, S. (2005). Work–family relations in transnational perspective: A view from high-tech firms in India and the United States. *Social Problems*, 52, 122–146.

Ramamurti, R. (2004). Developing countries and MNEs: Extending and enriching the research agenda. *Journal of International Business Studies*, 35, 277–283.

Roberts, K., Kossek, E. E., & Ozeki, C. (1998). Managing the global workforce: Challenges and strategies. *Academy of Management Executive*, 12(4), 93–106.

Roehling, M. V., Boswell, W. R., Caligiuri, P., Feldman, D., Graham, M. E., Guthrie, J., Motohiro, M., & Tansky, J. W. (2005). The future of HR management: Research needs and directions. *Human Resource Management*, 44, 207–216.

Schuler, R. S., Dowling, P. J., & De Cieri, H. (1993). An integrative framework of strategic international human resource management. *Journal of Management*, 19, 419–460.

Shapiro, A. & Noble, K. (2001). A work–life lens helps bring a global workforce into focus. *It's About Time*, 2 (Spring), 1–2.

Sheridan, A. & Conway, L. (2001). Workplace flexibility: Reconciling the needs of employers and employees. *Women in Management Review*, 16(1), 5–11.

Spinks, N. (2003). Work–life around the world (Building a global work–life strategy). Paper presented at the Designing the Future, 7th Annual Work–Life Conference, Orlando, Florida.

Spinks, N. (2005). *Work–Life Around the World: Building a Global Work–Life Strategy*. Toronto: Work–Life Harmony Enterprises.

Stroh, L. K. & Caligiuri, P. M. (1998). Increasing global competitiveness through effective people management. *Journal of World Business*, 33(1), 1–16.

Thompson, M. A. & Richter, A. S. (1998). Using culture principles to resolve the paradox in international remuneration. In R. Platt (ed.), *The Best of Global HR*. Scottsdale, AZ, WorldatWork.

Turnbull, P. (2000). Contesting globalization on the waterfront. *Politics & Society*, 28, 273–97.

Vincola, A. (1998). How to set a global work–life strategy: Work–Life Matters. (www.bcsolutionsmag.com/Archives/special_sections/global_work_life.htm).

Welbourne, T. (2005). Editor-in-chief's note. *Human Resource Management*, 44, 113–114.

Working Mother Magazine, www.workingmother.com

Yang, N. (2005). Individualism–collectivism and work–family interfaces: A Sino–U.S. Comparison. In S. A. Y. Poelmans (ed.), *Work and Family: An International Research Perspective*. Mahwah, NJ: Lawrence Erlbaum Associates.

Yin, R. (2003). *Case Study Research: Design and Methods* (3rd ed.). Thousand Oaks, CA: Sage.

Zhu, C. J. (1997). Human resource development in China during the transition to a new economic system. *Asia Pacific Journal of Human Resources*, 35(3), 19–44.

Zikmund, W. (2000). *Business Research Methods*. Sydney: Harcourt College Publishers.

PART III

Cultural change

8 | Barriers to the implementation and usage of work–life policies

CYNTHIA A. THOMPSON
Baruch College, CUNY, USA

Work is taking over the lives of many employees in today's fast-paced, global environment, and organizations are increasingly offering work–life programs to help employees manage the conflicts and stress resulting from long hours and workload escalation. For some firms, work–life programs are having their intended effect: absenteeism declines, loyalty and retention increase, the ability to recruit talented employees improves, and many employees report that their productivity improves. However, for other firms, work–life programs are not successful, or do not reach their potential for enhancing work–life balance for employees. In some cases employees may not be aware the programs exist, in other cases employees are fearful that their careers will suffer if they participate in the programs. Further, programs sometimes fail because they are not implemented properly, as when employees are not given the necessary technical and management support to work from home.

The purpose of this chapter is to discuss potential barriers that may impede the successful implementation and utilization of work–life programs. I will begin by discussing the underlying assumptions and values that influence the way employees and employers think about work and family. For example, I will discuss the ways in which organizations and individuals define success, and how these traditional definitions limit their ability to think creatively about new ways of working. I will next discuss specific barriers that may occur at the planning and implementation stages of work–life programs, as well as barriers to usage as perceived by employees (e.g. fears of committing career suicide if they take advantage of programs like telecommuting). Finally, to help those in charge of implementing and managing work–life programs, I will present a model (see Figure 8.1) that portrays barriers that may occur at each of the following levels: organization level (e.g. organizational culture), work-group level (e.g. supportiveness

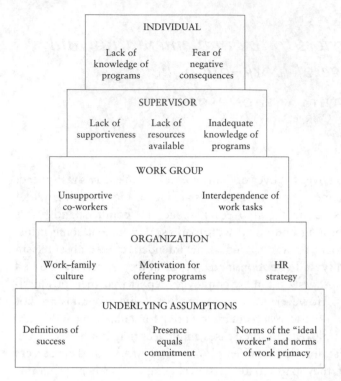

Figure 8.1 Five-level model of potential barriers to the success of work–life programs.

of co-workers), supervisor level (e.g. level of supportiveness), and individual level (e.g. knowledge of work–life programs, resentment among employees without families), as well as examples of barriers related to underlying assumptions. A checklist is also included for program planners to use as a guide to examine potential roadblocks that may interfere with the successful implementation of work–life initiatives (see Table 8.1).

Underlying assumptions

The culture of an organization has a powerful influence on the way employees and managers think and behave at work (Schein, 1992). As described in Chapter 6, organizational culture – broadly defined as the implicit assumptions, social norms, and expectations that govern the work environment – has a major impact on how easily an organization can effect a positive change towards a more supportive work–life culture. More specifically, the supportiveness of a firm's *work–family* culture is shaped by shared assumptions, beliefs, and values regarding the extent to which an organization should support and value the integration of employees' work and family lives (Thompson, Beauvais, & Lyness, 1999). To begin to understand potential barriers to the implementation and utilization of work–life programs, one needs to get at the heart of the firm's culture, and this requires diagnosing the underlying assumptions of the culture (Lewis, 1997; Schein, 1992).

There are several important assumptions that influence the way employees and employers think about work and family. The first and probably most important assumption is that there is only one definition of success: firm performance, measured by, for example, profit margin, return on equity, sales growth, and shareholder payout. Success at the firm level is centered on pleasing a subset of stakeholders (e.g. managers and investors), and ignores other possible stakeholders such as employees themselves, their family members, their children, and the larger community (Cleveland, 2005). As with environmental contamination, stress and heavy time demands from work can spill over and negatively affect family functioning, thus creating "social contamination" that may damage a central institution in our society (Poelmans & Sahibzada, 2004). However, minimizing the intrusion of work on employees' home lives, while possibly viewed as a worthy goal for the organization, is not typically included in management discussions on increasing profits and shareholder value. As a result, programs for improving work–life balance are not connected to strategic planning and therefore not likely to be considered important to the firm's mission, despite evidence that work–family conflict and role overload are related to outcomes at least indirectly if not directly related to the bottom line (e.g. absenteeism, stress-related illness, burnout; see Eby, Casper, Lockwood, Bordeaux, & Brinley, 2004; Thompson, Beauvais, & Allen, 2005).

Definitions of success at the firm level influence employee definitions of success, which typically center around movement up the managerial hierarchy (Bailyn, 1993). Incentive systems and career paths reinforce this singular definition of success. For example, employees who prioritize work over family personify the "ideal worker," that is, "someone for whom work is primary, time to spend at work is unlimited, and the demands of family ... and personal life are secondary" (Rapoport, Bailyn, Fletcher, & Pruitt, 2002, p. 29; Williams, 2000). These ideal workers are likely to be rewarded with the promotions they covet. Employees who do not fit the mold of the ideal employee are often viewed as less serious about their careers (Bailyn, 1993), and thus are less likely to be chosen for career advancement. After all, why invest in an employee who is unwilling to put the company first, especially when there are other employees willing to do so? This assumption of what makes an ideal employee thus limits the ability of an organization to value the contributions of employees who may not be career primary, and it makes it difficult for career-primary employees who would like to incorporate time for non-work activities without fear of losing career opportunities.

Vertical movement up the hierarchy is predicated not just on an employee's competence but an employee's ability to show high levels of commitment to work. Because job performance is difficult to measure in many professional and managerial jobs, managers often expect their employees to show their dedication by putting in long hours, going beyond the call of duty, and always putting the firm's or the client's needs first. The underlying assumption is that there is only one way to show commitment, and employees who can put their jobs first are the ones who should be retained and promoted. Even in blue-collar jobs, employees are expected to agree to last-minute requests for overtime, and saying no to the boss may hurt their chances for wage increases or promotions. Inflexible assumptions about what it takes to be successful at work create a critical barrier for employees who want to thrive at work without jeopardizing their own and their family's health and well-being (Bailyn, 1993; Cleveland, 2005).

In some organizations, the norms for long hours may encourage ostentatious displays of work primacy. For example, in one financial services firm, a senior officer who was a member of a cross-departmental task force, boasted at a meeting that "we are committed to the business and to making money for the bank, and have the divorce rates to prove it!" Attitudes about the importance of prioritizing work over family slip out in other somewhat more subtle ways. In the same organization, a candidate for an internal transfer and promotion described an interview in which the interviewer, who was responsible for a global business, was "downright gleeful" when he realized that the candidate was divorced and had a child who lived with his mother in another state. The interviewer clarified the candidate's status by asking, "Oh, so there is no one that cares how much traveling you do?"[1]

Another important assumption that influences the way we think about work and family is the assumption that paid work is the main responsibility of men and caregiving is the main responsibility of women (McDonald, Brown, & Bradley, 2005; Simon, 1995). Despite the fact that more women than ever are working, we still expect that for women, work will take a back seat to home when there is a conflict between the two. And despite the fact that men appear to be taking on an increasing share of the chores and responsibilities of home and child raising, they still average 4.7 hours per day, compared to women's 6.5 hours (Bond, Thompson, Galinsky, & Prottas, 2003). Because of these underlying expectations for gender roles, organizations continue to structure work based on the assumption that employees will be able to, and should be able to, meet all job demands placed on them. Women are often relegated to lower-paying or lower-status jobs that allow them to put family first, further reinforcing the notion that women don't have, or don't want, what it takes to be an ideal worker. In fact, while some women appear willing to give up the fast track, modify their career goals, or quit altogether to spend more time with their children, many women prefer to continue working, but at a reduced schedule, in the profession for which they were trained (Lewis & Cooper, 2005; Williams, 2000). However, women (and men) who choose to work in non-traditional ways, such as reduced hours or telecommuting, are often penalized because they no longer fit the image of the ideal or "work-primary" worker.

In summary, assumptions about how success should be defined and measured, assumptions about what an "ideal worker" is, and assumptions about the importance and strength of gender roles continue to influence the way employers and employees think about work and family. These assumptions underlie many of the barriers to the planning, implementation, and use of work–life programs that will be discussed in the next two sections.

---

[1] Prottas, David. Personal communication. January 3, 2003.

Barriers to program planning and implementation

Lack of support from top management

Some CEOs appear to fully support the idea, at least in theory, that employees should have a life outside of work. Phil Laskawy, former CEO of Ernst & Young LLP, was concerned about the high attrition rate among his employees, and hired Deborah Holmes to create new programs to help retain employees (Friedman, Thompson, Carpenter, & Marcel, 2001). She determined that one of the main reasons for attrition was job burnout, which resulted from employees struggling to balance the heavy demands of work with the need to have a life outside of work. With the full support of Laskawy, she experimented with numerous initiatives to increase work–life balance for all employees. Laskawy said, "this is not about being a nice guy, it's about doing the right thing" (Friedman *et al.*, 2001, p. 6). His support could be seen clearly by all employees: he addressed the issue of work–life balance regularly through his firm-wide voice messages, and he created the Office for Retention, with Deborah Holmes as director. She reported directly to him, and kept him abreast of the progress the firm was making toward work–life balance. Evidence of success can be seen in the higher retention rates in the parts of the organization that participated in work–life initiatives. For example, the San Jose/Palo Alto tax-and-audit practice, one of the firm's most profitable offices, saw its staff turnover decrease by 15 percent after implementing several initiatives (Kruger, 2000).

At Sony Corporation, top management made it clear to employees that they did not condone working long hours, and reinforced this message through their reward system. A recently hired MBA graduate, for example, was told that his long hours at work were excessive, and that his promotion would be suspended until he learned how to work differently. Management was concerned that rewarding his long hours would send the wrong message about what it takes to succeed at Sony. After the employee acquired the new habit of leaving work at a reasonable hour, he was promoted (Chinchilla, Poelmans, Leon, & Tarres, 2004).

---

[1] Prottas, David. Personal communication. January 3, 2003.

In contrast, many CEOs and top managers simply pay lip service to the issue of work–life balance, or disparage the idea altogether. As Jack Welch, former CEO of General Electric, famously said: "People who publicly struggle with work–life balance problems and continually turn to the company for help get pigeonholed as ambivalent, entitled, uncommitted, incompetent—or all of the above."[2] In fact, in his mind, managers should make their employees' jobs so interesting that employees would rather be at work than at home:

To make the choices and take the actions that ultimately make sense for you, you need to understand that reality: your boss's top priority is competitiveness. Of course he wants you to be happy, but only inasmuch as it helps the company win. In fact, if he is doing his job right, he is making your job so exciting that your personal life becomes a less compelling draw.[3]

His attitude may be more representative than many CEOs and top managers let on. Joan Kofodimos, a consulting psychologist who worked for the Center for Creative Leadership, counseled many executives about work and work–life imbalance. She found that while the executives complained about the long hours, the pressures of their jobs, and the way their jobs wreaked havoc in their personal lives, they admitted that they evaluated their own subordinates partially based on their willingness to work long hours. According to Kofodimos, many executives derive their self-esteem and identity largely from their accomplishments at work, which then leads them to internalize and elevate the value of achievement. Because they have lived their work lives prioritizing work over family so that they may be successful at work, they come to believe that the only way to succeed is to put the job first. As a result, they expect their subordinates to make work their primary life priority, even if it involves sacrifices (Kofodimos, 1995). While these executives may support the idea of work–life balance for lower-level employees who are not career primary, they rarely support it for employees who expect to move up the corporate hierarchy.

Lack of first-line support

Whether or not top management supports work–life programs, the support of first-line supervisors and managers is essential (see Chapter 3 for a detailed discussion). According to employees at a large international

[2] Jack Welch on work and family. *Newsweek*, April 4, 2005.   [3] Ibid.

consulting firm, "abstract pronouncements of support" from top management are no substitute for a supportive supervisor (Nord *et al.*, 2002). Unfortunately, it is often the case that first-line supervisors are not adequately represented in the planning stage of program development, and as a result, do not fully understand the need for, or the value of, work–life programs. As supervisors are evaluated based on meeting goals, increasing productivity, reducing inefficiencies, etc., they may feel that these programs will make their jobs more difficult and as a result, actively (or passively) resist their implementation. For example, unsupportive supervisors have been known to limit access to flexible work arrangements or make it more difficult for employees to use them (Brewer, 2000).

In addition, some work–life programs such as telecommuting can change the power balance in the employee–supervisor relationship. As employees gain control over where and when they work, supervisors lose control. Many supervisors find this threatening, or at least disconcerting, as they are no longer able to judge the employee's performance based on observing the employee at work. Interestingly, according to recent research, managers' fear of loss of power or control is just as prevalent today as it was twenty years ago (Brewer, 2000), when telecommuting was a relatively new option for work.

Perception that work–life programs do not add value

Recent research suggests that employees who work in family-supportive work environments are more satisfied with their jobs, more committed to their employer, and less likely to quit (Bond *et al.*, 2003; Thompson, Jahn, Kopelman, & Prottas, 2004), and employees who use family-friendly benefits are absent less frequently, experience lower levels of conflict between work and home, and are less stressed (Lapierre and Allen, 2006; Thompson *et al.*, 1999). In addition, companies with extensive work–family programs report higher levels of perceived organizational performance (Perry-Smith & Blum, 2000) and productivity (Konrad & Mangel, 2000). One study found that firm announcements of work–family initiatives that appeared in the *Wall Street Journal* (e.g. "IBM began a child care referral service for its employees") resulted in a significant increase in the price of shares (Arthur, 2003).

A recent report on the business impact of introducing greater schedule flexibility further documents the impressive gains that firms can make by being more accommodating of employees' lives outside of work. This report, prepared by Corporate Voices for Working Families (2005), provides many persuasive examples of the power of flexibility, including:

- IBM found that employees who scored higher on an index of work–life balance (which included indicators of flexibility) were significantly more satisfied with their jobs, IBM in general, their sense of accomplishment at work, and their willingness to give extra effort at work, compared to employees with lower scores.
- JPMorgan Chase found that support for work–life integration, including increased flexibility, was a key driver of employee satisfaction.
- At Bristol-Myers Squibb, employees who use flexible work arrangements were less likely to report feeling stressed or burned out.
- At Ernst & Young, employees who perceived they had flexibility were more committed to the firm, and commitment in turn was predictive of revenue per person as well as retention
- Watson Wyatt's Human Capital Index shows that firms with high employee satisfaction have higher market value, and that a flexible workplace is associated with a 9 percent change in market value.

Despite these positive findings, many managers continue to believe that work–life programs are too costly and are unrelated to firm productivity. Further, these programs are rarely viewed as an investment in human resources (HR) (Poelmans & Sahibzada, 2004). And because there are few studies in which the costs of such programs are examined in relation to the benefits achieved, it is difficult to argue the point with financial data, the lingua franca of top-level managers. As a result, they remain skeptical about the supposed benefits of such programs, despite evidence that these programs are related both directly and indirectly to the bottom line.

The perception that work–life programs do not add value was demonstrated at Proffirm, a consultancy practice that is part of an international professional services firm. In this company, managers collaborated with researchers to uncover inefficiencies and unproductive work practices, as well as the assumptions underlying them. Top management rejected the resulting recommendations to improve the situation, as these practices were not considered to be business related and therefore not worth the time and financial resources required to implement the changes (Lewis & Cooper, 2005).

Inadequate needs assessment

For organizations considering work–life initiatives, one of the first steps is to conduct an assessment of employees' work–life needs and concerns. Needs assessments are often conducted by Human Resources or by a task force formed for the purpose. The methodology usually involves employee surveys and focus groups, and the questions revolve around employee demographics (e.g. number of employees who are parents), work–life balance needs of employees (e.g. need for reduced hours, childcare, elder care), and employee health and well-being (e.g. stress and burnout, work–family conflict, ill health). Some organizations monitor the psychosocial work environment to determine which business units have high levels of stressed or burned-out employees (Shain, 2005).

The importance of a thorough needs assessment was demonstrated in a company that, based on an analysis of employee demographics, built a million-dollar, state-of-the-art daycare facility. Unfortunately, the needs assessment did not uncover the fact that although the employees had childcare needs, they did not necessarily want to bring their child to an on-site daycare center. As a result, very few employees signed up to use it.

While factors such as employee demographics, work–life balance issues, and employee health and well-being are certainly important to assess, they do not get at the underlying, or root cause, of the work–life issues facing employees (Rappaport, Bailyn, Fletcher, & Pruitt, 2002; Thompson, 2005). For example, what exactly is causing the imbalance? Is it the unpredictability of workloads? Unreasonable workloads? Poorly designed jobs? Is it over-reliance on face time to measure employee performance? Or perhaps the inability of the supervisor or manager to trust the employee to get the job done without constant oversight?

Needs assessments that focus on employee demographics or attitudes will likely miss the deeper, underlying reason for employees' work–life imbalance. As a result, companies end up developing popular but inadequate "band-aid" solutions to assuage employee distress over work–life imbalance. Flextime, for example, is not helpful when the real problem is that employees are struggling under the weight of having too much to do and too little time. Flextime may help "at the margins" (Lewis, 1997) but does nothing to change the fact that employees have unreasonable workloads or unrealistic deadlines, which in turn spill over and create havoc in the employees' personal lives.

Inadequate alignment with HR system

Once the decision to implement work–life programs has been made, there is often too little attention paid to whether the new programs fit with existing human resource or management systems. In particular, HR managers sometimes neglect to rethink how jobs are designed, how work should be distributed, how performance should be measured and rewarded, how employees should be compensated, and whether career paths as currently defined continue to make sense for all employees (Bailyn & Fletcher, 1997; Nord *et al.*, 2002). Further, without proper management training in how to best manage employees who work in alternative work arrangements, managers or supervisors may under-utilize these workers or devalue their contributions (Nord *et al.*, 2002).

When work–life programs are not incorporated into the HR systems in general and into the mindset of managers and HR decision-makers in particular, the organization may be sending mixed signals to employees. For example, in a financial services firm that prides itself on being supportive of families, HR planned a management retreat for a weekend that fell on Mother's Day. Not surprisingly, many of the employees questioned the company's commitment to its mission of supporting work–life balance for all employees. In contrast, companies that reward managers for being supportive of their employees' work–life needs are sending the signal that family and personal life matter, and that the company values the health and well-being of employees. Happy Ltd, an award-winning training company in London, for example, holds managers accountable for being supportive of their employees' work–life needs, and includes a question on work–life balance in managers' performance evaluations[4].

Inadequate internal and external communication

Inadequate communication with external clients may also create barriers to effective implementation of work–life programs. Clients have expectations about employee availability and can be highly resistant to

---

[4] www.businesslink.gov.uk/bdotg/action/detail?r.s=sc&type=CASE%20 STUDIES&itemId=1075431613#

changes in that availability. However, it is not impossible to get the clients on board. At Ernst & Young (E&Y), for example, a new work schedule was implemented for consultants from the New York office who worked at a Chicago engagement during the week. Labeled the "3–4–5 schedule," the schedule involved four days on-site rather than five, and allowed the New York consultants to fly home on Thursday nights so they would have a day at the home office plus a full weekend with their families. Although the client's managers initially resisted, they understood that E&Y's turnover problem was their problem, too, and began to appreciate the value of the new schedule. In addition, the E&Y consultants liked the 3–4–5 schedule so much that they now include it as part of their upfront negotiations with new clients (Friedman *et al.*, 2001).

Another barrier to the successful implementation of work–life programs is inadequate internal communication specifically, and information about new programs or policies often is not well disseminated nor fully explained to employees or supervisors. In fact, research suggests that employees have limited or inaccurate knowledge of the various work–life benefits, programs, and policies offered by their employers (e.g. Prottas, Thompson, Kopelman, & Jahn, 2007). Clearly, without knowledge of these programs, neither the employee nor the organization can benefit. In addition, when supervisors are not informed about the nature and function of the programs, the likelihood that they will allow their employees to participate is reduced.

Inadequate training for supervisors and managers

Even when supervisors and managers know about the various work–life programs, they may not be adequately trained to implement them. New flexibility policies, for example, sometimes require managers to change the way they allocate tasks or the way they measure performance (Nord *et al.*, 2002). Managers who previously evaluated their employees based on the amount of time they spent at the office, for example, need to learn how to evaluate *results* rather than "face time." In addition, questions of eligibility and fairness arise: Who is eligible? How many of my employees are eligible? How do I choose which employees can participate? These issues need to be nailed down before rolling out the new programs, and managers need to fully understand not only *why* the organization is implementing them but *how* to implement them. Otherwise, untrained managers may apply work–life policies capriciously or inconsistently, thus potentially creating resentment among employees (Hyman & Summers, 2004; Poelmans, Chinchilla, & Cordona, 2003; Poelmans & Sahabzada, 2004; see also Chapter 6 of this volume). As one branch manager from a large Scottish retail bank noted: "There is a wide variation in how these policies are implemented because there is no training in this at all and no HR involvement" (Hyman & Summers, 2004, p. 422).

Inadequate consideration of suitability of employees for work–life programs

When implementing work–life programs that allow employees to work at home for at least part of the time, there is often little thought paid to which employees are likely to succeed. Because working at home requires discipline and focus, not all employees are suitable. If an employee is easily distracted, for example, the messy kitchen, the overgrown lawn, or the children in the next room may be too much of a pull. Other considerations include the employee's level of intrinsic motivation, the adequacy of their skills to perform the work alone, and their relationship with their supervisor (Ertel & Pech, 2006). For employees with young children at home perhaps the most important consideration is the availability of external childcare, or at a minimum, a babysitter who is able to occupy the children while the parent employee works in the next room.

Although there is little research examining which employees are most successful at telecommuting, several discrete and measurable traits may be relevant. For example, employees who are conscientious, tolerant of ambiguity, and have a low need for affiliation as well as a high internal locus of control, may be more likely to succeed in their telecommuting arrangement than employees who do not have these traits. In fact, one study found that telecommuters who have strong self-management skills and low affiliation needs were more likely to perform well (Haines, St-Onge, & Archambault, 2002) than those with weak self-management skills and high affiliation needs.

Barriers to program usage

Once an organization has implemented work–life programs or has created new work–life policies, there are several barriers that may keep employees from fully taking advantage of the new programs or policies. In fact, usage rates for work–life programs are often quite low, suggesting either that barriers to usage are very strong or the programs as designed are inadequate to solve the problems associated with work–life balance (Frankel, 1998). Some of these barriers arise from underlying assumptions of what an "ideal" and successful employee looks like, as discussed earlier, and some of the barriers are more structural in nature (e.g. inadequate technology).

Work–family culture

The most important barrier, and probably the most difficult to overcome, is an unsupportive culture created by underlying assumptions of the primacy of work (Lewis & Cooper, 2005; Thompson *et al.*, 1999). As discussed earlier, these underlying assumptions create a work culture that prioritizes work over family, that rewards the "ideal worker" who will work long hours and meet client demands at all costs, and that equates productivity with time expended (Bailyn, 1993; Williams, 2000). Employees who strive to be considered ideal workers are reluctant to acknowledge that they have any personal or family-related needs, much less take advantage of any work–life program that reduces their visibility. In some cases, employees feel that they have to meet all work demands not just to compete for limited promotions but simply to keep their jobs. As a result, many employees feel unable to take advantage of work–life initiatives offered by their employer, and instead feel obligated to prioritize work over family or personal life, work long hours to enhance their visibility, and in short, *be* the ideal employee their employer prefers.

There are at least five dimensions of work–life culture that affect whether employees feel comfortable using work–life benefits: (1) managerial support for work–life balance; (2) perceptions of potential career consequences for participating in work–life programs; (3) perceptions of heavy time demands; (4) perceptions that work–life programs are primarily for women; and (5) co-worker support for using work–life programs (McDonald *et al.*, 2005; Thompson *et al.*, 1999; Thompson & Prottas, 2006). Although lack of managerial or supervisor support is probably the most immediate deterrent to participation, the other aspects of culture certainly create a dampening effect on program usage. If employees believe that participating in a flexible work hours program, for example, will threaten their chances for promotion, then it is unlikely that they will feel comfortable using the program. In fact, as described in Chapter 3, research shows that there are often negative career consequences associated with using various work–family programs, suggesting that their fears are not unfounded.

Similarly, when employees perceive that long hours are required to show one's dedication and commitment, even when long hours are not truly necessary to complete the work, they will be less likely to participate in any work–life program that reduces their visibility to management. Further, resentful co-workers, as well as employee perceptions that work–life programs are for women, make it difficult for men or career-minded women to participate. These and other barriers to program usage are described below.

Supervisors as gatekeepers

First-line supervisors are the gatekeepers to work–life programs. Without their support, it is very difficult for employees to take advantage of work–life programs sanctioned by the firm. In fact, recent research suggests that supervisor or managerial support is a major factor in employees' decisions to use work–life programs and benefits (Allen, 2001; Brewer, 2000; Thompson *et al.*, 1999).

For several reasons, supervisors may resist allowing their subordinates to participate (Lapierre & Allen, 2006; Thompson, Beauvais, & Allen, 2006). As discussed above, they may fear losing control over their employees, especially when the level of trust is low. More to the point, because many employees work in jobs that are difficult to measure, supervisors often rely on what they can observe the employee doing rather than what they produce. In addition, supervisors may resent the additional administrative work involved with work–life programs, work that often comes on top of an already heavy load. They may also resist allowing their subordinates to participate because they hold traditional views of how work and family should be separate, and because they believe that the only way to show commitment and dedication is for employees to be available at all times. Finally, supervisors may resist because they don't have the resources to support a subordinate who wants to telecommute, or the coverage needed if an employee wants to reduce his or her hours to part time.

In a study investigating factors that may influence whether employees use work–family programs and policies, researchers examined the social context of the work environment in a highly regarded global financial services institution (Blair-Loy & Wharton, 2002). The researchers found that the extent to which an employee's supervisor was powerful – they argued that men tend to be more powerful in most organizations – was predictive of employee use of flexibility policies, whereas employee need was not. They suggested that powerful supervisors may be able to protect employees from potentially negative career consequences often associated with using work–life benefits such as flextime or flexplace. Further, employees whose supervisors lack organizational power may have greater difficulty getting permission to take advantage of certain work–life programs.

Resentful co-workers

Unsupportive or resentful co-workers may discourage employees from using work–life programs (Parker & Allen, 2001; McDonald *et al.*, 2005; Rothhausen & Gonzales, 1998). In *The 1997 National Study of the Changing Workforce* (Bond, Galinsky & Swanberg, 1998), a representative survey of workers in the US, researchers found that 22 percent of American workers strongly agreed that they would resent family-friendly initiatives if they felt the initiatives did not benefit them personally. Further, 16.5 percent said they would resent having to do extra work occasionally to accommodate co-workers' personal or family-related needs. Resentful co-workers can make it very uncomfortable for employees to take advantage of work–life programs. At Marriot International, for example, managers used to tease other managers who left "early":

In the past, when someone left at five o'clock, a co-worker might remark, "working just a half day?" Such comments reinforced our culture of face time, and they certainly made people feel guilty about the time they put in. (Bill Munck, Vice-President and Market Manager for Marriot; Munck: 2001, p. 6)

Marriot implemented a pilot program called Management Flexibility and coupled it with strong messages about the need to change their culture of face time. They attempted to eliminate the assumption that managers had to be at the hotel for a certain number of hours rather than when they were needed. When not needed, according to Munck, managers were expected to go home and have a life.

Perception that work–life programs are for women only

Despite greater societal acceptance of women working, the belief continues to persist that women are (and should be) more committed to family than to work, and that men are (and should be) more committed to work than to family. As a result, family-supportive policies continue to be seen as policies primarily designed to "help" women (Lewis, 2001; McDonald *et al.*, 2005). This can make it difficult for career-minded women to use the policies as they may fear management will think of them as less serious about their careers, and it makes it doubly difficult for men because they not only worry about being perceived as uncommitted to their career, but also as being unmasculine (Pleck, 1993). As described by Lotte Bailyn, a professor at MIT who has had a tremendous impact on the field of work and family, separate role expectations for men and women are at the heart of how work and family issues are currently framed (Bailyn, 1993), and as such create a psychological barrier to usage for both women and men.

Encouraging men to use family-supportive benefits and openly participate in childrearing is an important step in overcoming the view that family issues are women's issues. Recent research conducted in Sweden found that men were more likely to use paternity leave when their performance was evaluated based on *results* rather than long hours at work and when the company was perceived as being committed to gender equality (Haas, Allard, & Hwang, 2002). In the US, Ernst & Young LLP is working to overcome the stigma associated with flexible work schedules, which had been viewed as an accommodation for women, by redefining the policy as a quality-of-life concern for everyone. They created an ad campaign highlighting successful men who had used flexible work arrangements (see Figure 8.2). Maryella Gockel, E&Y's flexibility-strategy leader, said that although the firm had a policy of flexibility, both women and men shied away from it because they feared it would hurt their career progress. She said the new campaign was designed to send the message that these programs are "gender neutral," so that more people would participate (Badal, 2006). Lehman Brothers has repackaged the issue by framing telecommuting as contingency planning for disaster. Lehman's chief diversity

Figure 8.2 In promotional materials, Ernst & Young LLP portrays men using flexible work options.

office, Anne Erni, is "committed to de-stigmatizing flex" schedules by describing them as gender neutral (Badal, 2006).

Perceived motives for offering work–life programs

There are several motives that an organization might have for offering work–life programs:

- to keep up with the competition;
- to improve recruiting and retention;

- for public relations, to increase likelihood that the company will be perceived as a caring organization, worthy of a "top 100" list of "family-friendly" companies;
- to accommodate employees' personal and family life needs so that they can achieve job-related goals without family interference;
- to facilitate the ability of employees to integrate or balance their work and family/personal lives so that employees feel valued and supported as people, rather than as employees only.

These five motives represent legitimate goals for any organization, although the first four may entail costs for the organization if not combined with the fifth. That is, if employees believe that work–life programs are offered only for the benefit of the organization rather than for the benefit of the employee, they may be less likely to trust the sincerity of the company's support. In addition, employees may erroneously believe that work–life programs are offered because they are required by law or government regulation, thus negating the possible goodwill motives of their employer (Prottas *et al.*, 2007).

To understand why perceived motives matter, social exchange theory from psychology is instructive (Eisenberger, Huntington, Hutchison, and Sowa, 1986). It teaches us that employees and employers are in an exchange relationship such that employers expect something back for a benefit given, and vice versa. That is, by giving employees benefits they desire (e.g. work–family programs), employees will perceive the organization as family-supportive and will reciprocate by putting forth more effort and by increasing their commitment to their employer (Thompson *et al.*, 2004). However, if employees believe that work–life programs are offered more for the benefit of the organization, they may feel less responsibility to "pay back" the organization through their greater commitment or hard work.

Most importantly, when career-minded employees do not trust their organization's motives for offering work–life programs, especially programs that involve reduced face time at work, they will most likely not want to participate for fear of jeopardizing the goodwill of their boss. Instead, they continue to work long hours to prove to their boss that they are committed to the organization and willing to do whatever it takes to succeed, thus nullifying the intended goals of the work–life initiatives.

Operational problems

Even when employees are enthusiastic about work–life programs (e.g. telecommuting from home), inadequate technological infrastructure can dampen their commitment to the new arrangement. For example, in one consulting firm employees complained of slow modem speed, inadequate software and hardware support, and inadequate teleconferencing support (Nord *et al.*, 2002). Others complained of inadequate technical support:

For the first six months, I was on the phone with our help desk, working to get access at least once per week – usually on the weekends, and the phone calls lasted sometimes four hours … It has been frustrating. (Nord *et al.*, 2002, p. 228).

In contrast, one large international corporation implemented a "follow-the-sun" system of on-call computer support for its employees throughout the world. At any time and in any time zone, employees can call for computer support and receive help from someone who is in their zone, alert, and wide awake (Lewis & Cooper, 2005).

Task interdependence and the design of work

When individuals in work groups are highly dependent on one another to get their jobs done, they may be less likely to support the use of work–life programs that reduce their ability to meet face-to-face (e.g. telecommuting). For example, an employee who must constantly interact with a large number of co-workers to get the job done may find that co-workers are impatient or downright hostile when the employee is not at the worksite for impromptu meetings. Certainly, co-workers are more likely to be supportive of a telecommuting employee who has only occasional task-related interactions with co-workers, rather than one who must constantly interact with a large number of co-workers to get the job done (Thompson, Andreassi, & Prottas, 2005). However, even in the former case, it is often unexamined assumptions about how work should be performed that creates the tension. At Xerox Corporation, for example, engineers in a product development team felt that interrupting their co-workers was a necessary and acceptable way of working, despite the long hours of work that resulted. In fact, the culture supported constant interruptions to the detriment of the

Table 8.1. *Checklist for program planners*

To avoid barriers at the planning and implementation stages

__ Conduct interviews and focus groups to examine underlying assumptions about:
  • what it takes to succeed.
  • what an "ideal employee" looks like.
  • the importance of face time.

__ Examine additional assumptions and fears that may interfere with managers' support for work–life initiatives:
  • fears of change in power balance?
  • fears of increased workload?

__ Examine CEO and top management's understanding of and attitudes towards the issue of work–life balance.

__ Conduct a needs assessment to determine the root cause of work–life imbalance:
  • unpredictability of work?
  • unreasonable workloads?
  • jobs with unnecessary but time-consuming tasks?
  • reliance on face time to evaluate performance?
  • lack of trust between supervisors and employees?

__ Conduct a needs assessment to determine specific needs of employees:
  • how many need help with childcare? elder care?
  • how many would like to work reduced hours?

__ Examine the fit of the new programs with existing human resources and management systems:
  • how should work be distributed?
  • how will performance be appraised?
  • do career paths and promotion criteria need to be changed?

__ Consider eligibility issues:
  • who will be eligible?
  • which jobs are amenable to participation?
  • are the selection criteria fair?

__ Determine what technology and infrastructure are necessary.

__ Determine best way to disseminate information about the new programs to employees, managers, and, if relevant, clients or customers.

__ Train supervisors and managers on the value of the work–life programs, how to implement the programs in their department, how to choose participants, etc.

To avoid barriers to program usage

__ Continually make the case for the value of work–life programs.

__ Monitor employee perceptions of how supportive the work culture is for balancing work and life (e.g. survey employees).

Table 8.1. *(cont.)*

___ Examine co-worker support for the work–life initiatives; monitor
resentment.
___ Provide training to supervisors and employees on how to use the new
programs.
___ Ensure adequate technology; solicit feedback from program users and
managers on difficulties using the program.
___ Evaluate initiatives, modify, and enhance as necessary.

employees' lives outside of work. With the help of researchers, managers
at Xerox Corporation confronted the underlying assumptions about
work and helped interdependent groups restructure their work to
allow for periods of quiet, uninterrupted work time. As a result, the
team was able to achieve its first on-time launch of a new product
(Lewis & Cooper, 2005; Perlow, 1997).

Bottom line: determine the root cause of work–life imbalance

The underlying barrier to the success of work–life initiatives is that they
often do not solve the root cause of employee work–life imbalance. To
be sure, employees who have access to certain work–life initiatives like
flexible work arrangements or flexplace tend to experience less conflict
between their jobs and family lives (Bond *et al.* 2003). But offering
these initiatives does not change the underlying structure of how work
is organized or executed, and does not change the underlying culture.
Flexible work hours may help employees manage the demands of work
and family, but do not change the total number of hours required,
unpredictability in work routines, unsupportive managers, last-minute
overtime demands, unreasonable workloads, etc. Work–life programs
make organizations look family-friendly without requiring them to consider deeper, more fundamental changes – how jobs are designed, how
work is coordinated, and how organizational rewards are determined
(Rapoport *et al.*, 2002; Thompson, 2005; Thompson *et al.*, 2005).

Conclusion

Although organizations spend time, money, and energy developing
and implementing work–life programs, low usage rates suggest that

employees do not need the programs, or do not use them for fear of career suicide or because their manager or the culture does not support the legitimacy of the programs. Given the increasing demands we place on our employees as well as their perceived need to protect their jobs by doing whatever it takes to get the job done, many employees experience overload, conflict, and burnout. As such, it seems unlikely that the programs are unnecessary. What is more likely is that the organization's culture does not support their use, and as a result, neither the organization nor the employee benefits from the much heralded work–life programs.

References

Allen, T. (2001). Family supportive work environments: The role of organizational perceptions. *Journal of Vocational Behavior*, 58, 414–435.

Allen, T. D. & Russell, J. E. A. (1999). Parental leave of absence: Some not so family friendly implications. *Journal of Applied Social Psychology*, 29, 166–191.

Badal, J. (2006). To retain valued women employees, companies pitch flextime as macho. *The Wall Street Journal Online*, p. B1, December.

Bailyn, L. (1993). *Breaking the Mold: Women, Men, and Time in the New Corporate World*. New York: Free Press.

Bailyn, L. & Fletcher, J. K. (1997). Unexpected connections: Considering employees' personal lives can revitalize your business. *Sloan Management Review*, 38, 11–19.

Blair-Loy, M. & Wharton, A. (2002). Employees' use of work–family policies and the workplace social context. *Social Forces*, 80(3), 813–845.

Bond, J. T., Galinsky, E., & Swanberg, J. E. (1998). *The 1997 National Study of the Changing Workforce* (Vol. 2). New York: Families and Work Institute.

Bond, J. T., Thompson, C. A., Galinsky, E., & Prottas, D. (2003). *Highlights of the 2002 National Study of the Changing Workforce*. New York: Families and Work Institute.

Brewer, A. M. (2000). Work design for flexible work scheduling: Barriers and gender implications. *Gender, Work and Organization*, 7, 33–44.

Chinchilla, N., Poelmans, S., Leon, C. & Tarres, J. (2004). Guía de buenas prácticas de la empresa flexible. Hacia la conciliación de la vida laboral, familiar y personal. www.iese.edu/icwf.

Cleveland, J. (2005). What is success? Who defines it? Perspectives on the criterion problem as it relates to work and family. In E. E. Kossek & S. Lambert (eds), *Work and Life Integration: Organizational, Cultural, and Individual Perspectives* (pp. 319–346). Mahwah, NJ: Lawrence Erlbaum Associates.

Corporate Voices for Working Families (2005). *Business Impacts of Flexibility: An Imperative for Expansion.* Washington, DC: Corporate Voices for Working Families.

Eby, L. T., Casper, W. J., Lockwood, A., Bordeaux, C., & Brinley, A. (2004). Work and family research in IO/OB: Content analysis and review of the literature (1980–2002). *Journal of Vocational Behavior, 66(1),* 124–197.

Eisenberger, R. Armeli, S., Rexwinkel, B., Lynch, P. D., & Rhoades, L. (2001). Reciprocation of perceived organizational support. *Journal of Applied Psychology, 86, 42–51.*

Ertel, M. & Pech, E. (2006). Success factors of teleworking in the public sector. Paper presented at the Sixth International Conference on Occupational Stress and Health, Miami, Florida, March.

Frankel, M. (1998). Creating the family-friendly workplace: Barriers and solutions. In S. Klarreich (ed.), *Handbook of Organizational Health Psychology: Programs to Make the Workplace Healthier.* Madison, CT: Psychosocial Press.

Friedman, S., Thompson, C., Carpenter, M., & Marcel, D. (2001). Proving Leo Durocher wrong: Driving work/life change at Ernst & Young. A Wharton Work/Life Integration Project (http://wfnetwork.bc.edu/template.php?name=casestudy_wharton).

Haas, L., Allard, K., & Hwang, P. (2002). The impact of organizational culture on men's use of parental leave in Sweden. *Community, Work and Family, 5,* 319–342.

Haines, V. Y., St-Onge, S., & Archambault, M. (2002). Environmental and personal antecedents of telecommuting outcomes. *Journal of End User Computing, 14,* 32–50.

Hyman, J. & Summes, J. (2004). Lacking balance? Work–life employment practices in the modern economy. *Personnel Review, 33,* 418–428.

Kofodimos, J. R. (1995). *Beyond Work–Family Programs: Confronting and Resolving the Underlying Causes of Work–Personal Life Conflict.* Greensboro, NC: Center for Creative Leadership.

Konrad, A. M. & Mangel, R. (2000). The impact of work–life programs on firm productivity. *Strategic Management Journal, 21,* 1225–1237.

Kruger, P. (2000). Jobs for life. *Fast Company,* May, p. 236.

Lapierre, L. M. & Allen, T. D. (2006). Work-supportive family, family-supportive supervision, use of organizational benefits, and problem-focused coping: Implications for work–family conflict and employee well-being. *Journal of Occupational Health Psychology, 11,* 169–181.

Lewis, S. (1997). "Family-friendly" employment policies: A route to changing organizational culture or playing around at the margins? *Gender, Work & Organisation*, 4, 13–23.

Lewis, S. (2001). Restructuring workplace cultures: The ultimate work–family challenge? *Women in Management Review*, 16, 21–29.

Lewis, S. & Cooper, C. (2005). *Work–life Integration: Case Studies of Organizational Change*. Chichester: John Wiley & Sons.

McDonald, P., Brown, K., & Bradley, L. (2005). Explanations for the provision–utilization gap in work–life policy. *Women in Management Review*, 20, 37–55.

Munck, B. (2001). Changing a culture of face time. *Harvard Business Review*.

Nord, W. R., S. Fox, A. Phoenix, & K. Viano (2002). Real-world reactions to work–life balance programs: Lessons for effective implementation. *Organizational Dynamics*, 30, 223–238.

Parker, L. & Allen, T. D. (2001). Work/family benefits: Variables related to employees' fairness perceptions. *Journal of Vocational Behavior*, 58, 453–468.

Perlow, L. A. (1997). *Finding Time: How Corporations, Individuals, and Families can Benefit from New Work Practices*. Ithaca, NY: Cornell University Press.

Perry-Smith, J. E. & Blum, T. C. (2000). Work–family human resource bundles and perceived organizational performance. *Academy of Management Journal*, 43, 1107–1117.

Pleck, J. H. (1993). Are "family-supportive" employer policies relevant to men? In J. C. Hood (ed.), *Men, Work, and Family* (pp. 217–237). Newbury Park, CA: Sage.

Poelmans, S., Chinchilla, M. N., & Cardona, P. (2003). The adoption of family-friendly HRM policies. *International Journal of Manpower*, 24, 128–147.

Poelmans, S. & Sahibzada, K. (2004). A multi-level model for studying the context and impact of work–family policies and culture in organizations. *Human Resource Management Review*, 14, 409–431.

Prottas, D. J., Thompson, C. A., Kopelman, R. E., & Jahn, E. W. (2007). Factors affecting employee knowledge of work–family programs. *Personnel Review*, 36, 163–189.

Rapoport, R., Bailyn, L, Fletcher, J., & Pruitt, B. (2002). *Beyond Work–Family Balance: Advancing Gender Equity and Workplace Performance*. San Francisco: Jossey-Bass.

Rothhausen, T. & Gonzales, J. (1998). Family-friendly backlash – Fact or fiction? The case of organizations' on-site childcare centers. *Personnel Psychology*, 51, 685–707.

Schein, E. H. (1992). *Organizational Culture and Leadership: A Dynamic View*. San Francisco: Jossey-Bass.

Shain, M. (2005) Benchmarking the psychosocial environment. *Journal of Employee Assistance*, 34, 32–33.

Simon, R. W. (1995). Gender, multiple roles, role meaning, and mental health. *Journal of Health and Social Behavior*, 26, 182–194.

Thompson, C. A. (2005). Work–life balance? Organizations in denial. *Journal of Employee Assistance*, 35, 2, 7–9.

Thompson, C. A., Andreassi, J., & Prottas, D. (2005). Work–family culture: Key to reducing workforce-workplace mismatch? In Bianchi, S. M., Casper, L. M., Christensen, K. E., & Berkowitz King, R. (eds), *Workforce/Workplace Mismatch? Work, Family, Health and Well-being*. Mahwah, NJ: Lawrence Erlbaum.

Thompson, C. A., Beauvais, L. L., & Allen, T. (2006). Work–life balance: An industrial-organizational psychology perspective. In Pitt-Catsouphes, M., Kossek, E., & Sweet, S. (eds), *Work–Family Handbook*. Mahwah, NJ: Lawrence Erlbaum.

Thompson, C. A., Beauvais, L. L., & Lyness, K. S. (1999). When work–family benefits are not enough: The influence of work–family culture on benefit utilization, organizational attachment, and work–family conflict. *Journal of Vocational Behavior*, 54, 392–415.

Thompson, C. A. Jahn, E. W., Kopelman, R., & Prottas, D. (2004). The impact of perceived organizational and supervisory family support on affective commitment: A longitudinal and multi-level analysis. *Journal of Managerial Issues*, 16, 545–567.

Thompson, C. A. & Prottas, D. J. (2006). Relationship among organizational family support, job autonomy, perceived control, and employee well-being. *Journal of Occupational Health Psychology*, 11, 100–118.

Williams, J. (2000). *Unbending Gender: Why Family and Work Conflict and What to Do About It*. New York: Oxford University Press.

9 How to become a family-responsible firm: proposing a model for cultural change

STEVEN A. Y. POELMANS and
OLENA STEPANOVA
IESE Business School, Spain

The previous chapters described different work–family policies used in companies in various contexts, the sources of resistance among employees that can arise when applying them, and the overall difficulties experienced when trying to introduce work–life balance. Therefore, an important question remains: *How* to introduce these practices in a successful way.

In today's world of growing competition and strife for occupying new markets, companies are facing various challenges, and in order to deal with them a sustainable advantage is needed – skillful and capable employees (Causon, 2004; Deloitte, 2005). The life of employees is also full of challenges: juggling personal and professional lives, and having interests besides work to which they want to devote time (continuing education, involvement in the community, hobbies, etc.) (Tombari & Spinks, 1999; Peper, 2005). Therefore, in order for the company to profit from the knowledge and skills offered by its employees, it has to create the environment for it and attend to their needs (Doorewaard & Benschop, 2003).

According to the literature, successful work–personal life integration is attained if it is regarded as a strategy by the company and not as a temporary solution for existing problems. The dual agenda approach (Rapoport, Bailyn, Fletcher, & Pruitt, 2002; Lewis & Cooper, 2005) further suggests that this strategy should be designed as a benefit for both the company and its employees. As these cases show, successful implementation of work–life practices takes place when the employer aims to improve the business situation and not when he is driven by the desire of ameliorating the life of its employees. The business situation can be improved through the work–personal life integration strategy. It gives employees the possibility of exploring together work inconveniences (e.g. fixed starting/finishing time, long working hours, etc.), underlying assumptions causing them, and the chance to design working conditions that meet their personal needs as well as their company's one. Nevertheless, proclaiming new policies and practices does not lead to their usage and achievement of the expected results, as discussed in Chapter 8. For change to occur, a company should undergo all the steps of the change process.

The purpose of this chapter is to propose a *model for cultural change*, which aims at achieving work–personal life integration that would satisfy both the employees' and company's needs. In contrast to the policy design and implementation described in Chapter 6, the emphasis in this chapter switches from top down to *bottom up communication*.

We begin the chapter by introducing the main concepts that support the process of cultural change. We then give an overview of what impacts the process of change and describe the existing models of cultural change. By addressing employees' assumptions regarding work–life balance, fears towards innovations, existing values, myths, and practices, and by working with resistance, we build a model for cultural change based on the Collaborative Interactive Action Research (CIAR) approach, explained below. To conclude, we stress the importance of working continually on change and provide some examples of practices to sustain the implemented changes.

Cultural change

Culture is defined by Schein (1997, p. 12) as "the pattern of basic assumptions that the group learned as it solved its problems of external adaptation and internal integration, and that have worked well enough to be considered valid and, therefore, to be taught to new members as the correct way to perceive, think, and feel in relation to those problems." In other words *organizational culture* can be defined through its values and behaviors that reflect how these values are recreated. Schein produced a set of categories to describe culture reflecting these two components (Molton Reger, 2006). Among them are: *observed behavioral regularities* when people interact (which includes language, customs, and traditions); *expressed group norms*; and *espoused values* – publicly announced principles that the group wants to achieve. Furthermore, the organizational culture can be defined through the formal philosophy – the ideological principles of the organization – as well as the implicit rules that support one's integration into the company. The climate, embedded skills, habits of thinking, mental models, and linguistic paradigms, which are transmitted from generation to generation, constitute the behavioral manifestation of cultures. Finally, during its life, a group creates shared meanings, formal rituals, and celebrations. We can think for example of the ritual of birthday and season holiday celebrations.

Cultural change is different from other organizational changes because the attention shifts from the structures and systems of an organization to the employees. "The shared beliefs, values and behaviours of organizational members become the target of the change process" (Waterhouse & Lewis, 2004, p. 354; Lewis, 1996). Therefore it requires leaders and employees to think differently about their work, thus changing their mindset.

The process of change can be described best by answering the following questions: what, why, who, and how? (Lewis & Cooper, 2005). In each organization the *focus* (*what?*) of change is different depending on the problems, needs, and characteristics of the organization. In this chapter, the focus is placed on the working practices that aim to accommodate both work and family demands.

The *reasons* for change (*why?*) are the modern world demands, the nature of the workforce, and working practices that impede the work–personal life integration. "For organizations to be motivated to change, however, there has to be recognition of a specific business-related problem" (Lewis & Cooper, 2005, p. 19). For example, a high staff turnover may either lead to the need of recruiting and retaining talented employees or run the risk of the company losing know-how. The tie between talent and financial results is a contemporary issue. As today's world faces the aging of the population and the decrease of births, companies no longer profit from the wide range of professionals to fill their ranks. The Deloitte study of talent management conducted globally (among 1,396 organizations in over sixty countries) showed that the discovery, attraction, and development of talented employees is critical for ensuring organizational performance (Deloitte, 2005). The practices that have been used in the past (like monetary incentives) no longer apply as strongly to the new setting and do not contribute to the resolution of the problem. Thus a solution to these issues needs to be sought.

The *agents* of change (*who?*) can be internal (managing directors, human resource (HR) officers, the workers themselves) or external to the company (external consultants helping in making the change). There are varying opinions about employing external consultants/researchers. The advantages of utilizing external resources are that they perceive better the different assumptions, values, and myths circulating in the company and they are more objective. They have an easier time asking questions since they ignore which topics are labeled as taboo within the company. On the other hand, the fact of not belonging to the power structure of the company might create barriers to introducing change as the decision-making is in somebody else's hands.

The change can be led by the HR department, which can be effective if it has power to make change. "But often, the change agent in HR lacks position power and is perceived as pursuing people issues rather than both people and strategic business issues" (Lewis & Cooper, 2005, p. 19).

An example of using an external agent is Printco, a small non-unionized company based in central England that manufactures labels and nameplates using screen printing, engraving, and vinyl graphics (Lewis & Cooper, 2005). This company was headed towards bankruptcy and needed urgent changes. The new managing director hired outside of the printing industry, had a fresh view of the existing situation, and promoted change.

There is also an option of combining both possibilities: HR and external agents. In the case of IBM, the internal professional research staff conducted the study of work and family issues (Kraut, 1990). Additionally, the IBM staff became closely involved by including a dozen employees into a so-called *steering committee*. They were responsible for bringing information on topics that would be useful to research, giving feedback on the drafts of the survey, reviewing the data analysis, and conducting special analysis on topics that would serve their needs.

According to Covin and Kilmann (1990), in order for change to be effective, management, and not external consultants, should be responsible for the process of change. Consequently, the change agents should be carefully chosen as a function of the unique situation of each firm. Nevertheless, as studies suggest, a certain amount of external help may provide significant insights and experience to help avoid the pitfalls and wasted resources.

An important point to take into consideration in the change process is the source of financing. Externally funded change agents like academics and governmental consultants tend to be more independent from the organization's influence and agendas. Moreover, the company might be more receptive to change implementation, since it does not represent any cost effect (Lewis & Cooper, 2005).

The question of *how?* to bring change will be described in the part devoted to the cultural change model.

To summarize, the process of change consists of the following *parts*:

- focus of change (what?): working practices, nature of workforce, etc.;
- reasons for change (why?): difficulties faced by the organization – current and future/perceived;
- agents of change (who?): internal and external to the company;
- process of change (how?).

What nourishes cultural change?

As with any complex process, cultural change encompasses several elements, which are essential for a successful outcome: communication, trust, collaboration, predictability of the change process, consistency, and climate of innovation.

Several authors consider *communication* as one of the vital instruments for implementing change (Waterhouse & Lewis, 2004; Lewis 1992; Putnam 1999). Communication is used throughout the stages of change: assessment of the situation, design and implementation of strategy, and finally feedback to determine effectiveness. In other words, communication is a way of preparing and shaping the change process as talk and action are hard to separate (Fairclough, 1992; Watson, 1994; Cameron, 2004). It helps to create a shared meaning for the action taken, part of which implies going through negotiation and conflict phases (Ford & Ford, 1995). A shared meaning is created when people adopt a common language and understanding of decisions that need to be taken in order to create change and achieve desired results (Ford & Ford, 1995). In the process of change, communication should be used as a fair tool of expression, meaning that the employees should not only be allowed, but also encouraged to state their opinions and share experiences. It should be a two-way interchange, a dialogue. Thus, it will also support the necessary change in mindset, such as perceiving employees as representing a collective knowledge rather than possessing trivial opinions. At one company with a "command and control" management style, junior-level employees were excluded from the design of change and the strategy implementation stage, which resulted in the emergence of various negative beliefs about the project and created barriers for brainstorming and further progress on change (Francis, 2003).

Communication is not only used for realizing the change process, but also for informing employees about the process of transformation, and for persuading both management and employees of its importance and usefulness for the company (Cameron, 2004). As one executive noted, when speaking about getting employees involved in the research project: "If you get them in the boat with you, they are less likely to try to sink it!" (Kraut, 1990, p. 116).

Based on the example of the IT staff at one company, Doorewaard and Benschop (2003) underline the importance of communication. They state that if the IT staff (which can be applied to the staff in any other industry) is able to understand the needs of the users and communicate with them, this will contribute to their work and to the whole project. In the same way, if the company is eager to learn about the needs of its employees and satisfy them, both sides will profit. "Research has shown that employees who feel their organizations care about them and their ability to balance work and family demands (e.g. supportive supervisors, part-time, or flextime work) have higher affective commitment, lower work–family conflict, and lower intentions to quit" (Forret and de Janasz, 2005, p. 479).

A possible way of establishing a two-way communication is the emerging broad-based participative techniques, such as IBM's Jam approach (Hemp & Stewart, 2004). IBM conducted a 72-hour experiment during which it proposed its employees discuss the company's values on the intranet. As the organization was going through a top-to-bottom review of its management strategies it was essential for the top management to have an insight into employees' perception of the organization.

Trust is critical for the usage of communication and as an instrument for change. If employees trust each other, they will be able to share much more information and experiences and will be less likely to restrict their behavior and expression. As stated by Bailyn, Rayman,

Bengtsen, Carré, and Tierney (2001), during the change process at Fleet Financial Group the main problem encountered was a lack of trust. The employees were suspicious of change due to the fact that they did not trust the good intentions of the managers and did not believe that the changes would not be used against them. In order to build trust, management had to emphasize the importance of the project's success. They allocated a certain amount of time during the work day to the project, so that no personal time of the employees was used. In this way workers would not think that it was an unimportant project and it did not demand time from them after work. If the employer behaves with respect and commitment towards the employees and their needs, the latter will also tend to reciprocate (Stavrou, 2005). In this manner, in organizational cultures which display and promote family-supportive policies, employees tend to be more confident of using them. They trust the initiatives taken by management without the fear of their negatively affecting their career. In return they manage their workload more effectively (van Doorne-Huiskes, den Dulk, & Peper, 2005). It should be noted that trust can be easily eroded by poor actions and therefore consistency is vital for the change process.

In the case of the Customer Administration Site in Xerox Corporation, though the company has had a range of work–personal life policies available, management was not eager to allow their usage, fearing that it would mean a drop in productivity (Lewis & Cooper, 2005). In other words, management adhered to the opinion that productivity was more important than these policies. While juggling personal life and work, the staff, comprised mainly of women, responded to the restrictions by taking sick leaves and vacations. This resulted in situations of insufficient work coverage. Once this pattern was discovered, management made work–life policies available to everybody and through team-work, more suggestions were made for meeting professional and personal needs. Consequently, the company changed its mindset, as it became clear that work practices were in conflict with the offered policies and therefore neither work–life initiatives nor productivity aspirations could be reached successfully.

Trust is essential for *collaboration* as well: personal information and experience can be shared only in an environment that disposes to doing so (Forret & de Janasz, 2005). For a fruitful collaboration, trust needs to be bilateral. Management should be able to listen to the suggestions of employees, take their ideas seriously and provide them with a sense of ownership of the change project (Bailyn *et al.*, 2001). In the case of Printco, employees were eager to enroll into the change process since they appreciated that their opinion was asked and that they could make a contribution to prevent the company from going bankrupt. Employees were encouraged to think about honest and mutually beneficial solutions. If they were continually not working their scheduled shifts, the manager would ask if there was a need of renegotiating hours or ask how else the person would make them up. As in the case of one worker who was absent in the morning, the manager asked for the reasons and he confessed to having had a hangover. They agreed that being paid for this was not fair. The manager suggested making up the hours over the following two weeks, which was also fair from the employee's point of view. As noted in the case of Fleet Financial Group (Bailyn *et al.*, 2001 p. 55), "The tool kit we use is really nothing more than common sense and people's ideas. That's the power, and you don't need lots of dollars in order to implement it." This power of collaborative work gives results and unites people.

Predictability is another important factor in the change process. "By making behavior predictable, cultural norms also prepare individuals to cope with the *unpredictable*, making them more adaptable to change than if they were to follow only specified rules" (Phelan, 2005, p. 53). Predictability also refers to a set vision for the change. If the company knows what it wants to achieve by the process of change (e.g. to create a new vision, a new workplace, a more family-friendly environment), then it knows where it is headed.

In the study of working mothers employed at a large Australian university, women were offered part-time work possibilities and management was flexible about their time. However, there existed an agreement that during peak times they would work extra hours. In this situation, both the company and the employees were flexible and aware that change would benefit both of them. This agreement could not be possible without the existing trust and collaboration between them (McDonald, Guthrie, Bradley, & Shakespeare-Finch, 2005). As an example, a woman working part-time stated:

I sometimes don't come in till 9.30 or if my child is sick or can I have this week off in the school holidays, or can I change my days because I want to go on an excursion on Friday, I really don't have a problem.

I think that's individual management as well. They respect that I am going to do the work whether I'm there on Wednesday or on Friday and that I'm going to get it done and I'm going to do a good job of it. (McDonald *et al.*, 2005, p. 486)

The absence of predictability of approaching events or tasks might create stress. Studies show that employees who do not suffer stress show better results, have a better relationship with their co-workers, and are more open for communication (Bailyn *et al.*, 2001). The nature of the job is not the index for stress, rather the fact of whether employees believe in their control over various aspects of their work or not. The feeling of losing or having no control leads to stress. The availability of flexible work arrangements diminishes stress and increases employees' commitment (Halpern, 2005).

Once the change is initiated, the company management needs to show *consistency* in aligning the desired and the existing values and in making sure the work–personal life policies are indeed well implemented. There needs to be coherence in the messages which are communicated and practices that are brought into place, otherwise the change initiative might not be successful. This is what happened in the Department of Main Roads, a large state government department in Queensland, Australia. The objective of moving to a state of change in the company failed:

due to a failure to address lower-level staff's need for a set vision and future direction, their perceptions of weaknesses in transformational leadership, inconsistencies and impreciseness in messages, a gap between messages and action and lack of communication between different areas of the department and with external stakeholders. (Waterhouse and Lewis, 2004, p. 355)

A *climate of innovation* is another key success factor for change. An emphasis placed on work–family issues can foster employees' involvement, motivation, and *creativity*. The company which creates an environment, which empowers employees, giving them the possibility to make a difference in their lives as well as in their organization, and which listens to the ideas expressed, receives a valuable input (Causon, 2004). In the case of Energyco, a large international industrial corporation in one of the Nordic countries, the articulation of *flexible work forms* resulted from creative thinking on flexibility. As a consequence the so-called "follow-the-sun" concept was introduced (Lewis & Cooper, 2005). In order to provide all employees with the best PC service, the Information Services Division introduced three IT-support offices, in the home country, the USA, and the Far East. In this way, any employee, regardless of location, could receive the services around the clock. It should be noted that these changes were possible because of the company's vision that managers should encourage discussions on existing practices and support innovations.

At Printco (Lewis & Cooper, 2005), employees were encouraged to express their ideas, experiment, and show creativity. They were trusted to make agreements among themselves that would accommodate their needs. For instance, when an employee in the print department wanted to change working hours, this was made possible by redesigning work. By focusing on preparatory work aimed at providing the printers with everything needed to ensure continuity, one woman was able to change from a five- to a four-day working week.

The management at Printco was also innovative. The new management director realized that some employees were working longer hours in order to receive payment for the extra time. He made a deal with them: if they were able to finish their work in thirty-nine hours, they would get paid for forty-five hours. Consequently it was emphasized that employees received pay for what was achieved during working hours (productivity and not just actual time physically at work). From the company's side, it reserved the right to call on these employees in case it needed these six hours. As the managing director commented: "We actually make a saving because we don't actually have to have anyone in on a Saturday morning and pay the lighting bill for it" (Lewis & Cooper, 2005, p. 81).

Covin and Kilmann (1990) conducted a survey among managers, consultants, and researchers aimed at finding out issues that positively or negatively influence the process of change. The content analysis of over 900 topics uncovered several issues. The process of change is influenced positively by management support, involvement, and their ability to act as role models; a careful preparation of change based on a thorough assessment of the organization, its needs and issues; participation of the employees, greater freedom of planning of their time; intense communication; a salient business need ("The more the program was directly tied to clear and well-understood business needs, the better" (p. 237)); and a reward system supporting the process of change.

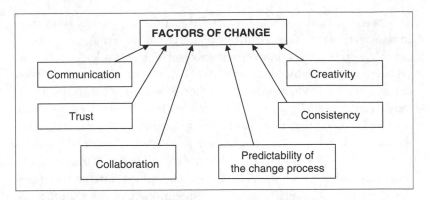

Figure 9.1 Factors of change.

The negative issues mentioned included a lack of consistency among managers' actions, wrongly set expectations, poor communication, and the absence of a clear end date of the program. These issues support the previously mentioned concepts that nourish cultural change and underline their importance.

Therefore, the change process, being complex, consists of several elements, which "nourish" or influence the successful outcome (as shown in Figure 9.1).

Models of change

Once the questions of "what" and "why" are answered, and the factors that nourish change are established, the next step for the change process is answering the "how" question. For this, we can rely on several models of change in the literature. Early models focused on the role of managers as the drivers of change. More than forty years ago, Likert (1961) suggested a "supportive model" of change, where change was viewed as a result of collaboration between the leader and the employees. From this perspective, cultural change occurs in a slow, non-forced way, under the guidance of a leader (Waterhouse & Lewis, 2004). In recent literature, there are descriptions of several models/steps of cultural change that further emphasize the idea of collaboration between management and employees. For example, Royal Bank Financial Group designed a program of "organizational work–life continuum" (Tombari & Spinks, 1999). It represents a five-stage model describing the development of an organization from an inactive state (disregarding the needs of its employees) to an interactive one (the executives not only implement work–life solutions in their companies by using employees' input, but also work on their design and introduction with other employers). Kropf (1999) introduced a model based on company goals to achieve change (build organizational support, support managers and employees, internalize the practice, sustain the commitment), which is illustrated by cases from Bank of Montreal and Deloitte & Touche. Another model proposed by Rapoport *et al.* (2002) is Collaborative Interactive Action Research (CIAR). Finally, the above-mentioned positive factors for successful organizational change introduced by Covin and Kilmann (1990), though not being a model itself, describe crucial issues to drive change.

These models have many common points. The company experiences a certain problem, which needs to be resolved. In order to do so, the consent for action from top management is necessary. Once obtained, a thorough analysis of the problems and needs of the company is carried out. Based on the results, new practices and policies are designed and implemented, often with intense collaboration between the researchers/consultants and the employees. Finally, the results of the implemented practices are measured. All models underline the importance of communication throughout the organization as well as the active participation of employees in the change process.

For this chapter, we have chosen the Collaborative Interactive Action Research approach as the basis for the proposed model of cultural change. This choice is explained by the fact that it is a comprehensive model, which includes significant issues for the change process described above. At the core of this research lies the concept of the *dual agenda*. "The dual agenda approach has two goals in mind at all times – increasing (or at least not harming) work productivity or efficiency and enhancing personal life, including gender equity. It connects humanistic values with facilitating people to work more effectively, thus linking the integration of personal life and the workplace" (Lewis & Rapoport, 2005, p. 302). It aims at increasing work effectiveness, which would allow employees to have more personal quality time. This vision coincides with our perception of change – as a way of benefiting both the employees and the company. In other words the beneficiation of both employees and the company creates a self-reinforcing "system," which helps to sustain the change and moreover can be improved over time as employees will be attracted to work in a company valuing their work–life balance. The emphasis on the concept of gender equity implies that the work situation of both women and men needs to be improved. For instance, women may gain equal access to management positions on the condition that they sacrifice their family lives. In this concept, gender equity involves equal career opportunities *for both men and women* who seek fulfilment through commitments in *both work and personal life* (equal to those who assign a central and dominant role to work in their lives) (Rapoport *et al.*, 2002). Gender equity also acknowledges the diverse ways of working, recognizing and rewarding the full range of skills and contributions of workers to the organization's success.

The CIAR method has been tested in several major companies, like Xerox Corporation, the Body Shop International, Hewlett Packard/Agilent Technologies (Rapoport *et al.*, 2002) and various non-governmental organizations. We would like to underline that the CIAR method differs from consultancy by the fact that it assumes mutual learning of the company and the researchers, while consultancy provides solutions to existing problems (Lewis & Cooper, 2005). In the CIAR approach the researcher represents an agent of change, since it is believed that he or she can bring a new outlook into the company and its practices. However, the employees play an active role and are empowered so that they can appropriate the change process.

In order to initiate change, the researcher works with existing beliefs and assumptions about work. Reflecting on these issues proves to be fruitful because the mindset shift gives the possibility to challenge the existing norms and consider different ways of working.

Rapoport *et al.* (2002) identified four categories constructed out of work norms mentioned by employees at different companies as possible areas of change. They encompass the following:

(1) *Use and politics of time*: e.g. it includes organizational cultures with long working hours with an important aspect of employees being visible at their working place;
(2) *Image of top performers*: e.g. organizations consider top performers as those employees who can invest many hours into work, being fully committed to it, and not taking into account other responsibilities;

(3) *Beliefs about real work*: e.g. in one organization this norm was reflected as being very complacent towards the clients, being always there for them, and not disturbing them even if additional information was needed;

(4) *Beliefs about hierarchy and control*: e.g. a firm where it was considered that unless controlled, employees would not work as expected. Therefore managers showed little trust and exercised a lot of control.

The authors recommend discussing these assumptions as a first step in initiating changes in supervisors' and employees' mindsets.

Right vs. Right approach

A way of addressing change in the above-mentioned areas can be the Right vs. Right approach, created by IBM (Moulton Reger, 2006). Due to the acquisition of PwCC by IBM, an integrated Consulting Business Unit was created and so there was a need to establish a new culture to unite both organizations. Despite the multiple guidelines developed to facilitate the process, conflicts remained during the integration process of the companies. The Right vs. Right approach emerged as an answer to the situation.

During a merger or an acquisition, management need to develop new guiding principles that will be used throughout the company. They can include: *customers are our top priority*; *we deliver our commitments, acting with integrity at all times*; *speed of execution is a key priority*, and so on (Moulton Reger, 2006, p. 69). Often there is an inherent conflict in "how" to do this. The conflict might not be evident to executives but appears in the day-to-day operations. The following illustration of the principle "customers are our top priority" best describes the existing conflicts – which represent different existing business practices. Company A sees it as a need to deliver certain services required by the customer, even if a customized solution has to be created. On the other hand, Company B, centered on standardization, focuses on providing the best quality and low-cost services, by helping the customer choose from a menu of options. Both companies are right when following the principle; still a choice needs to be taken or the conflicts may cause delays, strife, and eroded business results.

Table 9.1. *The Right vs. Right approach: five-point uneven scale*

1	2	3	4	5
100%	99%–51%	50% / 50%	51%–99%	100%
The option to the left is always the answer	The answer is the left-hand option most of the time	The answers on the left and right are equally split	The answer is the right-hand option most of the time	The option to the right is always the answer

The Right vs. Right approach was designed to help reconcile these dilemmas, raise realistic solutions, and make the decision-making process more flexible (Moulton Reger, 2006). The Right vs. Right five-point uneven scale was introduced to put away precisions, leading to misunderstandings and rigid choices, and assure an answer that everyone can "live with." As shown in Table 9.1, the percentage distribution helped to guide the decision.

The approaches advocated as the "right" ones by both parties were included when using the scale. Right vs. Right consists of issues identified as dilemmas, operational preferences, or mindsets/existing beliefs. Only viable options are considered. Table 9.2 represents an example of a possible dilemma regarding the usage of family-friendly policies employees can face.

The decision on the course of action is taken during a Right vs. Right reconciliation session. Since the group is split, as shown above, the facilitator encourages the participants to share their experiences on the issue (Moulton Reger, 2006). In the example above, the participants expressed the importance of having the family-friendly policies accessible to all employees. From the other side, it is also important to coordinate their usage with the departmental activity assuring that it doesn't undermine the working process. After the discussion, the group takes a decision on the course of actions. The facilitator reminds everyone that the company supports a practical approach and they need to ask themselves the question: "Can I live with this? Not (*seek*) perfection" (emphasis added; Moulton Reger, 2006, p. 77). The final decision is taken through an open vote and the discussion points are documented (as shown in Table 9.3).

After the session, all the information is documented and eventually used to design Outcome Narratives (discussed later in this chapter).

Table 9.2. *The Right vs. Right data collected prior to reconciliation*

	100%	99%–51%	50%/50%	51%–99%	100%	
The usage of family-friendly policies is the right of all employees. Every employee is entitled to file a request for their usage and have it approved.		PR TS MD KT	FS ET	KC AD		Allowance of family-friendly benefit is a departmental (managerial) decision.
		Letters above are participant initials				

Table 9.3. *Results of Right vs. Right reconciliation session*

	1	2	3	4	5	
	100%	99%–51%	50% / 50%	51%–99%	100%	
The usage of family-friendly policies is the right of all employees. Every employee is entitled to file a request for their usage and have it approved.			X			Allowance of family-friendly benefit is a departmental (managerial) decision.

All employees within the specified categories can file a request to use family-friendly policies, but each request will be discussed within the context of the performance and quality standards of each department. In case of conflict, the HR department will mediate between the employee and the supervisor.

The Right vs. Right approach has several benefits identified by the research team, such as:

(1) Mere usage of the terminology Right vs. Right is constructive and creates a good start for the reconciliation process.

(2) The fact that all the answers are "right" diminishes arguments and guarantees success independent of the answer chosen.

(3) The focus placed on conflict areas can generate new ideas and ways out of the situation. The presence of a group with different mindsets can bring variety to the solutions.

Cultural change model

The cultural model we introduce follows the steps of the CIAR method. Figure 9.2 presents an overview of the main steps of change of the CIAR method. Our model represents a synthesis of different modes and practices applied in various companies that exemplify these steps. We consider it to be of interest to the practitioners as it offers illustrations of emerging difficulties and successes during the change process (see Figure 9.3).

The way of *bringing about the change* (*how?*) is different in all cases (Lewis & Cooper, 2005). The common way of addressing change is to identify a problem and find ways of resolving it. It is nonetheless clear that even if work–life policies are chosen to address the problem, the mere proclamation of their usage will not help to reach the desired goal. Several studies have shown that the company culture and more specifically the attitude of the supervisors toward company policies play an important role for the successful implementation of work–family policies (Thompson & Prottas, 2005; Mennino, Rubin, & Brayfield, 2005). Cultural change, being a process, demands time and commitment for the long term. For change to happen it is essential to experience it. Taking this into consideration we divide the change process into two parts: first, *preparing change*, which describes what needs to be done for making change possible, such as data collection, data analysis, and feedback; second, *implementation of change*, which includes brainstorming, planning, implementing action, and measurement. The general way of introducing change includes active and attentive listening, the need of reflecting and bringing up assumptions and fears, and the importance of participation and collaboration of people involved in the change. It is essential to experiment, and to work on the dissemination of the process of change (for details of the model consult Figure 9.3).

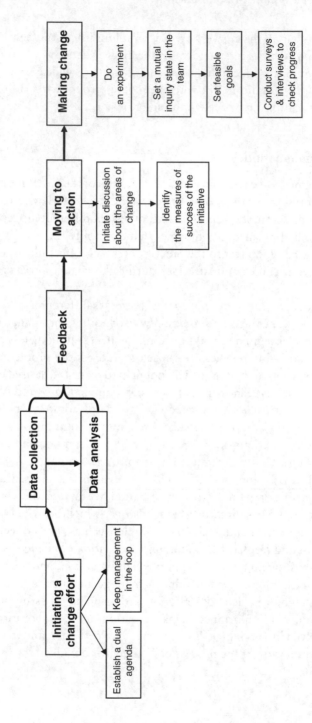

Figure 9.2 CIAR method: main steps of change.

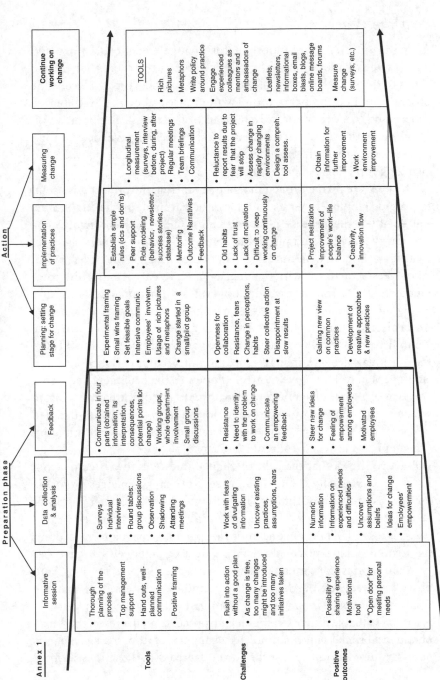

Figure 9.3 Process of change.

Preparing change

All parts of CIAR are important for change: research, action, and interactive collaboration. As with any project, the process of change needs to be well planned; moreover, all the participants of the change process should be prepared for it (Waterhouse & Lewis, 2004). Before proceeding to begin the research of an organization, Rapoport *et al.* (2002) suggest several steps that need to be taken to pave the way for a successful change. It includes establishing the *dual agenda* and engaging top management in the process.

The CIAR team mentioned that before starting the project it is useful to provide employees with a certain informational, *intellectual frame*, thus making the process of change more clear and predictable. As previously stated, a certain predictability of actions reduces the level of fears as well as the initial resistance to change. In order to get employees acquainted with the dual agenda, researchers start by communicating general information, holding informational sessions, and giving more detailed explanations in small groups. In this way, before the project starts it already has a certain frame. For example, when the flexibility program was to be introduced at Procter & Gamble (P&G), the national general managers communicated the policies to the employees in order to give more credibility to the program. They were given a three-month period to disseminate the information, during which the employees were shown a video and provided with detailed information about the policies and sources of further information (Poelmans & de Waal-Andrews, 2005).

Practice shows that the call for change does not always come from *top-level management*. Often the need for change emerges from the lower ranks and is brought up to the executive level. The latter might not be willing to become closely involved in the change process. Nevertheless, it is essential for change agents to keep management informed about the actions taking place, through conducting interviews to uncover personal stories concerning existing issues, giving presentations, and providing feedback on the conducted studies. It is essential that the concept of *joint learning* is fully comprehended – the managers are receiving valuable insights in the change process and the researchers also obtain additional information. The support of top management is necessary also because in case they do not agree with the visions adopted for the change, they possess enough power to stop the process or make changes they consider necessary. Much damage can come from initiating a process and stopping it mid-term or after roll-out. As even starting the process will raise expectations and the closure may actually erode employees' perceptions of their importance in the eyes of senior managers, making the conditions worse than in the beginning.

The idea of *positively framing* the project is closely connected with top management support (Doorewaard & Benschop, 2003). Though employees might not be fully aware of it, emotions have an influence on the professional life and work relationships. According to the relational theory of emotions, emotions are involved in the process of organizational change in two ways: "First, emotions function as implicit subroutines or feeling frames and, second, they do so in non neutral, often hegemonic power processes"(Doorewaard & Benschop, 2003, p. 280). For example, one especially successful project was carried out in a supportive atmosphere. The HRM officer, the equality officer and the top manager were enthusiastic and supportive of the project. Therefore there was a suportive subroutine to change. This was also the case at Printco, where they could implement change due to a positive environment. Another project, which turned out unsuccessful, was surrounded with resistance from the management team, who were preoccupied with the financial issues and were overall suspicious of the contribution coming from HR.

Data collection

In order to uncover the existing assumptions and beliefs in the organization, the researchers use different methods of data collection, such as surveys, observation, shadowing individual employees, attending technical and staff meetings, and interviews with managers, supervisors, and line workers, conducting field observations of work, document collection, and round tables. They ask questions such as: What is recognized as a competency here? What is viewed as real work? How is time used? How is commitment assessed? Does this affect men and women differently? How? Also, discussions are held about personal lives in order to uncover the importance of this part in employees' life (Lewis & Cooper, 2005). It should be noted that the data collection process, especially if carried out at all levels in the organization, is likely to surface Right vs. Right options. Researchers should be alert to them as this information will be very useful during subsequent steps of the change process.

A *survey* is an effective way to obtain initial information. Moreover one can present the information in figures to support the need of working on work–personal life integration. At DuPont, a big chemical company, a survey of 20,000 employees in four different sites showed that 70 percent of employees who had children used childcare services outside their homes (Kraut, 1990). This allowed management to become aware that this was a big issue for the employees, something that even if they suspected before, they could not assess. In this situation the presented data might have aroused resistance, as it presented information which some might have wished to keep concealed. However, since the figures spoke for themselves, this data presented a good ground for discussion and action.

Besides the survey, the researchers can conduct *individual interviews* among employees, management, and also sometimes among partners of the employees. The interviewer can create a complex opinion about the situation from different sources. A researcher can ask questions about how a typical day looks and what a person would change in the company to make the work–personal life balance possible. Another technique used in interviewing consists of reframing the questions from an individual to a systemic level. The interviewer would ask questions about the workload, amount of traveling, demands for presence in the office and for meetings.

Round-table discussions are used for checking whether the ideas and assumptions expressed by a sample of employees pertain to the larger group. Proffirm, a consultancy practice part of a large international organization providing professional advice and services, had a culture of "super-pleasing" the client and working long hours (Lewis & Cooper, 2005). It meant that the client was not to be disturbed even if the consultants needed additional information. After gathering data the consultants formed a two-hour round-table meeting to confirm the relevancy of the data gathered before proceeding to the next stage of data analysis. The participants were surprised to find out that "although all the issues had consequences for work–personal life integration, there were a greater number of negative consequences for organizational performance and professional service and this was an incentive to think about changes" (2005, p. 67).

Data analysis

The analysis begins with studying all the data while keeping in mind the following questions: "What does an ideal worker look like here? What do people do to demonstrate competencies here? What kind of behavior gets recognized here?" (Rapoport *et al.*, 2002, p. 93). The responses of the interviewees are used to formulate existing assumptions and to identify existing problems. At an NGO, data analysis revealed that working on new projects and demonstrating creativity was highly praised. This assumption was called "competence equals new ideas." In terms of work effectiveness, it translated into neglecting ongoing projects and continuing work on essential strategically important tasks. In this way older projects were not carried out to their completion. "The workload implications of the pressures on grant-making staff to keep producing new ideas and launching new projects, including the heavy travel requirements entailed by that kind of work, made this NGO an unfriendly environment for people with significant outside commitments" (p. 97). Women were underrepresented among the staff. These revelations of existing assumptions and expectations gave the possibility to reflect on the situation and come up with creative solutions. As a result, *mere information* turned out to be a significant source for change.

Feedback

Feedback is an essential part of the change process. Depending on the way it is done, the presented information can be accepted positively, motivate people to change, give a feeling of empowerment, or provoke negative feelings and total rejection. Therefore feedback should be prepared very carefully. The suggested way to start is by preparing formal feedback from the data analysis to management, which can include quotes from participants. This is a way to engage top management and to prepare them for the changes ahead. This format also offers an opportunity for management to provide some ideas on how to present the results and a trigger for discussion or deeper exploration.

When it comes to giving feedback to the entire company, it is important that all working groups including entire departments are present. It is very important to convey the information to as many

Table 9.4. *Main steps to take during preparation phase*

⇒ Hold information sessions:
  • Thorough planning of the process.
  • Thorough top management support.
  • Distribute hand-outs, well-planned communication.
  • Positive framing.

⇒ Collect and analyze data:
  • Surveys.
  • Individual interviews.
  • Round tables: group discussions.
  • Observation.
  • Shadowing.
  • Attending meetings.

⇒ Provide feedback:
  • Communicate in four parts (obtained information, interpretation, consequences, potential points for change).
  • Working groups, whole department involvement.
  • Small-group discussions.

employees as possible. The dual agenda proves to be most powerful when the feedback is presented to the whole company. One of the suggested ways of presenting the feedback is to divide it into four parts: "(1) This is what we heard. (2) This is what we think it means. (3) This is what we think the consequences are. (4) These are potential leverage points for change" (Rapoport *et al.*, 2002, p. 100). In order to work through the information it is also useful to break into small groups for more detailed discussions. Nevertheless it is possible only in the case when employees seem receptive to the information and are willing to identify with it. There are instances when big-group discussions are initiated right after the feedback. If there is an atmosphere of trust, the ideas and discussions flow easier. During the discussion of assumptions, one senior manager explained that in their company "time is no obstacle" and he received a feedback that the employees actually felt that their time was perceived as commodity. This discussion led to introducing change where people's time would have a higher value (p. 100).

In such a way, the main steps taken during preparation phase of the process of change can be summarized as shown in Table 9.4.

Designing practices

Planning: setting stage for change

After collecting general information about the state of affairs in the company, researchers work with employees on finding ways to address the presented issues. "The real challenge is to tap into individuals' increased capacity and openness and translate that into collective action plans for change that are concrete and doable and that can be experienced and evaluated on both dimensions of the dual agenda" (Rapoport *et al.*, 2002, p. 103). Collaboration gives employees the possibility to experience new ways of doing things, and to reflect on issues that seem to be set in stone in order to gain a new view on common practices. It develops their creativity and leads to the creation of new practices. Most importantly, it is a guarantee for employee buy-in and commitment to the action plan.

One of the ways to support the design of new practices is to use *experiments*. Experiments allow employees to freely express themselves and bring new ideas as they do not have the pressure of following a policy. Nevertheless, the responsibility of working on an important project is not set aside since people are working for a common goal that will bring advantages to their work and life. Experiments imply the idea of achieving small goals and small wins. It does not oblige the participants to achieve results from the very beginning of the project.

At Proffirm, a decision was made to give a project the small-win framing, meaning setting small goals, celebrating the achievement, and then moving onto the next objectives. This resulted in the design of a pilot experiment (Lewis & Cooper, 2005). At Fleet Financial Group (Bailyn *et al.*, 2001) it was emphasized that mistakes or undesired outcomes are a part of the process and so they would not carry negative consequences. On the contrary, the view was that mistakes would contribute to the success of the project and would make it well rounded. As noted by a director of planning & governance in the Department of Education, Science, and Training for Australia, when change was initiated "we had to be careful that there wasn't executive overreaction when something didn't go as planned. We had to eliminate a culture of blame" (Greengard, 2005, p. 33).

CIAR underlines the importance of being in a mutual inquiry state – meaning that during continuous interaction, workers exchange opinions, doubts, and ideas. It is an ongoing experiment.

Change should not be initiated at once in the entire company. It is recommended that *change begins in one department first* to experiment with possible improvements and to monitor advantages and disadvantages. Like at Energyco, the senior management together with the working units selected pilot projects where the main change would be conducted (Lewis & Cooper, 2005). Management gave the vision of the project but the piloting units (comprised of IT support, resource and consultancy units, and two units dealing with technology and communication) ran the project themselves. Management support was very useful since it provided employees with a sense of safety to continue with projects even though they might not be successful. Recruitco (a small recruitment company with around forty employees) decided on a slow change process within a limited time frame by launching a pilot project among the administrative staff for a three-month period (Lewis & Cooper, 2005).

When starting a change process, another important point for discussion is the *outcomes* of the projects. There need to be realistic expectations. The members should determine goals that they want to reach in order to make an appropriate evaluation of the project, as well as a realistic time frame to measure the results. By deciding the measurement time frame in the beginning, before implementation, the change agents avoid the likelihood of leaders expecting measurable results before it is reasonable that they can be achieved (Lewis & Cooper, 2005).

During the process of change, *resistance* arises towards the new ways of doing things and towards innovation in general. This can distract from an already established way of actions and slow down the initiated project. Rapoport *et al.* (2002) perceive resistance as a positive force which can be turned from resistance to innovation and resistance to existing practices that impede successful work–personal life integration. Among the sources of resistance are: (1) *concerns about performance* – whether the newly implemented changes will not harm productivity or career advancement; how one can be professionally successful if spending more time on this (Doorewaard & Benschop, 2003; Thompson, Beauvais, & Lyness, 1999; Allen, 2001); and (2) *resistance to change on a structural level* – the perception of full-time work as the "right" schedule, which makes the introduction of flexibility difficult. It also includes the perception or directive that beyond the regular eight-hour working day people have to be paid, which hampers the introduction of four ten-hour days or other non-regular hours. In addition, space can also restrict flexibility; e.g. cubicles impede the creation of shared spaces, where employees can interact, exchange ideas, and work collaboratively. Another issue can be that the computer system does not admit changes for flexibility. "In most cases, these sources of resistance emerge only as work groups actually begin to change the work practices in which these barriers are embedded" (Rapoport *et al.*, 2002, p. 110).

Using the "experimental framing" of change helps to counter resistance and fears. In a software engineering group with a culture of working under strain, individual work was considered to be the "real," correct one, while sharing information with colleagues and working together was not (Rapoport *et al.*, 2002). In this case, it was acceptable to interrupt colleagues for the need of urgent information. Since it was a non-stop crisis mode type of culture, all kinds of information was considered urgent, resulting in longer working hours. The solution for this problem was the introduction of "quiet time," when interruptions occurred only in cases of extreme urgency. As a result, employees reported that they were working more productively, they started to set priorities, and since they could not interrupt their colleagues whenever it suited them, they became more at ease with scheduling meetings only when they were available. It should be emphasized that this project could be developed and implemented because it was framed as an experiment limited in time, and not as a rule to follow, which put less pressure on the participants.

The method of rich pictures and metaphors offers a possibility to facilitate the brainstorming process. It is also a way to generate a more holistic approach to organizational change (Ragsdell, 2000). Rich pictures and metaphors provide the opportunity to talk about organizational topics from a new perspective, it contributes to creating relationships among people who did not have the chance to previously interact, and finally it fosters participation. Moreover, talking about the organization with the help of pictures makes expression easier and takes attention away from specific people.

As change typically aims at replacing the current state of things with an improved one, the method of rich pictures and metaphors supports the exploration of the "before" and "after" desired state. In order to assess the "before" state of things, the researchers propose drawing a common picture of the organization, while thinking about questions such as: What sort of organization are we?, What are we doing? and Where are we now?

In one case, the last question was discussed in a group of engineers *to frame the before scenario* of the company. At the beginning of the exercise there was reluctance to draw, since it was perceived as lacking an element of seriousness (Ragsdell, 2000). Nevertheless, after the initial uneasiness was overcome, it produced fruitful results allowing the emergence of various interpretations of the organization with deeper and more sincere answers than expected. Another benefit was the encouragement of cohesion between the participants. To illustrate, the engineers were coping with a constantly increasing number of tasks assigned by the senior management. The situation created the image of knights running a race to the castle of their lord. The entrance to the castle was through a drawbridge, which could be put up or down according to the senior management's will. There were also two ways leading to the castle. One was easy, with direction signs posted and supplies along the way. The knights on this road were easily seen and welcomed by management. The second way was a hard one with no available supplies and with a cloud that obscured the route to the castle. Sometimes travelers on the second road were not seen by management and did not reach the castle. Through these pictures the engineers tried to convey their overwhelming job demands and management's responses to it.

It should be emphasized that the rich picture has meaning only to the group who created it or was present at the moment. Also, the picture reflects the state of affairs at the given moment and is subject to change as time passes by. An interesting aspect was that during these sessions, senior managers experienced a new role of not being obliged to stand out as experts with all the answers and were able to participate with everyone on the same level and seek advice from their subordinates, something which would be considered as a sign of weakness in a standard work day.

The "after" scenario (the desired state of affairs) was also constructed by the help of metaphors. The participants had to answer the question: Where do we want to be? The use of metaphorical descriptions allowed the emergence of various solutions to dealing with the situation and also created new insights. For instance, one group of engineers referred to the saying "striking while the iron is hot" as a way of communicating that there was an urgent need for change. Another group adopted the metaphor "voyage to the moon" to reflect their vision of how their organization should be. It described what the team needed in order to reach their goal for change, which included the following characteristics: sufficient resources, respect for each member's contribution, and usage of new technologies. Thus the metaphor permitted their model to encompass the elements of structure, processes, and culture and present a holistic vision of future change (Ragsdell, 2000).

Implementation of the practice

After discussing existing issues and defining a way to accommodate the needs of both the employees and the company, the group is now at the implementation phase. The implementation of ideas needs sufficient time and demands effort from all the participants. The challenges that are faced at this stage include the reccurrence of old habits and the lack of trust from some members who may find change difficult to accept. Therefore the team needs information, training, and perhaps coaching and other support for adapting to the usage of these practices. The implementation of simple rules to follow, designed by participants of change can help to facilitate the transition. Simple rules encompass the things that need to be done, those that are prohibited, and those that are allowed (NHS, 2005). Having these basic rules provides employees with a necessary guideline of action in the new culture.

Outcome Narratives

Structured mini-stories implemented at IBM to define expectations is a good example of such a frame (Moulton Reger, 2006). The integrated Consulting Business Unit of PwCC and IBM needed a new vision and culture which would support its successful functioning. The management had already been using story-telling as one of the tools for communicating the new culture. A "day in the life" description reflected the typical day from an employee's role perspective. Nevertheless, it was not sufficient in the new situation. There was a need to address the issue of overlapping responsibilities and ways to deal with disagreements between employees from the two companies. Management started the design of the new culture by identifying potential problems employees would experience in situations where the two companies handled matters differently. For example: "After approval of proposal terms, the client requests some last-minute changes outside of the partner's level of authority to approve. What should happen?" (p. 53). Upon identifying an issue, the expert team worked on creating desired outcomes and analyzed how the two companies would deal with the issue in order to identify gaps and design an action plan. Then, the schema of outcomes turned into a more complex one since different roles and behaviors were added.

The Outcome Narratives focus on business outcomes and provide people with information on possible actions within identified limits; they help reach the desired goal in the best way possible. Besides, they are flexible for global requirements, such as legitimate differences across countries and business units. For example, in BCS (the integrated business unit of the two companies), Outcome Narratives were first designed globally and then were submitted to regional units for adjustments to local practices, cultures, and regulations (Moulton Reger, 2006, p. 56). They also provide information about possible gaps in managing various situations and their assessment and evaluation of objectives. Through rich and detailed stories, Outcome Narratives help provide employees with valuable information in an easy-to-remember format.

The Outcome Narratives consist of the following elements:

(1) *Situational statements*: description of a problem.
(2) *Desired outcomes*: statements about how to resolve a problem, while encompassing various values, principles, and policies.
(3) *In-scope roles*: identification of employees who would help to achieve the desired outcomes – this piece of information is very valuable, since it allows the involvement of the right people to resolve the current issue.
(4) *Role behaviors and actions*: involves the description of how each person should contribute towards reaching the goal.
(5) *Other considerations*: additional information is provided in order to allow users to handle situations in a context with some different details.

Table 9.5. *Outcome Narratives: first iteration*

Situation	Two leaders, a partner from BCS* and an executive from another IBM business unit, both hold responsibility at an account. They cannot agree on how to handle a client situation. What should happen?
Desired outcome	The answer could depend on the details, but an escalation mechanism is needed to resolve issues that cannot be resolved quickly across business units.
Current outcome for BIS**	Hierarchy resolves these situations. Escalations ultimately lead to the sector decision-maker, but issues are often resolved at lower levels.
Current outcome for PwCC	Assigned client ownership makes this situation relatively rare.

*BCS: Business Consulting Services, is IBM's current integrated consulting business unit.
**BIS is the consulting business unit that existed within IBM before the PwCC acquisition.

(6) *Reference*: provides information that explains the commonly used concepts, principles or competency definitions.

Outcome Narratives may be used in different settings and for various reasons:

(1) when employing new people it can serve as a vehicle for communication and job support reasons;
(2) when a change in business function is initiated which requires managing some situations differently, it can be used as a communication and job-support tool, but also as a gap assessment and progress evaluation – how far/close are people to reaching the desired state;
(3) When two companies are brought to work closely together as a result of an acquisition or a merger, Outcome Narratives can also be used for establishing the expectations, which is very important for successful outcomes, for assessing the gaps, and identifying the changes to be made.

Table 9.6. *Outcome Narratives: second iteration*

Situation
A disagreement exists between a relationship manager who wants approval for a contract and the finance manager who needs to approve it. The disagreement is about authority levels since the contract value exceeds what the relationship manager can approve.

Desired outcome
The relationship executive is responsible for the ultimate decision. Exceptions would be the contracts $X or X percent outside the established levels of authority for that position. The escalation process should be used for exceptions and unusual circumstances, with the answer communicated within forty-eight business hours.

In-scope roles	Role behaviors and actions
Relationship manager	Needs to work with the intent of true resolution to understand the reasons for objections, and what is best for both the client and company. Needs to help mitigate the risks and impacts by working collaboratively with finance. Needs to seek other help to mediate the issues before escalation. Should ensure the next higher-level client-facing leader concurs before taking action if mediation has not resolved the issues. As appropriate, needs to support the escalation process and constructively implement the decision from it. Should work to restore any relationships strained during the situation.
Business advisor (for example, finance)	Needs to be objective and ensure that the risk/issue is serious enough to warrant continued discussion. Needs to work collaboratively to mitigate the risks/issues while meeting the client and company requirements. Should engage in mediation and support the escalation process, as appropriate. Should support and enact the final decision, whether it is made by the relationship manager or the escalation process. Should work to restore any relationships strained during the situation.

Outcome Narratives are beneficial in various ways.

They help to reduce delays, inconsistencies, and rework – and employee frustration from being accountable for expectations but not understanding them. They provide needed information to systematically identify the gaps and what to do about them ... They provide tangible, objective basis for evaluating progress over time. (Moultan Reger, 2006, p. 62)

Besides the Outcome Narratives, there are different ways to support the adaptation to the change process, like peer support, role modeling, and mentoring.

Peer support

Peers play an important role in an employee's life: they create the social environment for interactions and represent the reference group that reflects the practices and the culture of the company, like for instance the use of flexible policies. As one study shows, if the peer group consists of employees who would be in favor of alternative schedules (women, those having family demands, etc.) there would be less group resistance to adopting these practices. Previous use of flexibility arrangements by peers is a stronger predictor of their use than amount of people who could "qualify" for their use (Kossek, Barber, & Winters, 1999).

Therefore peers can play an important role in the change process. In the case of previously mentioned Energyco, work on the change project was publicly maintained. "Making the pilot participants visible to others created a commitment to the process and a sense of pride among participants. It also strengthened accountability" (Lewis & Cooper, 2005, p. 52). Later on, the pilot participants supported other projects through their experience, advice, creativity, and their solution-oriented approach; all elements that are representative of a role model.

Role modeling

This can enhance the process of change as well. Role modeling consists of adopting a certain type of behavior and bringing the behavior into public awareness. For example, if a company provides access to different flexible policies and verbally encourages employees to use them, it might not reach its goal. On the other side, when a manager or an employee implements flexibility in their own working schedules and manages to achieve work–life balance, this is a role to be followed because desired behaviors and practices are reinforced. Besides, the use of flexibility opportunities by managers is also good for their own life quality. For example, the head of the sales department of P&G in Spain uses a flexible schedule 100 percent of the time. He testifies that in this way he spends a lot of time with his two sons. Being a divorced father, his flexible working schedule allows him to pick them up from school, help with classes, play and spend more time with them. Moreover, his supervisor is satisfied with the results he achieves and he feels happier with his personal and professional life (Chinchilla, Poelmans, León, & Tarrés, 2004).

However, if a company views itself as being flexible, but managers and executives never use this opportunity, the message sent to employees is that these new practices are not welcomed and that their usage might have an impact on their career (Kossek *et al.*, 1999). As mentioned before, here again the support of executives, and their behaviour according to the new policies, is essential to the success of the project.

Information about role models can be disseminated in various ways. Observation is one of the easiest, but may affect only a few workers. Newsletters featuring success stories of managers and executives using flexible policies (for various reasons, like family issues, recent birth, hobbies, volunteering) can be a more powerful means (Kossek *et al.*, 1999). As noted by Barbara Spitzer, a senior consultant at Watson Wyatt Worldwide, "organizations that provide ongoing progress reports and celebrate their successes are far more likely to keep project participants on track" (Greengard, 2005, p. 30). At this company, employees are already taking part in the design of the role models by participating in the research project, and by working with metaphors on where they would like their organization to be. The process of empowerment can be enhanced by involving employees in the design of the newsletter, and in the dissemination of knowledge about work–life balance. Their motivation for doing so should be high, since these actions contribute to their well-being too.

Deloitte & Touche introduced a new way of finding role models among their employees by creating a database (Halpern & Murphy, 2005). This database was designed especially for women at high leadership levels where it is hard to find role models. Each woman can enter her profile into the database. Then through a search tool, one can find a person with a similar profile, for example, by typing in a search for a woman occupying a management position with two children, using a flexible schedule in a certain department. Having many things in common, these individuals can create a network or a mentoring relationship to share experiences about similar situations.

Mentoring can also be a way of assisting the implementation of change. Mentoring consists of providing career and psychological support to employees, also called protégés. Studies have shown that this interaction supports the professional and personal success of employees (Kram, 1985; Scandura, 1992). Mentoring is a way to reflect the family-friendliness of the organization, since it aims at providing employees with resources, like information and support, that would help them to reach their goals. It can be of great assistance for the introduction of the new work–life practices. For instance, mentors can provide general information about policies offered within the company, and about overcoming existing assumptions; they can give examples of practices that contribute to work–personal life integration, and finally provide personal testimonies (Forret & de Janasz, 2005). It should be underlined that trust is of paramount importance to the relationship between the mentor and the protégés. Within a trustful relationship, employees can share very personal information and worries and, this way, they can benefit from the advice and experience of the mentor on work–personal life integration.

Ernst & Young uses the system of professional mentorship in order to transmit family values. The mentor follows the professional development of the new employees and transmits the company's values to them. Mentors work in teams with the HR director, and by monitoring different parameters they obtain information on the integration of work–family balance (Chinchilla *et al.*, 2004).

Mentoring can take place between one person higher in rank and a subordinate, but also between colleagues at the same level. As in the example of one CEO, Dan Caulfield (CEO of HQ Group in Oceanside, California) asked another CEO on how to achieve work–personal life balance. As a result of their interaction, he opted for a new working style. "Now I work a three-and-a-half-day week ... I never work on the weekends anymore ... I'm so in love with the business, I could end up talking about it all the time ... What's amazing is that I get a lot more work done this way" (Maxwell & Hopkins, 2002, p. 40). (Refer to Chapter 3 for more details on mentoring programs.)

Measurement of change

While planning a project it is important to define how it will be measured. At the Royal Bank Financial Group (Tombari & Spinks, 1999) the key indicators for change are employee retention, absenteeism, productivity, performance, employee satisfaction and commitment, stress, work–life conflict, role overload, and organizational climate. The changes are assessed though statistics and trend reports, employee surveys, and employees' demographic profiles. The usage of more subjective "measures," inquiring about what people say about the organization and what they "feel" about it, can complement "objective" measures. Though difficult to measure, this qualitative information can reflect the changes in employees' perception of change, while retention, absenteeism, and productivity indicators may not change because of other confounding factors.

The concepts that are crucial for change can also be considered points for measurement. *The investors in people guide to helping organizations manage work-life balance* (2003) suggests checking if the main values announced as critical to the company are also perceived this way by the employees. A survey is probably the best tool for this, as it encompasses the most information and makes the presentation of results easier as well. The survey should examine whether:

(1) both managers and employees can confirm that the implemented practices oriented to satisfy people's needs are being used and are equally available to all employees;
(2) employees can confirm that there are clear policies and practices put in place in order to reach work–personal life balance;
(3) managers of all levels support these practices;
(4) there is a continuous supervision of whether employees are reaching this balance in reality;
(5) good and successful practices are being circulated around the company. It is also important to include in the survey questions that would address difficulties and resistances encountered during the process of implementation and actual usage of the practices.

At Fleet Financial Group (Bailyn *et al.*, 2001), the measurements of change followed the following principles:

(1) They had to be longitudinal: information was collected before, during, and after the implementation of change, like absenteeism, turnover (quits, discharges, layoffs), family, and medical usage.
(2) They reflected the opinion of several key participants, from employees taking part in the project, to co-workers, immediate supervisors, managers, and some customers. A special survey that reflected opinions and attitudes towards work–family issues and general demographical data was designed.
(3) They had to be designed collaboratively: the Radcliffe Public Policy Institute committee worked with the employees to design measure of satisfaction and work performance and to assess those factors proposed by the Radcliffe team.

The surveys proposed along the project focused on two points: whether employees could meet their work goals and whether they could balance their work and life. The surveys were anonymous and the results were communicated at each of the stages to the units. In addition to the surveys, individual interviews were conducted with employees, supervisors, and managers at different stages of the project in order to obtain personalized opinions about the change process. Finally, a general study of individual and group production was conducted using a collectively designed measurement tool.

Another form of assessment is continuously checking employees' satisfaction through meetings and communication with managers. An example is Dormer Tools' workshop factory, guided by the philosophy of continuous improvement. There were monthly team briefings, presentations to the employees held by the managing director four times a year, weekly cell meetings, and regular team meetings to work on improvement of the existing practices (Sanford, 2005). Changes were visible and successes were communicated.

Rapoport *et al.* (2002) bring up some difficulties, which can arise when researchers want to measure change. They note that while the experiment was in progress, employees were eagerly communicating their satisfaction and personal-life improvements, but they were not as eager filling out any surveys that would document the change. As it turned out, they were afraid that the common results might not reflect to the full extent their satisfaction, which might lead to the cancellation of the experiment by the management. This also needs to be taken into

Table 9.7. *Introduction of change: main steps to take*

⇒ Plan the process of change:
- Experimental framing.
- Small wins framing.
- Set feasible goals.
- Intensive communication.
- Employees' involvement.
- Usage of rich pictures and metaphors.
- Change introduced in a small group (pilot projects).

⇒ Implement the designed practices:
- Establish simple rules (dos and don'ts).
- Peer support.
- Role modeling (behavior, newsletter, success stories, database).
- Mentoring.
- Outcome Narratives.
- Feedback.

⇒ Measure change:
- Longitudinal measurement (surveys, interview before, during, after project).
- Regular meetings.
- Team briefings.
- Communication with management.

consideration and the importance of measurement should be widely communicated among the employees.

The introduction of change is a complex process which requires thorough preparation. To conclude, we present in Table 9.7 the important steps to take when bringing change into the company.

Conclusion

Successfully carrying out the process of cultural change is difficult and tedious but nevertheless a vital task. The dual agenda approach is a supportive tool: when the interests of both the company and the employees are being considered and are regarded as interrelated for the success of the project, it motivates people to apply their skills and knowledge. Moreover, a positive attitude and experimental framing create grounds for innovation and makes one feel comfortable if things do not turn out in an expected way. The positive outcomes achieved through a well-planned and well-implemented change process are the best reward for the company.

Figure 9.3 presents our vision of the process of change: the tools used at each phase, the challenges faced, and the positive outcomes. As seen, change is a process that requires continuous work. It demands close collaboration between top management and employees and also a trustful two-way communication once the new practices are implemented. Some of the tools described above can support this process. The tool of rich pictures, used for uncovering existing assumptions, can be used for ongoing work on change if it is adopted by the company (Ragsdell, 2000). As evidence shows, companies that applied these practices kept on using them after the project was over. For instance, one company applied them for initiating a discussion between an external customer and the engineering department. It resulted in creation of two rich pictures, "Them by us" and "Us by them" developed independently by each group, which contributed to the dialogue about the possible improvement of the situation between the two groups.

An important step that needs to be taken after ensuring that the introduced practice brings the desired change and fulfills the set goals is to write a policy for it and to spread it around the company. The agents of change can be the ambassadors for innovations in other departments and the mentors for their colleagues. The way the process of change works should be made public also in a written format (leaflets, newsletters, informational boxes, email, blogs, online message boards, forums). This gives employees additional exposure to the information as a reference to consult. At Royal Bank Financial Group (Tombari & Spinks, 1999), information about work–family–life policies and flexible alternatives was available on the website, in the recruitment literature, and also on the intranet. Additionally, in the Career Navigator section, employees could find work–life related resources. Again, it should be emphasized that change is a process and that the members of the department where practices will be implemented have to go through the same phases as the pioneering team.

To conclude, we would like to summarize the crucial elements for the change process in Table 9.8.

Table 9.8. *Crucial elements for the change process*

✓ The support of the top management is essential.

✓ Both parties need to see the importance of the changes for their interests; it has to be a win-win situation (e.g. the dual agenda approach).

✓ Collaboration is crucial for success. Employees, who take an active part in the project, feel more involved and more responsible about the results, and thus take ownership.

✓ Constant communication and interaction of opinions gives the possibility of constantly working on improvement.

✓ Measurement of change is the source of additional information about change as well as for reflection on areas which need further development.

✓ Finally, careful planning of the change process as well as the ability to be flexible when designing flexibility and attending the work–personal life balance needs are the prerequisites of a successful outcome of the project.

References

Allen, T. (2001). Family-supportive work environments: The role of organizational perceptions. *Journal of Vocational Behavior, 58*, 414–435.

Bailyn, L., Rayman, P., Bengtsen, D., Carré, F., & Tierney, M. (2001). Fleet Financial and Radcliffe explore paths of work/life integration. *Journal of Organizational Excellence*, summer, 49–64.

Cameron, E. (2004). *Making Sense of Change Management: A Complete Guide to the Models, Tools and Techniques of Organizational Change.* London: Kogan Page Limited.

Causon, J. (2004). The internal brand: Successful cultural change and employee empowerment. *Journal of Change Management, 4(4)*, 297–307

Chinchilla, N., Poelmans, S., León, C., & Tarrés, J. (2004) Guía de buenas prácticas de la empresa flexible. Hacia la conciliación de la vida laboral, familiar y personal. www.iese.edu/icwf

Covin, T. J. & Kilmann, R. H. (1990). Participant perceptions of positive and negative influences on large-scale change. *Group and Organization Studies, 15*, 233–248.

Deloitte, 2005. Becoming a magnet for talent: Global and Luxembourg Talent Pulse Survey Results 2005. Deloitte SA.

Doorewaard, H. & Benschop, Y. (2003). HRM and organizational change: An emotional endeavour. *Journal of Organizational Change Management, 16(3)*, 272–286.

Fairclough, N. (1992). *Discourse and Social Change*. Cambridge: Polity Press.

Ford, J. & Ford, L. (1995). The role of conversations in producing intentional change in organizations. *Academy of Management Review*, 20 541–571.

Forret, M. & de Janasz, S. (2005). Perceptions of an organization's culture for work and family: Do mentors make a difference? *Career Development International*, 10(6/7), 478–492.

Francis H. (2003). HRM and the beginnings of organizational change. *Journal of Organizational Change Management*, 16(3), 309–327.

Greengard, S. (2005) Agents of change. *PM Network*, November, 27–34.

Halpern, D. F. (2005). How time-flexible work policies can reduce stress, improve health, and save money. *Stress and Health* 21, 157–168.

Halpern, D. F. & Murphy S. E. (2005). *From Work–Family Balance to Work–Family Interaction: Changing the Metaphor*. Mahwah, NJ: Lawrence Erlbaum Associates.

Hemp, P. & Stewart, T. A. (2004). Leading change when business is good. *Harvard Business Review*, 82(12), 60–70.

Investors in People (2003). *The Investors in People Guide to Helping Organisations Manage Work–Life Balance*. London: Investors in People.

Kossek, E. E, Barber, A. E., & Winters, D. (1999). Using flexible schedules in the managerial world: The power of peers. *Human Resource Management*, 38(1), 33–46.

Kram, K. E. (1985). *Mentoring at Work: Developmental Relationships in Organizational Life*. Glenview, IL: Scott Foresman.

Kraut, A. I. (1990). Some lessons on organizational research concerning work and family issues. *Human Resource Planning*, 13(2), 109–118.

Kropf, M. B. (1999). Flexibility initiatives: Current approaches and effective strategies. *Women in Management Review*, 14(5), 177–185.

Lewis, D. S. (1992) Communicating organizational culture. *Australian Journal of Communication*, 19(2), 47–57.

Lewis, S. (1996). Rethinking employment: An organizational culture framework. In Lewis, S. & Lewis, J. (eds), *The Work–Family Challenge. Rethinking Employment*. London: Sage Publications.

Lewis, S. & Cooper, C. (2005). *Work–Life Integration: Case Studies of Organizational Change*. Chichester: John Wiley & Sons.

Lewis, S. & Rapoport, R. (2005). Looking backwards to go forwards: the integration of paid work and personal life. In Peper B. (ed.) *Flexible Working and Organizational Change: The Integration of Work and Personal Life* (pp. 297–311) Cheltenham: Edward Elgar Publishing Limited.

Lickert, R. (1961). *New Patterns of Management*. New York: McGraw-Hill.

Maxwell, J. H. & Hopkins, M. (2002). Who do you call when no one has the answers? Where the smartest CEOs turn for guidance and perspective when company building gets personal. *Inc.*, September, 40.

McDonald, P., Guthrie, D., Bradley, L., & Shakespeare-Finch, J. (2005). Investigating work–family policy aims and employee experiences. *Employee Relations*, 27(5), 478–494.

Mennino, S. F., Rubin, B. A., & Brayfield, A. (2005). Home-to-job and job-to-home spillover: The impact of company policies and workplace culture. *The Sociological Quarterly*, 46, 107–135.

Moulton Reger, S. J. (2006) *Can Two Rights Make a Wrong? Insights from IBM's Tangible Culture Approach*. Crawfordsville: IBM Press.

NHS (2005). *Improvement Leaders' Guide: Managing the Human Dimensions of Change, Personal and Organisational Development*. London: HMSO.

Peper B. (2005). *Flexible Working and Organizational Change: The Integration of Work and Personal Life*. Cheltenham: Edward Elgar Publishing Limited.

Phelan M. W. (2005). Cultural revitalization movements in organization change management. *Journal of Change Management*, 5(1), 47–56.

Poelmans S. & de Waal-Andrews, W. (2005). Launching flexible work arrangements within Procter & Gamble EMEA. In Poelmans, S. (ed.), *Work and Family: An International Research Perspective*. Mahwah, NJ: Lawrence Erlbaum Associates.

Putnam, L. (1999) Shifting metaphors of organizational communication: The rise of discourse perspectives. In P. Salem (ed.), *Organizational Communication and Change*. Cresskill, NJ: Hampton Press.

Ragsdell, G. (2000). Engineering a paradigm shift? An holistic approach to organizational change management. *Journal of Organizational Change Management*, 13(12), 104–120.

Rapoport, R., Bailyn, L, Fletcher, J., & Pruitt, B. (2002). *Beyond Work–Family Balance: Advancing Gender Equity and Workplace Performance*. San Francisco: Jossey-Bass.

Sanford, A. (2005). Lean-driven cultural change. *MWP*, March, 20–22.

Scandura, T. A. (1992). Mentorship and career mobility: An empirical investigation. *Journal of Organizational Behavior*, 13, 169–174.

Schein, E. (1997) *Organisational Culture and Leadership*. San Francisco: Jossey-Bass.

Stavrou, E. T., (2005). Flexible work bundles and organizational competitiveness: A cross-national study of the European work context. *Journal of Organizational Behavior*, 26, 923–947.

Thompson, C. A., Beauvais, L. L., & Lyness, K. S. (1999). When work–family–personal life benefits are not enough: The influence of work–family–personal life culture on benefit utilization, organizational attachment and work–family–personal life conflict. *Journal of Vocational Behavior*, 54, 392–415.

Thompson, C. A. & Prottas, D. J. (2005). Relationships among organizational family support, job autonomy, perceived control, and employee well-being. *Journal of Occupational Health Psychology*, 10, 100–118.

Tombari N. & Spinks N. (1999). The work/family interface at Royal Bank Financial Group: Successful solutions – a retrospective look at lessons learned. *Women in Management Review*, 14, 186–193.

van Doorne-Huiskes, A., den Dulk, L., & Peper, B.(2005). Organizational change, gender and integration of work and private life. In Peper B. (ed.) *Flexible Working and Organizational Change: The Integration of Work and Personal Life* (pp. 297–311). Cheltenham: Edward Elgar Publishing Limited.

Waterhouse, J. & Lewis, D. (2004). Communicating Culture Change: HRM implications for public sector organizations. *Public Management Review*, 6(3), 353–376.

Watson, T. J. (1994). *In Search of Management*. London: Routledge.

Epilogue: flexibility and diversity in the twenty-first century – the responsibility of human potential managers

STEVEN A. Y. POELMANS and
ALINE D. MASUDA
IESE Business School, Spain

We can compare the impact that firms will have on the social fabric of society in the twenty-first century with the impact firms had in the twentieth century on the natural environment and will continue to have in the next centuries. Firms, among the most powerful and influential institutions of our society, have the potential to transform our way of living, even our way of thinking, for the better and for the worse. They are generators of wealth and waste. The emergence of corporate social responsibility, often as a response to much of the waste created, holds the promise that company owners, executive boards, and CEOs are starting to understand the constructive and destructive power of the institutions they create.

One of the major challenges or types of waste companies will have to learn to come to terms with is *stress*. There is ample evidence showing how stress impacts the health and well-being of individuals, and that work-related stress is one of the major causes of strain. In the US, 43 percent of adults suffer adverse health effects from stress, and 75–90 percent of all physician office visits are for stress-related ailments and complaints. Stress is linked to the six leading causes of death: heart disease, cancer, lung ailments, accidents, cirrhosis of the liver, and suicide (American Psychological Association, 1997). People who experienced stress typically go through different stages and degrees of suffering and along the way they pass on their stress to their direct environment, their families, their co-workers, and their friends. Research in the field of work and family has well established the spillover and crossover effects of stress, affecting co-workers, spouses, children, and the community at large (Allen, Herst, Bruck, & Sutton, 2000). The waste is immeasurable.

In order to understand the causes and consequences of stress in managers, we have been collaborating with Paul Spector and Tammy Allen (both University of South Florida), Cary Cooper (Lancaster University), Michael O'Driscoll (Waikato University), Juan Sanchez (Florida International University), Laurent Lapierre (University of Ottawa), and many other researchers in five continents around the globe, as part of the Collaborative International Study of Managerial Stress (Spector *et al.*, 1999, 2001, 2002, 2004, 2005, 2007). The leading question in this research is: what universal laws and what cross-cultural differences govern the way stress affects managers' well-being? First, the answer is clear: stress affects managers' well-being across the globe. We have found support for the hypothesis that having a sense of control of events in the workplace (i.e. internal work locus of control) is a universal factor to enjoy better physical and mental health and job satisfaction, even in collectivist countries where we can expect that having too much of an internal locus of control can be looked upon as individualistic. That suggests indirectly that individuals in regions, cultures, or religions with an important component of fatalism, or external attribution of the success of work, would suffer worse health. It also means that health and stress management programs designed to improve employee health do good simply by being organized, as they create increased awareness of the possibilities employees have to improve their own health, despite high pressure or unfavorable circumstances at work or at home.

In another study we have been able to observe that individuals in different cultures experience something as fundamental as working hours very differently, at least when we focus on the impact of working hours on work–family conflict. In the collectivist cultures (Latin-American, Eastern European, and Asian) the effect of working hours is not as disruptive as for managers working in individualistic, Anglo-Saxon cultures. This is fascinating data supporting the idea that work and family ethos means something fundamentally different in different cultures. It is possible that in individualistic cultures work and family compete for time. Men and women compete for time. In collectivistic cultures working more hours *serves* the family; it represents a sacrifice for the family. An interesting fact is that, according to the data collected among Spanish executives, we see a rapid evolution from collectivism to among the highest levels of individualism worldwide in a matter of twenty years. This rapid cultural transition that we can observe in many countries transitioning from a more traditional/family oriented culture to a more Western/free-market/consumption/individual oriented culture around the globe, like Spain, Turkey, Argentina, or Taiwan, holds some strong risks. It suggests that we would observe more inter-generation and marital conflicts (indeed, in Spain domestic violence mainly directed against women is in the center of the news and public debate), but also more inter-motivational conflicts in terms of prioritizing family or work, in men as well as in women. This is probably one explanation why we have found that Spain has the highest level of work–family conflict compared to several of the twenty-six countries studied (Poelmans, Spector, & Allen, 2006). This in turn is probably why Spain has one of the lowest fertility rates in the world (INE). Not having children or keeping them to a minimum seems to be a strategy to avoid or to minimize conflict.

We can realistically anticipate that in the decades to come work pressure will only continue to rise as a consequence of imperative economic growth, intensifying competition on a global scale, a push towards consumerism, scarcity of qualified employees, and continuing organizational surgery (mergers, acquisitions, and downsizing) to keep growth up and costs down. The combined effects of cost reduction and the war for talent will lead to further polarization between the haves and have-nots, as limited company resources to retain employees will be targeted to limited segments of high potentials and high achievers with skills that are scarce in the labor market. Those who do not belong to the center core of the firm will have to suffer the abuse and waste of human potential and health, and with them, so will their families.

On the one hand we have the vast majority of low-skilled workers and the new workforce of immigrants that will take most of the abuse, working without or on temporary contracts for low wages and in precarious conditions. Delocation, resourcing, or simply a change of temporary work provider can leave them without jobs overnight. Those who take over their jobs in some remote developing country will work in even more precarious conditions for even lower wages. Their will to survive and take care of the most basic needs of their families will leave them with no other choice than accepting these jobs, and so growth will be sustained, to the detriment of their and their families' health. Obviously, firms concerned with profit and shareholder value only will not allocate resources to meet the needs and caring responsibilities of these workers. They will create flexible work schedules purely out of considerations of customer responsiveness and efficiency. They will have increasing problems though to undo their reputation in the labor market, and that reputation is without any doubt a powerful weapon in the war for talent.

As noted by Paula Caligiuri and Nicole Givelekian in Chapter 1, with the tight labor market, the battle for qualified professional and managerial personnel will be waged, and all kinds of perks and benefits will be generously but exclusively offered to compensate for the increasing responsibilities and pressures that these talented professionals have to carry on their shoulders. Hence, we can draw two conclusions: stress will continue to spread to affect all levels of society, but the danger is that only the upper layer and those working in healthy organizations, which are organizations with the vision to improve both employee well-being and productivity and are characterized by having supportive environments, meaningful jobs, and accessible and equitable opportunities for career and work–life balance, will have access to benefits to offset the negative effects (Wilson, Dejoy, Vandenberg, Richardson, & McGrath, 2004). This situation brings to mind ethical questions and the role of corporate responsibility to employees' well-being. That is, is it part of corporate responsibility to promote employees' physical and mental well-being? Most importantly, should all employees have the right of benefiting from working conditions that promote a healthy and balanced life? More than ever, the challenge will be to craft organizational visions that ensure corporate competitiveness and inspire performance-driven behaviors without creating a destructive organizational environment. This challenge can be easily resolved if corporate leaders became aware that fulfilling corporate responsibilities is financially advantageous. For example, the fact that corporate image has important consequences for company performance is a fundamental reason for organizations to become aware of the fatal consequences of stress in the workplace. Many still remember the damaging consequences for Nike's reputation after an article appearance in 1992 at Harper's Magazine about Nike's sweatshop conditions at some suppliers and factories overseas. The destructive consequences of Nike's public relations crisis are exemplified by the fact that given public protests, some universities cancelled their orders with Nike to produce collegiate athletic products. Luckily, Nike did an excellent job recovering its public image. By creating the first department to exclusively handle labor standards, Nike promoted and invested in initiatives to improve worker conditions in global supply chains. As Simon Zadek (2004), a senior fellow at Harvard University's John F. Kennedy School of Government in Cambridge stated, "beyond getting their own houses in order, companies need to stay abreast of the public's evolving ideas about corporate roles and responsibilities" (p. 125).

Working conditions have always been in the center of corporate image. However, with the sweeping changes in demographics, such as more dual-career couples and rising numbers of working mothers with young children (Bond, Galinsky, & Swangberg 1998), promoting a workplace environment where employees are able to balance several domains of their lives will be perceived by the public as part of corporate responsibility. Hence, a company that promotes a climate suitable to work and family conciliation will be viewed more favorably in the eyes of employees and customers compared with companies that promote an unhealthy environment. Unfortunately, work–family balance issues, or eliminating stress in organizations, is still viewed by corporate leaders as a luxury and sometimes as a roadblock to attain corporate objectives. The belief that promoting a family-friendly culture impedes productivity is very common among corporate executives. Further, employees and firms are not aware of the impact that work pressure, stress, and conflicts can have on individuals and their direct social environment, and how one day the stress accumulated at home may spill over to work in an acute and fatal way with severe consequences to company performance. This has already been observed by academics studying stress and safety issues in the workplace (Frone, 1998; Zohar, 2000). Most notably, research shows that healthcare professionals who experience stress at work are more likely to have accidents with their patients (Elfering, Semmer, & Grabner, 2006). For example, loss of sleep and long working hours in nurses can have severe safety implications for patients. Additionally, doctors who experienced high workload are more likely to be accused of medical malpractice.

Public awareness is unfortunately often created by a severe problem or crisis affecting a whole region. For example, the 23 March 2005 explosion in the British Petroleum (BP) refinery in Texas City that claimed the lives of fifteen employees and injured 170 others is a tragic example of this type of contamination. Reports suggest that during the day of the accident, several employees were working thirty straight 12-hour days with some employees commuting an additional two hours. Additionally, workload was evident with a single control board operator responsible for running the controls of three different complex process units (Operating Experience Summary, 2006). This example illustrates how stress at work can contaminate the life of employees, that of their co-workers, and their entire community.

In the case of environmental contamination disasters can be extreme, such as Bhopal and Chernobyl. In the case of human contamination the waste is distributed in much smaller portions and is sufficiently "common" to pass unnoticed, like for instance the loss of a valuable manager because of "private reasons." That loss can be physical (e.g. death caused by a heart attack), psychological (e.g. strain caused by a divorce), economic (e.g. turnover caused by unsolved conflict or opportunistic bosses), or in the worst case existential (e.g. suicide, burnout, sabotage, fraud), where we see employees losing purpose and spiraling down into destructive behaviors towards themselves or others. In the case of Procter & Gamble (Poelmans & Andrews, 2001, 2005) exit interviews revealed that female managers were not leaving the labor market altogether as was thought, but went to competitors and other high-demanding jobs offering more autonomy or flexibility. Now, after many years of experimenting with different work–life benefits as part of their global diversity program, and carefully deploying the policies in different regions, they are one of the companies admired for their respect for the caring responsibilities and diversity of their employees.

We anticipate that awareness, as in the case of environmental contamination, will most probably come once three critical conditions are met. First, a critical number of individuals need to be confronted on a large scale with the waste in their immediate, local environment (as in massive lay-offs). Second, they need to become aware they are picking up others' waste and have to become resentful about it. This effect was ironically observed in the work–family backlash, i.e. employees without families feeling resentful about being discriminated in comparison with employees with families and demanding fair treatment (Young, 1999). Third, they have to get organized to form a sufficiently powerful pressure group to demand changes, as in labor unions demanding universal work–life benefits in collective agreements.

We expect this trend to emerge in the next decade, especially in the European Community. Obviously, unwilling response to pressure is not the most desirable way of going about things. A more recommendable way would be to take a proactive approach to avoid resentment and painful negotiations with increasingly aware labor unions.

Awareness in a certain domain often is a reflection of a "Zeitgeist," an awareness awakened through changes happening in other domains of social life. Some of the trends that are highly related with work–family conflict are changing work and family values, changing career expectations, and familiarity with new technologies. First, unlike previous generations who put a high priority on a career, today's youngest workers or Generation Y are more interested in making their jobs accommodate their family and personal lives. Second, they have more individualistic values, as they often grew up in nuclear families or as single children (Armour, 2005). Generation Y has been pampered, nurtured, and programmed with a slew of activities since they were toddlers, meaning they are both high-performance and high-maintenance. Third, they believe in their own worth. They are technologically savvy; they literally grew up with computers, the Internet, and personal mobile phones, and they will simply not expect anything else than jobs offering autonomy and flexibility, telecommuting options, and flexible leave arrangements. They will have a strong negotiation power to simply ask to work part-time or leave the workforce temporarily when they want to travel around the world or when children come in the picture. Fourth, the computer game generation likes change. Generation Y-ers do not expect to stay in a job, or even a career, for too long. They like to collect their bonuses and move on to the next "level." They can be skeptical when it comes to such concepts as employee loyalty. This will result in an intriguing new state of affairs: stress and pressure will clash with the values of this new generation, to reach a point where stress is no longer a problem of the unhealthy and weak employee, but a problem of unhealthy and weak companies and those who choose to work for these companies. We can already observe this effect in MBA students preferring jobs in the industry instead of in investment banking and consulting, very often because they had some bad personal experiences working in those industries before doing an MBA. For example, many MBA students with previous experience as consultants report the negative consequences of working long hours, traveling often, and having to be available for the client and employer all the time. Unhealthy companies that operate under a vision of optimizing growth and paying off the waste (like for instance tolerating high turnover among eager young employees) will have to pay increasingly high salaries to keep that talent sufficiently long enough in order not to erode their customer base. Companies that wait for a crisis to act will lose precious time to develop a sustainable strategic advantage in the labor market, and indirectly with a lapse of probably three to six years, in the consumer market. Strong and healthy firms on the other hand are already anticipating evident shocks in the labor market and are starting to invest their wealth in waste management. If they keep up the efforts they will survive and succeed tomorrow thanks to their proactive behavior today. Procter & Gamble (P&G) now ranks twenty-fourth on the Fortune 500 and sixty-eighth on the 2007 ranking of the Best Companies to Work For. The case of flexible work arrangements at P&G Europe, Middle East, and Africa is publicly available (Poelmans & Andrews, 2001, 2005). The company does not fear giving away its competitive advantage. It knows it takes at least a decade to develop. We expect that soon their competitors will start realizing their losses due to invisible "opportunity costs" and knowledge drain, and so P&G, as many other pioneering organizations mentioned in this book, will have to anticipate the next "level," in order to keep their strategic advantage.

One shock all firms will have to confront is the growing diversity in their workforce, not just in terms of cultural diversity, but as a logical consequence of the migration trends described earlier. Generation Y in the US, for instance, is one of the most diverse demographic groups – one out of three is a minority. Another type of diversity that can be expected to be at least as problematic as well as potentially enriching, is diversity in family compositions. This is a direct consequence of the earlier described trends of individualism, need for change, and easy access to alternative partners in life or on the Internet: more people get separated or divorced, fewer people get married or live together in a long-term relationship, and together they have fewer children. This is resulting in many new family forms, some of which we might not recognize, but which certainly flourish, such as one-person, mono-parental, dual-earner and dual-career, childless, adoptive, blended, mixed, and homosexual families, with adults, children, the elderly, friends, and pets living together in all possible configurations.

The conclusion is clear: increasingly, human resource managers will have to face a vast diversity in their workforce, with each employee representing unique caring responsibilities. Migration will also affect the cultural composition of families, to make things even more complex, and the expectations of employees will vary in function of their blended values, that are mostly invisible to the supervisor or employer. The development and promotion of cultural intelligence (Early, 2002; Thomas & Inkson, 2004; Thomas, 2006) seems one of the most probable industry moves to deal with diversity in this new century.

A lesson we can draw from research up to date, is that building a flexible and family-responsible organization, and developing a culture supporting these new realities, takes a lot of time and effort. These efforts need to be carefully planned at the highest levels of the organization and implemented throughout the whole organization, department by department, region by region, country by country, to be truly global in outlook. Reading through the different chapters of this volume, there are many instances where we realized that the processes for successfully managing cultural change to create flexible and family-responsible firms are equally valid for creating diverse, culturally intelligent, and truly global firms.

The mere concept of cross-cultural intelligence represents a paradigmatic leap in cross-cultural research and the way we think about diversity in general. Under the previous paradigm, investigators sought universal dimensions that would permit them to differentiate among cultures, thus reducing people to representatives of their cultures. In the new paradigm we seek individual universal character-istics that permit people to be adaptive to cultural differences universally. We challenge you: do you believe there exists a universally acceptable, that is to say, culturally neutral wisdom, on how two people can interrelate without offending the other, on the contrary, how they can encounter trust and respect with the objective of working and living together? And if this wisdom exists, would we be able to recompile and organize this wisdom? Can we teach it and learn it? And would it really result in more healthy relationships between people, their families, their organizations, and their communities?

Companies that start today to apply and develop their cultural intelligence to figure out ways to cater to this wide diversity in needs will be able to attract and retain the most valuable employees tomorrow. Their workforce and values will mirror the diversity in the population and thus in their customers, who are also becoming increasingly demanding in terms of expecting unique answers to unique needs. As such, firms leading the way in becoming flexible, family-responsive, and culturally intelligent, have greater chances to thrive and survive, socially and economically. They are doing well and doing good. Given a choice, wouldn't you prefer to work for such a firm?

This chapter goes out to a new breed of human *potential* managers and consultants, researchers, and students, who understand and anticipate the changes in our society. Human potential managers or researchers no longer think of people in terms of resources, to be assigned as a function of short-term fluctuations in the market, but rather think in terms of long-term potential, and gaining competitive advantage by unleashing entrepreneurial, innovative, and responsible behavior in their employees. They proactively think of ways of facilitating *positive* spillovers between work and family, taking advantage of competencies developed as parents, spouses, partners, and caring children. They include employees' spouses in vital career decisions, regardless of whether it concerns a modest promotion, or a more risky expatriation or repatriation, because they acknowledge research findings that spouses' and families' well-being are a critical success factor for adjustment and performance. They develop and coach employees beyond the strict boundaries of their job. They counsel them to become healthy, equilibrated persons, to drive their firm to be healthy and profitable. This is the new deal: companies who want to have employees that give the best of themselves, will have to invest a considerable part of their wealth and give the best of themselves, as enlightened visionaries, strategists, planners, human potential managers, and coaches. Organizational and professional evolution cannot be separated from personal evolution and the universal and timeless cycles of birth, immaturity, maturity, and decline. Human potential managers show respect for both high potentials and vulnerable segments in their workforce. They focus on what will be, in addition to what is already there. This is not a utopia, it is a hard reality. And the future has already begun.

References

Allen, T. D., Herst, D. E. L., Bruck, C. S., & Sutton, M. (2000). Consequences associated with work-to-family conflict: A review and agenda for future research. *Journal of Occupational Health Psychology*, 5, 278, 308.

American Psychological Association. (1997). How does stress affect us? APA HelpCenter. Retrieved 7 January 2003 from http://helping.apa.org/work/stress2.html

Armour, S. (2005). Generation Y: They've arrived at work with a new attitude. *USA Today*. www.usatoday.com/money/workplace/2005-11-06–gen-y_x.htm. (Ms. Armour quotes Bruce Tulgan, a founder of New Haven, US-based RainmakerThinking, which studies the lives of young people.)

Bond, J. T., Galinsky, E., & Swangberg, J. E. (1998). *The 1997 National Study of Changing Workplace*. New York: Families and Work Institute.

Early, P. C. (2002). Redefining interactions across cultures and organizations: Moving forward with culture intelligence. *Research in Organizational Behavior*, 24, 271–299.

Elfering, A., Semmer, N.-K., & Grebner, S. (2006). Work stress and patient safety: Observer-rated work stressors as predictors of characteristics of safety-related events reported by young nurses. *Ergonomics*, 49, 457–469.

Frone, M. R. (1998), Predictors of work injuries among employed adolescents. *Journal of Applied Psychology*, 83, 565–576.

INE www.ine.es

O'Driscoll, M., Poelmans, S., Spector, P. E., Cooper, C. L., Allen, T. D. & Sanchez, J. I. (2003). The buffering effect of family-responsive interventions, perceived organizational and supervisor support in the work–family conflict–strain relationship. *International Journal of Stress Management*, 10(4), 326–344.

Office of Environment Safety and Health (2006). Operating experience summary, Preliminary findings of fatal explosion at Texas refinery. http://hss.energy.gov/csa/analysis/oesummary/oesummary2006/OES2006-05.pdf

Poelmans, S. & Andrews, W. (2001). Launching flexible work-arrangements within Procter & Gamble EMEA. *FH 716 (A) and FH 717 (B)*. Barcelona: IESE Publishing.

Poelmans, S. & Andrews, W. (2005). Launching flexible work arrangements within Procter & Gamble EMEA. In Steven A. Y. Poelmans (ed.), *Work and Family: An International Research Perspective* (pp. 357–384). Mahwah NJ: Lawrence Erlbaum Associates.

Poelmans, S., Spector, P., & Allen, T. (2006). A 26-nation comparative study of work/family demands, resources, and conflict. Paper presented at the 2006 International Association of Applied Psychology.

Poelmans, S., Spector, P. E., Cooper, C. L., Allen, T. D., O'Driscoll, M. & Sanchez, J. I. (2003). A cross-national comparative study of work/family demands and Resources. *International Journal of Cross-Cultural Management*, 3(3), 275–288.

Spector, P. E., Allen, T. D., Poelmans, S. Cooper, C. L., Bernin, P., Hart, P., Lu, L., Miller, K., Renault de Moraes, L., Ostrognay, G. M., Pitariu, H., Salamatov, V., Salgado, J, Sanchez, J. I., Siu, O. L., Teichmann, M., Theorell, T., Vlerick, P., Widerszal-Bazyl, M., & Yu, S. (2005). An international comparative study of work/family stress and occupational strain. In S. A. Y. Poelmans (ed.), *Work and Family: An International Research Perspective* (pp. 71–84). Mahwah, NJ: Lawrence Erlbaum.

Spector, P., Allen, T. D., Poelmans, S., Lapierre, L., Cooper, C. L., O'Driscoll, M., Sanchez, J. I., Abarca, N., Alexandrova, M., Beham, B., Brough, P., Ferreiro, P., Fraile, G., Lu, C., Lu, L., Moreno-Velázquez, I., Pagon, M., Pitariu, H., Salamatov, V., Shima, S., Suarez Simoni, A., Siu, O. L., & Widerszal-Bazyl, M. (2007). Cross-national differences in relationships of work demands, job satisfaction and turnover intentions with work–family conflict, *Personnel Psychology*, 60, 805–835.

Spector, P. E., Cooper, C. L., Poelmans, S., Allen, T. D., O'Driscoll, M., Sanchez, J. I., Siu, O. L., Dewe, P., Hart, P., Lu, L., Renault de Moraes, L. F., Ostrognay, G. M., Sparks, K., Wong, P., & Yu, S. (2004). A cross-national comparative study of work/family stressors, working hours, and well-being: China and Latin America vs. the Anglo World. *Personnel Psychology*, 57(1), 119–143.

Spector, P., Cooper, C. L., Sanchez, J. I., Sparks, K., Bernin, P., Büssing, A., Dewe, P., Hart, P., Lu, L., Miller, K., Renault de Moreas, L., O'Driscoll, M., Ostrognay, G. M., Pagon, M., Pitariu, H., Poelmans, S., Radhakrishnan, P., Russinova, V., Salamatov, V., Salgado, J., Shima, S., Ling Siu, O., Stora, J. B., Teichmann, M., Theorell, T., Vlerick, P., Westman, M., Widerszal-Bazyl, M., Wong, P., & Yu, S. (2001). Do national levels of individualism and internal locus of control relate to well-being: An ecological level international study. *Journal of Organizational Behavior*, 22, 815–832.

Spector, P., Cooper, C. L., Sanchez, J. I., Sparks, K., Bernin, P., Büssing, A., Dewe, P., Hart, P., Lu, L., Miller, K., Renault de Moraes, L., O'Driscoll, M., Ostrognay, G. M., Pagon, M., Pitariu, H., Poelmans, S., Radhakrishnan, P., Russinova, V., Salamatov, V., Salgado, J., Shima, S., Ling Siu, O., Stora, J. B., Teichmann, M., Theorell, T., Vlerick, P., Westman, M., Widerszal-Bazyl, M., Wong, P., & Yu, S. (2002). A 24 nation/territory study of work locus of control, well-being, and individualism: How generalizable are western work findings? *Academy of Management Journal*, 45(2), 453–466.

Spector, P., Cooper, C. L., Sparks, K., Bernin, P. B., Dewe, P., Luo, L., Miller, K., Renault de Moraes, L., O'Driscoll, M., Pagon, M., Pitariu, H., Poelmans, S., Radhakrishnan, P., Russinova, V., Salamatov, V., Salgado,

J., Sanchez, J. I., Shima, S., Ling Siu, O., Stora, J. B., Teichmann, M., Theorell, T., Vlerick, P., Westman, M., Widerszal-Bazyl, M., Wong, P., & Yu, S. (1999). An international study of the psychometric properties of the Hofstede values survey module 1994: A case of poor internal consistency. *Applied Psychology: An International Review*, 50(2), 269–281.

Thomas, D. C. (2006). Domain and development of cultural intelligence: The importance of mindfulness. *Group & Organization Management*, 31 (1), 78–99.

Thomas, D. C. & Inkson, K. (2004). *Cultural Intelligence: People Skills for Global Business*. San Francisco, CA: Berrett-Koehler.

Wilson, M. G., DeJoy, D. M., Vandenberg, R. J., Richardson, H. A., & McGrath, A. L. (2004). Work characteristics and employee health and well-being: Test of a model of healthy work organization. *Journal of Occupational and Organizational Psychology*, 77, 565–588.

Young, M. B. (1999). Work–family backlash: Begging the question, what's fair? *The Annals of the American Academy of Political and Social Science*, 562(1), 32–46.

Zadek, S. (2004). The path to corporate responsibility. *Harvard Business Review*, 82, 125–132.

Zohar, D., (2000). A group-level model of safety climate: Testing the effect of group climate on microaccidents in manufacturing jobs. *Journal of Applied Psychology*, 85, 587–596.

List of website references

Corporate

Alliance for Work–Life Progress:
www.awlp.org
College and University Work–Family Association:
www.cuwfa.org
Corporate Voices for Working Families:
www.cvworkingfamilies.org

Public policy

Take Care Net:
www.takecarenet.org
Labor Project for Working Families:
www.working-families.org/
National Partnership for Women and Families:
www.nationalpartnership.org/site/PageServer
Institute for Women's Policy Research:
www.iwpr.org/index.cfm
Boston College Center for Work and Family:
www.bc.edu/centers/cwf/
Work–Family Newsgroup:
http://lser.la.psu.edu/workfam/history.htm
Sloan Work and Family Research Network:
http://wfnetwork.bc.edu/
Families and Work Institute:
http://familiesandwork.org/site/research/main.html
ICWF: International Center of Work and Family:
www.iese.edu/en/RCC/ICWF/Home/Home.asp
IFREI (diagnostic tool):
www.iesedti.com/ifrei2006/ifrei.htm

The Clearinghouse on International Developments in Child, Youth, and Family Policies at Columbia University:
www.childpolicyintl.org/
Case Studies of Flexible Work:
www.flexibility.co.uk/cases/index.htm
Great Place to Work Europe:
http://greatplacetowork-europe.com/
Project "Households, Work and Flexibility" funded under the Fifth Framework Programme of the European Union:
www.hwf.at/
Work–Life Research Center:
www.workliferesearch.org/wl_site/hp_main.htm
Employer and Work–Life Balance:
www.employersforwork-lifebalance.org.uk/

Index of subjects

3M 106

absenteeism 27, 28, 33, 51, 64
Accenture 60
ACREW key performance indicators of
    work–life best practice 190–201
adoption decision 39, 40–3
    factors affecting 41, 43–4
Africa 126–7, 127–9, 184
Agilent Technologies 247
Allianz 54, 57
allowance decision 40, 133, 135,
    154–61
    factors influencing 157–61
    group-level factors 159–60
    individual factors 157–9
    organizational-level factors 160–1
    reactions to 161–2
American Institute of Stress 20
Aon Consulting 33
assumptions about work 148, 209,
    210–13, 222, 228, 257
AstraZeneca 27
Australia, Department of Education
    Science and Training 259
Australian Centre for Research in
    Employment and Work 190–201
Austria 49, 56
Avon Cosmetics 56, 64

Banesto 152
Bank of America 86
Bank of Montreal 246
BASF 106
BMW 62
Body Shop International 247
Bosch Group 57, 61
Boston College Center for Work and
    Family 169
BP see British Petroleum

brain drain 83
Bristol-Myers Squibb 48, 217
British Airways 106
British Petroleum (BP) 67, 282
BT 83, 106
Burlington Northern Santa Fe
    Railway Co. 84
burnout 19, 34, 35, 214
    definition 20
    executive level employees 20
business travel 8–9, 34, 60, 124; see also
    global assignments, flexpatriates

Caja Madrid 136
Canada 174
careers 49, 78–88
    attitudes towards success 1
    backlash against 79–81
    development programs 8, 58, 65, 78
    flexibility in 82
    integrated systems 85–6
    organizational career systems 78,
        81–2
    recommendations for integrating
        personal life with 82–8
    stages of 81–2, 137, 211
Castle Press 60
Catalyst 79
Center for Creative Leadership 215
change: see also cultural change
    agents of 167, 238–9, 254, 273
    capacity for 124
    categories of 247
    financing for 239
    focus of 237–63
    implementation of 251
    model of 245–51
    organizational 237, 287
    planning stage 251, 254–8
    positive framing of 255

Index of authors